This book belongs to:

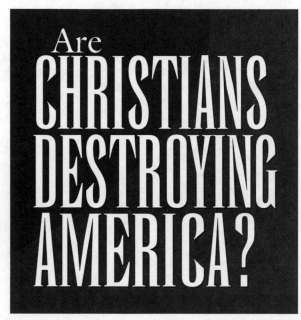

How to Restore
A Decaying Culture

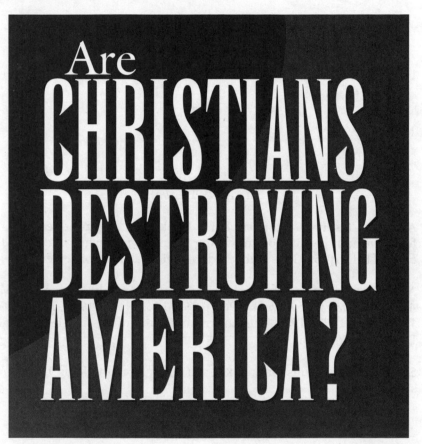

Are
CHRISTIANS
DESTROYING
AMERICA?

Tony Evans

MOODY PRESS
CHICAGO

ISBN: 0–8024–3920–9

1 3 5 7 9 10 8 6 4 2

Printed in the United States of America

Dedicated to my most trusted friend,

Martin Hawkins,

whom God has uniquely used to give me

a clearer picture of church ministry.

Only eternity will fully testify to

how much his love, friendship, wisdom, and camaraderie

have meant to me, my family, and my ministry.

TABLE OF CONTENTS

WITH GRATITUDE

I want to thank the people who helped make this book a reality: Greg Thornton, Bill Thrasher, Cheryl Dunlop, and the rest of the Moody Press team, and my editor and friend, Philip Rawley.

INTRODUCTION

On January 31, 1996, Pastor Joe Wright of the Wichita Central Christian Church was asked to give the invocation for the Kansas state legislature. According to radio commentator Paul Harvey, this is what Pastor Wright prayed:

Heavenly Father, we come before You today to ask Your forgiveness and to seek Your direction and guidance. We know that Your Word says, "Woe be to those who call evil as good," and that's exactly what we have done. We have lost our spiritual equilibrium, and we've inverted our values. We confess that we have ridiculed the absolute truth of Your Word in the name of moral pluralism. We have worshiped other gods and called it multi-culturalism, and we've endorsed perversion and called it alternative lifestyle. We have exploited the poor and called it a lottery. We have neglected the needy and called it self-preservation. We have rewarded laziness and called it welfare.

Father, in the name of choice, we've killed our unborn, and then in the name of right-to-life we've executed the abortionist. We have neglected to discipline our children and called it building esteem. We have abused power and called it political savvy. We have coveted our neighbors' possessions and called it taxes. We have polluted the air with profanity and pornography and called it freedom of expression.

We have ridiculed the time-honored values of our forefathers and called it enlightenment. Search us, O God. Know our hearts today. Try us, and show us any wickedness in us. And then cleanse us from every sin, and set us free!

Guide and bless these men and women who have been sent here by the people of Kansas and who have been ordained by You to govern this great state. Grant them Your wisdom to rule, and may their decisions direct us to the center of Your will. I ask it in the name of Your Son, the Living Savior, Jesus Christ. Amen.

What took place after this eloquent, biblically based prayer was an outburst of indignation. Many of the Kansas legislators stormed out, while others angrily condemned the prayer as blasphemous, ignorant, overbearing, and an attempt at political subversion.

The governor of Kansas mounted the podium and apologized for the pastor's inappropriate use of prayer to make political statements. Local and national talk shows took up the debate of the legitimacy or illegitimacy of the prayer.

This incident is a clear illustration of how far our American culture has wandered from its moral moorings. There was a time when pastors and churches were sought out for moral guidance and critique by leaders at the community, state, and national level.

But today the Christian frame of reference is all too often either ridiculed, criticized, rejected outright, or simply ignored in the public square. And this is happening at the same time as acceptance for humanistic and non-Christian religious worldviews is growing.

It is the contention of this book that the hostile reception Pastor Wright received was not just the result of the failure of non-Christians to take the Person and Word of God seriously. It also reflects the Christian community's seeming inability to impact our culture for Christ at the deepest levels.

It is my contention that Christians have contributed to the spiritual decline of American culture. While we have done an admirable job of cursing the darkness, we have done a poor job of spreading the light.

While we have talked about being the family of God, we have been a family in crisis unable to provide spiritual leadership to our unbelieving neighbors. Rather than being the church in the world, we have allowed the world to invade the church and help determine our thinking, actions, and lifestyle.

The price tag for this drive-through, "McChristian" spirituality has been weak Christians leading weak families, bringing about weak churches resulting in a weak nation. I believe the church's greatest need today is not for sinners to accept our worldview, but for us to accept our worldview and make it the modus operandi of our daily lives.

It is not until Christians take the lead that the culture will have something to follow. It is our failure to live out our faith in the marketplace that has kept us weak and ineffective in this culture, despite a staggering proliferation of evangelical books, tapes, television programs, conferences, conventions, churches, and schools from kindergartens to seminaries.

How can we have all this Christian activity and yet have all this cultural mess? As we used to say, there's a dead monkey on the line somewhere!

I'm convinced that until Christians change, the culture won't change, no matter how much we lament the violence and immorality and long for the good old days. To conduct business as usual in the church is to aid and abet the continued downward spiral of America.

Are Christians destroying America? In many ways the answer is yes. Can Christians save America? Not by our own works, but by the power and grace of God, we can be instruments in His hands to salvage our culture. If we don't, I don't see anyone else around able to do the job.

I pray that this book will help Christians accept our share of the responsibility for the demise of our nation and challenge us to begin taking responsibility for the aggressive spiritual restoration of our decaying society.

CHAPTER 1

A CASE OF SPIRITUAL AIDS

Anyone who can read a newspaper or operate a TV remote control knows that something is slowly destroying America. Some kind of hideous virus, some sort of deadly disease, is racing through our cultural bloodstream.

What are the symptoms of this sickness? A society that legally authorizes the killing of its young before they are even born. A generation of young men drowning in their own blood on the streets of our cities. A culture that values personal profit over justice and mercy. And an entertainment establishment doing all it can to promote our moral bankruptcy.

But instead of becoming mired in the symptoms, I prefer to search for a solution.

If I were an attorney, I might search for answers in judicial reform. I might insist that our justice system be overhauled to make it more even-handed and see to it that the lady holding those scales of justice stops peeking out from behind her blindfold.

If I were an economist, I would search for new ways to carve up the American pie so that everyone would get a fair slice. Perhaps we could relieve the frustration of the have-nots who feel trapped and victimized by economic disparity.

If I were a politician, I would chase after legislative solutions. I would try to rewrite laws to make them more just and redraw political boundaries to assure equal representation.

However, I am not an attorney, an economist, or a politician. And while all of the solutions I just proposed have some validity, I must look elsewhere for the diagnosis and cure of America's deadly disease, because I am, in my heart of hearts, a preacher of the good news of Jesus Christ. Therefore, like all Christians, I have access to a perspective on the problem that is not universally recognized: the infallible Word of God.

When you bring the Bible to bear on the crises facing our country, you don't have to spend much time with the television or the newspaper. We have a sure word from God.

A BIBLICAL DIAGNOSIS

When you pass America's problems through the filter of faith and the screen of Scripture, it becomes painfully clear that the problems spring from a common cause, from a spiritual problem deep within society's system. In fact, the symptoms of our society look like the beginning of AIDS.

When a human body is afflicted with AIDS, the immune system is incapacitated. It can't fight off the bacteria and viruses attacking the body, so even fairly minor ailments can mushroom into life-threatening diseases.

Our society has fallen victim to a disease I call "spiritual AIDS." The bacteria of sin and the virus of lawlessness are running rampant through our cultural system without being seriously challenged, because society's immune system, the church, has been badly weakened. Our country's ills are not merely the result of corrupt politicians, militant feminists, or hateful racists. Our troubles can be traced directly to ineffective Christians.

The tragedy today is not that sinners sin; that's what they're expected to do, since mankind is born in sin and shaped in iniquity (Psalm 51:5; Ephesians 2:1–3). The real tragedy is that the church as a whole has failed to act as salt and light in this society.

When Christians fail to live out their faith, then their families fail to function as Christian families. Failed Christian families make for ineffective churches. And ineffective churches make no impact on the communities they have been called to serve and change.

You can find a church building on nearly every corner in urban America, yet these communities are being systematically destroyed by violence as people languish in poverty and despair. It's obvious that the church is not having the influence that God created and intended it to have.

If we who name the name of Jesus Christ are going to do something for America, judgment must begin with the household of God (1 Peter 4:17). Let me suggest a few of the viruses afflicting our society that the church needs to attack.

The Virus of Selfishness

We live in a world where people's first priority is looking out for number one. We can't solve marriage problems because husbands and wives care more for themselves than they do for each other. We can't solve community crises because many ethnic and special-interest groups care only for their own agendas. We can't put an end to deficit spending because many politicians insist that the cuts take place in somebody else's district.

Now don't misunderstand. It's not necessarily selfish to be concerned for your own well-being. Selfishness is making someone else pay the price for your well-being. If I want a new VCR or compact disk player, for example, that would not necessarily be selfish. However, if you have the VCR or disk player that I want, and I reach for the .45 pistol tucked into my belt and blow you away, that would be selfish.

That sounds ridiculous, and it is. But people lose their lives every day over some piece of merchandise. That kind of stuff can only happen in a culture where *things* have become more important than people.

When we apply a biblical diagnosis to the problem, the selfishness around us should not surprise us. Paul told Timothy that in the last days, people would be "lovers of pleasure rather than lovers of God" (2 Timothy 3:4). Our world is addicted to pleasure. For many, life is a constant quest for something that gives them that good feeling. And Satan is happy to oblige.

An insidious form of selfishness is polarizing the African-American community today as the gap widens between the underclass and the middle class. If upwardly mobile people and the poor don't work together, our communities are doomed. As long as we remain selfish we will remain divided, unable to move toward a common goal.

Unfortunately, too many selfish Christians are unwilling to invest in their families and their communities for the cause of Jesus Christ. Christians are succumbing to the selfishness about them, falling into the deadly trap of immediate gratification. Self*less* living must start with the church if it is to expand to the community.

The Virus of Racism

Like selfishness, the virus of racism develops and grows in the sinful heart.

When I came to Dallas Theological Seminary in 1972, my wife, Lois, and I visited a well-known Bible church. The pastor was one of my seminary professors. But some of the members let us know in no uncertain terms that we were not welcome as visitors or members. The tragedy is that this was a Bible church, known for its teaching and preaching of the Word of God.

How can we overcome racism in the world when, as one well-known Christian leader observed, 11:00 Sunday morning is the most segregated hour in America? If suburban and urban churches can't join together for the kingdom, why should we expect the unregenerate to get along?

The church in South Africa has been a major player in the racist system of apartheid. The theology of the Dutch Reformed Church has perpetuated the myth of racial superiority, effectively suppressing the freedom of millions of people. But lest we be too quick to point an accusing finger, remember that there is a similar skeleton in America's closet. The church held its tongue in 1857 when the Dred Scott decision was rendered by the Supreme Court, declaring people of African descent in America to be not persons, but property.

Slavery in this country was allowed to exist because it was theologized. The so-called doctrine of Ham asserted that Canaan, the son of Ham (believed to be the father of black people), was cursed to be a servant for the rest of his days because Ham saw his father Noah's nakedness after the Flood (Genesis 9:20–25).

Through misguided theological maneuvering and horrendous hermeneutics, many whites used this teaching to support the conclusion that all blacks were cursed—a proposition that has no support in Scripture and no place in the body of Christ.

But to this day, the church in America has maintained a mentality of white superiority over blacks. And blacks have often responded with an unbiblical Afro-centrism, which at times rejects anything white despite its value or veracity. As I often say, black is only beautiful if it is biblical. And white is only right if it agrees with Holy Writ.

The Virus of Classism

James writes, "Do not hold your faith in our glorious Lord Jesus Christ with an attitude of personal favoritism" (James 2:1).

Many Christians look right past the color issue only to stumble in the area of class distinctions. Class distinctions can separate believers of the same race, in the same neighborhoods, and even in the same churches.

James hits this issue head-on. He describes a man who walks into church wearing a gold ring and fine clothes. I can imagine this guy in his Avanti suit, twirling the key to his $70,000 sports car on his finger as he walks down the aisle.

The deacons spot him at once, realize that we're talking big donor, and usher the man to the best seat in the house. At the same time, a beggar walks into the building and is forced to take a seat in the last row, hidden behind a post.

Those who make such distinctions are called "judges with evil motives" (James 2:4). Many upscale blacks have no problem coexisting with whites. However, they want nothing to do with their brothers from the inner city where they grew up. But how can we look down on others because their paychecks are smaller, their clothes are less stylish, or their homes are less elegant? Everything we have is by God's grace. Apart from His goodness, we are all one payday away from the streets.

Whenever I go home to Baltimore, I go past a fast-food restaurant where, as a child, I was not allowed to eat in the dining room because I was black. The restaurant was pleased to take my money at the take-out window, but eating in was definitely out.

Though I didn't fully understand it at the time, I was still angered by that restriction. Thank God for my father, who interpreted everything spiritually. "Boy," he would say, "you're a child of the King. If they don't want royal blood in their restaurant, then don't go in there."

GOD'S JUDGMENT

James 2:13 says, "Judgment will be merciless to one who has shown no mercy." God's judgment is the only outcome for a society suffering from spiritual AIDS unless there is a revival and turning to God.

I am convinced the Civil War, which cost more American lives than any other war in our history, was the result of this country's failure to abolish slavery.

The undoing of Adolf Hitler was not the result of Britain's stiff upper lip or America's "Yankee spirit." God responded to Hitler's cruelty and hatred by putting the "master race" in its place.

Leviticus 25 describes the Year of Jubilee. In the Year of Jubilee, Jews in bondage to their countrymen for any reason (i.e., slaves) would be set free. Ancestral land was restored to those who had been forced to sell out due to poverty. In other words, those in need among the people of God were given freedom and economic opportunity.

The primary job of caring for those in need was never intended to be a function of government. Can you imagine Paul going to Caesar and asking for a federal grant to fix the problems of poverty within the church in Jerusalem? God called the church to care for its own and set an example of compassion that compels the rest of society to do the same.

America is ripe for judgment by God because it perpetuates a system of injustice, inequality, and lack of concern for the poor or defenseless. Can God find among us enough serious saints to revive His spiritual immune system and hold back His judgment? A strong church is the only way to counteract the spiritual AIDS which threatens the very survival of our culture.

WHERE THE CHURCH HAS FALLEN SHORT

But where did we fall short? Do we not have enough money or programs or buildings or leaders?

No, none of these really explains why the church is failing as God's immune system to keep the viruses of sin from destroying America. Our problem goes much deeper than these outward things, and we'll get to that later.

But I want to illustrate one result of our problem before I

describe the problem. One big result of the church's failure is that the world doesn't take us seriously anymore.

Not long ago, the city of Dallas asked me to come and speak to a task force of business, civic, and educational leaders on ethics. But they didn't want to include God in the discussion. I told them that's crazy. Ethics are impossible without absolute standards. And if you're going to have absolute standards, you have to have an absolute base—God.

This didn't play downtown. I will not be needed to speak on this issue in the arenas of power. God has been dismissed because His church has been dismissed in the public square—except for a harmless invocation, of course.

So those in power dismiss God, and then they try every which way to address the problems that are destroying us. The same is true of people on the personal level. People don't understand that if they don't get to the root, they will never fix the problem.

When people refuse to deal with the root of society's problems, which is spiritual, all they have left to deal with are the symptoms of the problem. I look at this issue in depth in chapter 3, so I'll leave it there for now.

Now as to the problems plaguing the church today, I find a perfect parallel in the situation in ancient Israel as described in chapter 15 of 2 Chronicles:

For many days Israel was without the true God and without a teaching priest and without law. . . . In those times there was no peace to him who went out or to him who came in, for many disturbances afflicted all the inhabitants of the lands. Nation was crushed by nation, and city by city, for God troubled them with every kind of distress. (vv. 3, 5–6)

These verses draw a picture of tremendous spiritual and social chaos, the breakdown of a society. And the stunning thing is that *God* was the cause of Israel's distress, not the sinners in that culture or the devil.

Why was God causing distress? Verse 3 gives us three reasons. Three crucial things were missing in the national life of Israel.

God Was Missing

The first thing missing was "the true God." The writer didn't say the Israelites no longer believed in God. He didn't say temple attendance was down. The sacrificial fires at the temple were smoking. But a correct view of God was lost.

The Israelites wanted a convenient God they could control and knock around. But if you have a God you can control, then you're god, not Him. Any god you can boss around isn't the true God. If your god adjusts to you, you don't have the true God.

A lot of what is done in God's name today has nothing to do with the God of the Bible. Israel didn't want the true God. Neither does our culture.

Sure, the world wants a nice little prayer before their meetings, but they don't want to hear about the true God. I'm afraid that sometimes the church isn't very interested in the true God either, because we have our own agenda. But any time the church fails to let God be God in its midst, we are helping to reinforce our culture's false view of God as a harmless deity who doesn't need to be taken seriously.

God's Teachers Were Missing

The second problem in Israel was a loss of teaching priests. Again, the text doesn't say there were no priests. They had just stopped teaching the truth. They traded enlightenment for entertainment. The people came to be entertained, and the priests obliged.

Don't get me wrong. There's nothing wrong with enjoying worship. There's nothing wrong with celebrating God, with expressing our emotions in worship. There is a place for that. But emotion is never to replace truth.

There was an absence of preachers who were true to the word of God. See, if you're going to know the true God, then you need a preacher who will give you the truth about God. The moment I leave the Bible, I am not a true preacher. I'm not smart enough—and neither is any other preacher—to tell anybody how to live without the Book.

Have you ever wondered how we can have all those churches on all those corners with all those preachers and all those choirs and all those deacons and all those ministries—and still have all this mess? There's a dead monkey on the line somewhere. The truth must be missing.

Someone will say, "Well, I didn't like that sermon." Wrong response. The issue is whether it was true, not whether it was popular. Politicians need to be popular. Preachers need to tell the truth.

God's Law Was Missing

When a culture has a false view of God built on bad information, God begins to remove the restraint of His law and evil begins to grow unbridled. In the rapid deterioration of our culture today, you and I are witnessing the reality that God is removing more and more of His restraint.

Even sinners who respect God won't do certain things. But once God is removed from a culture because of the failure of the church, then the standard for a society is gone, and God becomes our worst enemy and our worst nightmare.

When the rule of God's law is missing, chaos replaces community. It is impossible to have order and structure in society without God.

Ungodly people in our culture want to intimidate the church into silence so they can rule by chaos. They don't want any divine standard to which they must be held accountable. So the church becomes intimidated rather than standing for God and for the truth.

But when God leaves a society, hope goes with Him. As long as you have God, you always have hope. He's the one thing you can bank on. If God is still in the picture, it's not over until it's over.

Even if circumstances collapse, God will keep you. As long as God is front and center in a culture, there's hope. But when God is pushed out to the outskirts of town, when He's confined to the "loop" around the city, hope is gone. Just like people and their taxes go to the suburbs, God goes to the spiritual suburbs and the culture deteriorates.

Actually, there is a law at work in our culture—the law of unrighteousness. It has become so strong that it almost seems as natural as the law of gravity. If you're going to buck the law of gravity, you'd better have a law more powerful than gravity going for you. The law of gravity can be "bucked" by the law of aerodynamics in flight.

In the same way, the law of unrighteousness can be bucked by the law of God if the church will power up the engine of God and start soaring. If we don't, this plane called American culture is going down—and we'll crash with it, because we're on board.

THE BREAKDOWN OF SOCIETY

Israel was minus a proper view of God, the teaching of His truth by the priests, and the restraint of His law. No wonder there was great turmoil in the land, as we saw above in 2 Chronicles 15:5–6. Let's talk about what was going on.

Social Chaos

"There was no peace to him who went out or to him who came in, for many disturbances afflicted all the inhabitants" (v. 5). That sounds like a high crime rate.

"Nation was crushed by nation, and city by city" (v. 6a). What a picture of conflict on both the local and the international level. Wars and urban conflict marred Israel.

But what I want you to notice is the end of verse 6: "For God troubled them with every kind of distress." In other words, God was behind the chaos in the society. He identified Himself as the responsible party.

Here is a crucial principle we so often miss. If God is your problem, only God is your solution. If God is the One who is ticked off, you had better assuage His anger.

I once went to Africa with Dr. Sonny Acho, a member of our pastoral staff in Dallas and a native of Nigeria. As we traveled together he shared his burden for his homeland, discussing very frankly the graft and other things that weren't complimentary about life in Nigeria.

One day I asked Dr. Acho, "What do you think should be done about Nigeria's problems?"

His answer was very insightful. "This mess is spiritual. Nigeria is rich in natural resources, and yet it has never fully developed because there are spiritual decisions being made by people in leadership that don't allow God to make the country all that it could be." Dr. Acho was describing 2 Chronicles 15. Israel's problem was spiritual, even though the symptoms of it were social and political upheaval. Israel's problem was God, but there was no one around to say so and to point to God as the answer.

The Real Solution

Do I need to say that America's problem is with God? That's why we'll never see solutions until we deal with God. But it's easier to blame the devil for our troubles.

See, verse 6 is surprising because it's not what you would expect to read. You would expect to read, "for Satan troubled them with every kind of distress." When you see disturbances in the land, you would expect somebody to say, "The devil is messing up America." The devil is busy, for sure, but he isn't our real problem.

To put it another way, when God is forsaken, unrighteousness dominates. When God is included, righteousness dominates. When God is left at the loop of the city instead of being brought downtown, we experience His judgment rather than His blessing, and deterioration sets in.

Now here's where the church could be making all the difference if we were really on top of things spiritually. The unregenerate don't know that God is their problem and their only solution, so they go around trying to fix problems using earthly means and earthly wisdom.

But we, the people of God, know that you can't use human, physical, secular means to bring about spiritual solutions. In 2 Corinthians 10:4, Paul writes: "The weapons of our warfare are not of the flesh, but divinely powerful for the destruction of fortresses."

We are supposed to offer a whole different approach, a whole different solution. We know the first issue that must be addressed is, What is God's approach to solving this problem? We as the people of God are called to bring the presence of God to a society that desperately needs Him.

So what are we doing using the same feeble, human approaches to our problems that the world uses?

God has made it unmistakably clear that He must be preeminent. He must be brought downtown in a culture if that culture would be preserved. But when a culture leaves God out, it deteriorates. God will always judge the culture that ignores Him.

That's why the Bible says, "Righteousness exalts a nation, but sin is a disgrace to any people" (Proverbs 13:34). The church has let the world marginalize God. Don't blame the schools for going downhill if righteous parents are never involved with the PTA. Their absence means the unrighteous can now dominate.

Don't blame the government for deteriorating if the church hasn't spoken up for righteousness in the public arena. We are the ones who take God to the culture. If we sit back and let the unrighteous dominate, they will control our lives. It is our role to bring God to the culture so that righteousness will pervade and God's blessing will be on the culture.

WHERE TO GO FROM HERE

So what is the church to do? Well, let's go back to our text in 2 Chronicles 15 and pick up verse 4: "In their distress they turned to the Lord God of Israel, and they sought Him, and He let them find Him."

Start Looking Up

That last line is critical. See, it is always God's prerogative when He is to be found and when He steps back and lets a society hit bottom. Israel didn't seek God until they were in distress. God will let you hit bottom, land flat on your back, if that's the only way you will be ready to look up.

Our society is going down. Our culture is collapsing. But we're still not looking up. And until we do, we'll keep going down.

That's where the church comes in. The church must penetrate the culture with the message, "You're going down, but look up. In your distress, cry to the Lord. Seek Him, and He will let you find Him."

It's not that God is playing hide-and-seek with America. He is wondering how long it will take us to look up, how long it will take us to come to Him. He's there, but we can't see Him until we look up.

Remain Faithful

You say, "But wait a minute, Tony. Suppose our culture

refuses to seek God. Suppose the people running our crumbling cities won't look up. Suppose even the church doesn't do what it's supposed to do. What about me?" God has a word for you. "But you, be strong and do not lose courage, for there is reward for your work" (2 Chronicles 15:7). That's good news for you. Even if nobody else goes with God, you go. Even if nobody else puts Him front and center, you put Him front and center, because He's going to take care of you.

I once knew a committed believer whose wife hated God and hated him and made life miserable for him. But he told her, "I am not going to leave you. I am going to love you and stay with you. If you choose to reject me and reject God, then I'll let you leave.

"But I'm going to hang in there and ask God to give me the strength when I can't take it anymore, and give me the love when I can't love anymore."

Well, she made it even worse for him. He prayed, "Lord, I deliver my wife into Your hands. I can't take it anymore, but she is in Your hands." He woke up the next morning, turned over, touched her, and she was dead.

You were probably expecting me to say that she got saved or she repented or something like that. God will save you if you let Him save you. But He'll judge you if He has to.

We have to make a choice. I like the way Joshua put it. "I don't know what the rest of you are going to do, but as for me and my house, we will serve the Lord, because we want His blessing" (Evans paraphrase of Joshua 24:15).

Satan is loose. He's wreaking havoc all around us. We can't control what everybody else does, but it's clear what the church needs to do. We need to serve the Lord.

We're not perfect. We're going to make mistakes. We're going to fail. But when we stumble, we're going to help each other up and keep on trucking for the Lord.

HOW LONG?

Billy and his sister Sally went to their grandparents' farm for the weekend. The grandfather had an old slingshot. He showed Billy how to shoot the slingshot, then told him to go into the woods and try it out. So the boy picked out a tree, but he kept missing it. He got frustrated and tired.

On his way back to the house, Billy saw one of his grandfather's ducks. So he decided to try the slingshot once more. Of course, he hit the duck in the head and killed it. He quickly grabbed it and buried it, but when he looked up, he saw Sally looking at him. She had seen the whole thing.

As they entered the house, Billy said, "Sh. Don't say anything."

Grandma said, "Sally, you need to wash the dishes."

Sally replied, "Oh, Billy would be glad to wash them for you today."

She went over to Billy and whispered, "Remember the duck." So he washed the dishes.

Later, Grandpa said, "Billy, let's go fishing. Sally, you stay here and cook dinner with Grandma."

But Sally replied, "Billy doesn't like to fish. I do. Besides, Billy is the cook in the family, aren't you, Billy?"

Billy said glumly, "Yeah, I love to cook." So Sally went fishing, and Billy stayed behind.

After dinner Grandma said, "Sally, it's time to clean up."

But Sally replied, "Billy would be glad to clean up. He loves to do it."

But this time Billy cried out, "No more! No more! Grandpa, I killed your duck."

His grandfather looked at him and said, "I know. I was looking out the window when you shot the duck. I just wanted to see how long you were going to let Sally make you her slave."

God wants to know, "Church, how long are you going to let the devil make you his slave? How long are you going to let him run the show and intimidate you and boss you around and destroy your society?"

What we have to do is stand up and say, "Yes, Father, I killed the duck. I know You saw me, so I confess. Now Satan, get off my back. I'm going to serve God."

That's what we need today, a church that is not going to let anyone or anything get in the way of serving God and standing up for heaven. We'll talk about how to be that kind of church in the chapters ahead.

CHAPTER 2

WHEN SAINTS LOSE THEIR SALTINESS

When you see a culture that's deteriorating, look closer and you will probably see a people of God who have withdrawn from the culture and turned it over to the unrighteous to rule. Consider:

When Christians began abandoning inner-city and urban neighborhoods, taking their skills, resources, and moral influence with them, those neighborhoods deteriorated.

When Christians left the public school system, moral values were systematically erased until they became almost illegal to teach.

When Christians vacated the media, then a spiritual approach to defining everything we hold dear went with them.

When Christians decided they ought to get out of politics, then righteous political decisions left with them.

These realities are magnified in minority communities. One of the beauties of integration is that minorities won the right to live anywhere they want. But one downside has been that much of the expertise and moral consciousness of the minority community left the inner cities, leaving behind an absence of the models who are desperately needed to give a community vision and stability.

God's people have been called to penetrate society. Don't get me wrong: Evangelism is always first because without forgiveness of sins, anything else we give a person is temporary. We have been called first and foremost to win people to Christ.

But having given a person Christ for eternity, we must also give him Christ in history. We must give him hope in time. The absence of righteousness in our culture has everything to do with the absence of God's people penetrating the culture. When there is no yeast the bread stays flat, and when there is no Christian influence the culture stays flat.

OFFERING AN ALTERNATIVE

That's why one of my favorite words is *alternative*. To me it embodies what we as the people of God ought to be offering our culture, a divine option. The idea is that Christian lawyers, for example, are God's representatives in the bar association, so the bar gets to see what God looks like when God tries a case.

The same is true for all Christians, whether they are surgeons in the operating room or typists in the clerical pool. Penetrating culture means that we represent in the marketplace the interests of the kingdom of God, not only in the excellence of our work but in the testimony of our character.

Far too many of us are like the Susan B. Anthony dollar of a bygone day. The Anthony dollar failed to catch on, one of the primary reasons being that it looked and felt too much like a quarter. People couldn't tell the difference, so the Anthony dollar fell into disuse and was soon taken out of active circulation.

A lot of us Christians are like that. We are worth a dollar, but we look like a quarter and live like "chump change." We have all the glories of Calvary and all the privileges that come with belonging to God, but we don't spend well in the marketplace where people need to hear, see, and feel the reality of Christ.

Jesus had some important things to say about the church's proper role in the world. In Matthew 5:13–16, He gave the distilled essence of His teaching on the subject. I want to focus on the first portion of His metaphor: "You are the salt of the earth; but if the salt has become tasteless, how can it be made salty again? It is no longer good for anything, except to be thrown out and trampled under foot by men" (v. 13).

Jesus went on to use the metaphor of light to explain the effect His disciples should have on the world, and we'll talk a little bit about that later. But first let's deal with what it means to be salt and how we can maintain our saltiness.

THE SALT OF THE EARTH

Notice first that Jesus said we are the salt of the earth, not the salt of the salt shaker. No homemaker buys salt so her family can stare at it in the shaker during dinner. The whole point of salt is to leave the shaker and penetrate the meat.

Gathered in the Shaker

You may say, "Tony, that's so obvious it hardly needs to be mentioned." I'm not so sure. See, we Christians are often at our best when we're all gathered together in the "salt shaker" at church on Sunday.

It's easy to be salt in church because you've got all these other grains of salt around you. Other people like you are the only ones you have to contend with. There is no real opposition, no one to try to silence or ridicule you when you name the name of Jesus Christ.

Being salty only in church is like playing basketball by yourself. It's a can't-lose deal! But the test of our salt as Christians is what happens when we hit the decaying piece of meat called the world.

Daring Us to Be Salt

You knew I wouldn't get very far without mentioning the Dallas Cowboys. People don't pay top dollar to see the Cowboys huddle. They want to know what difference the huddle is going to make. They want to see whether, having huddled, the 'Boys can now score.

What Cowboys fans pay a lot of money to see is the answer to the question, What are you eleven guys going to do about those eleven guys on the other side of the ball daring you to execute in public the play you called in private?

Those defensive players are saying to the Cowboys by their menacing presence, "We dare you to penetrate our defense. Go ahead, just try it and see if we don't take your heads off."

The question on the field is not necessarily how exciting the play is, how good the play-caller is, or how good the other players are. The question is, Can the Cowboys get by eleven other men daring them to run a play?

This is the situation we are in when it comes to the world, the flesh, and the devil. They are daring us to do something. But that's OK, because Jesus told us to expect opposition. The thing is, the church is supposed to be calling the plays and controlling the game, not getting high about its huddle. But we're not moving the ball.

God didn't save you or me so we could sit, soak, and sour. He saved us to infiltrate and penetrate the world the way salt soaks into a piece of meat.

No One Else But Us

Now when Jesus said, "You are the salt of the earth," He put the word *you* in the emphatic position. This phrase could be accurately rendered, "You, *and nobody else but you*, are the salt of the earth." It's you and me, the church, plus nobody.

Why? Because the people of God are the only ones who have been endowed with the spiritual resources necessary to do God's work God's way.

That means it's not you and the government, for example. Now don't get me wrong. I just said that Christians' withdrawal from the political process has contributed to our problem. What I'm talking about here is the difference between involvement and the attitude that politics is the answer, that somehow our problems could be solved by the arrival of Air Force One.

Our elected officials are called by God to be servants, but politics is not the salt of the earth. You can't substitute any other earthly organization or group of people into Jesus' statement and come up with the salt of the earth. When Jesus told His disciples, "You and you alone are the salt of the earth," He meant it!

The Kingdom Agenda

Jesus is saying that His kingdom agenda cannot be held hostage to any human agenda. I love Joshua 5, where my man Josh was getting ready to go into battle:

He lifted up his eyes and looked, and behold, a man was standing opposite him with his sword drawn in his hand, and Joshua went to him and said to him, "Are you for us or for our adversaries?" He said, "No; rather I indeed come now as captain of the host of the Lord." And Joshua fell on his face to the earth, and bowed down. (vv. 13–14)

This tells you that Joshua's mama didn't raise any dummies. Joshua did his sentry thing: "Halt. Who goes there, friend or foe?" That's a good idea when you're about to go into battle.

But when the man replied, "You are confused. I am captain of the Lord's army. I did not come to take sides; I came to take over," Joshua prostrated himself on the ground.

God will never allow His agenda to be held hostage to the agendas of men. That is why the church must always rise above current opinion or fashion in politics or anything else.

We are to inform culture from a biblical perspective, not just choose sides. To say it another way, God is neither a Republican nor a Democrat. He doesn't ride the backs of donkeys or elephants.

That means no matter how we vote, when we go into the booth and when we come out of the booth we should live kingdom. We should reflect a divine frame of reference. If we really want to change our communities, we should just get Christians to be Christians.

People say, "Boy, this world would sure be better off if sinners didn't sin." Well, that may be true, but what else do you expect sinners to do? For people who are born in sin and shaped in iniquity, sin is natural.

Some can do it better than others, but all sinners sin. It's their job description. Our problem isn't that sinners sin. Our problem is that the saints who are not supposed to be like sinners are often more sinful than the sinning sinners who sin. Instead of reversing this agenda, we support it by our compromise.

Our problem is that we as the people of God aren't living up to *our* job description. We have allowed the world to secularize us. So we have Christian businesspeople with no ethics in the marketplace, Christian spouses who renege on their vows, and Christian ministers who put financial gain above feeding God's flock.

And adding to the problem is that we have Christians who

know Christians living like that, but won't lovingly confront them so they can repent and get their lives on target. If we don't love each other enough to hold each other responsible, nobody else will. Why? Because we and nobody else are the salt of the earth.

The Preserving Quality of Salt

Salt was a very important commodity in Jesus' day, even more than it is today. In fact, if you have parents or grandparents who live in the country they may still salt down their food. The reason is, of course, that salt is a preservative. It's designed to repel bacteria and preserve food.

That was crucial in Jesus' day because they didn't have refrigeration. Salt was so valuable in the ancient world that it was often traded ounce for ounce with gold. Roman soldiers were paid in salt. In fact, the word *salary* is derived from the concept of paying for work with salt.

If a Roman soldier didn't do his job, he would not get all of his salt. That's where we get the phrase "so-and-so is not worth his salt" if he doesn't do a good day's work.

Believers are going to have to become worth their salt. We are going to have to live up to Jesus' expectations if this world is going to be preserved from decay. There's no one else around to fill the job description of being the salt of the earth.

You can see a graphic example of this truth in action in the story of Sodom and Gomorrah, the twin cities of the plains that were filled with every form of wickedness.

God came to Abraham and said, "The outcry of Sodom and Gomorrah is indeed great, and their sin is exceedingly grave. I will go down now, and see if they have done entirely according to its outcry" (Genesis 18:20–21).

God was saying, "Abraham, the sins of those two cities are screaming for punishment. I'm going down to check things out. Then I'm going to destroy them."

But Abraham said, "God, You can't do that." Whenever you tell God He can't do something, you'd better know what you are talking about. So Abraham continued, "If You destroy the wicked, You will destroy the righteous too. Suppose You find fifty righteous people there. Would You kill those righteous people along with the wicked? That's not how the Judge of all the earth does things" (see vv. 23–25).

Do you get the picture here? Abraham's nephew Lot and his family lived in Sodom, and Abe didn't want to see the in-laws killed. He was adding up the number of people in Lot's family in his head, but he must have figured they had done some evangelism since he picked the number fifty.

So Abraham was asking God, "Will You spare these cities if You can find just a remnant, a down payment, a little group of people who are doing it Your way?"

We don't know how many people lived in Sodom, but fifty believers out of a city is not many. But that's all of the "salt" it would have taken to spare Sodom because God accepted Abraham's deal (v. 26).

In fact, God would have spared Sodom for a lot less salt than that. The remaining verses of Genesis 18 tell the incredible story of Abraham doing his Monty Hall thing, saying, "God, let's make another deal."

Apparently Abraham got to thinking about those fifty righteous people and realized he was a little high. So he came down to forty-five, forty, thirty, twenty, and finally ten people. God said, "Yes, if I can find ten people who are going to live My way, I'll save the culture. But don't ask again, because I have My minimum quota. Ten is as low as we go."

So why was Sodom destroyed? It wasn't destroyed just because the sinners were sinning, but because God couldn't find ten righteous people. He couldn't find a remnant that made the culture worth saving. The few believers weren't salty enough.

We know Lot was righteous because the angels warned him to flee Sodom (Genesis 19:15). Peter says Lot's righteous soul was "tormented day after day" by the unrighteousness of his neighbors in Sodom (2 Peter 2:8).

But Lot apparently suffered from the American disease of personal peace and affluence. He was into "my world and my life and my cattle and my business." Lot's influence was so invisible that when he went to warn his family to leave Sodom, his sons-in-law thought he was joking (Genesis 19:14).

Lot's two daughters and his wife went with him, but on their way out of town, Mrs. Lot started thinking about the Sodom Mall. Her heart was still in Sodom, so she looked back and became a pillar of salt (how ironic!) as God judged her. And the girls later seduced their father (vv. 30–38). They had been co-opted by the immorality of the culture.

If Lot had been salt to his family, that would have been at least six righteous people. And if each family member had won just one other person to the Lord, that would have been twelve. Abraham would have had his ten righteous people, and Sodom and Gomorrah might still be on the map.

So again, Sodom wasn't destroyed only because the sinners were sinning. It was destroyed because the saints were nowhere to be found. If we are going to preserve our communities, our cities, and ultimately our nation, we have got to get out of the shaker and onto the meat as the preservative.

The Thirst Salt Creates

Another thing salt does is create thirst. Once when I was at the airport, I sat down at a counter and ordered a Coke. The waitress said, "That will be one dollar." So I pulled out a dollar and gave it to her.

She came back with my Coke and something I did not order, a little bowl of peanuts and pretzels. I didn't ask for peanuts and pretzels. Neither was she charging me for peanuts and pretzels. There is only one reason she brought them to me. They are full of salt.

The waitress knew those snacks were irresistible. And she knew that when I began to chew on them, the salt would interact with my taste buds and dry out my mouth so that when I finished my Coke, I would reach back into my wallet, pull out another dollar, and say, "Hit me again, Sam!"—or, rather, Samantha.

She brought me peanuts and pretzels to make me thirsty so I would order again. People should find us and our impact so irresistible that they just have to chew on our lives. And when they chew, they should get so thirsty that when we offer them the living water, Jesus Christ, they will gladly gulp Him down!

Losing Your Saltiness

But look back at Matthew 5:13. Jesus said, "But if the salt has become tasteless, how can it be made salty again? It is no longer good for anything, except to be thrown out and trampled under foot by men."

This is an interesting phrase because Jesus is not saying that you can have "saltless salt." There is no such thing. Salt is a solid compound. The only thing that makes salt salt is the compound of sodium and chloride. If you extracted either element, what's left would not be salt. So believers cannot become "unsalt."

But we can become "tasteless" salt, and Jesus' phrase "trampled under foot by men" explains how it can happen. In ancient Israel, the homes had flat roofs. People would go up on the rooftop at night to relax or entertain friends or pray or whatever.

The Israelites held wedding receptions on their rooftops. Kids played on the roofs. So there was a lot of walking around on the roof. And sometimes as a roof got trampled upon, a hole would get punched in the roof and the rain would leak into the house. So they would have to patch the hole.

This was done by mixing the mineral gypsum with water, creating a paste, and then thickening it with salt. The mixture was put on the hole in the roof, and the sun would harden it to form a seal and keep the rain out of the house.

But the salt used this way wasn't good for anything else, because gypsum is bitter. The bitterness of the gypsum would overpower the saltiness of the salt, and the salt would lose its taste. It was good only as a roof sealant to be "trampled under foot."

That's a good description of contemporary Christianity. We've become so mixed up with the "gypsum" of this world's way of thinking and living that people can't taste the Christianity in the culture anymore.

So what is the world doing? Walking on us. The world doesn't take the church seriously. It knows we are no risk to them. Why? Because all we are going to do is cluster in our buildings a couple of times a week and not do much of anything when we leave.

THE LIGHT OF THE WORLD

Now I want to pick up the second of Jesus' metaphors in Matthew 5: "You are the light of the world," He told His disciples (v. 14).

The last time I checked, lights have one purpose: to shine. That's all they do. People say, "This world is dark." Well, we can expect the world to be dark. It's supposed to be unclarified in its direction because the world is not the light.

Nobody But Us Again

We are the light—and the construction in the original is the same here as we saw earlier. That is, *you* is in the emphatic position. So guess what? When it comes to giving light, it's Christians like you and me and nobody else!

Jesus likened us to "a city set on a hill [that] cannot be hidden" (v. 14b). Buildings in biblical days were often made of white limestone, which would reflect the light of the moon. So if you were traveling by night in those days, you would know you were near a city when you saw the reflection.

And since many cities in New Testament days were built on hills, their higher elevation and white limestone made them even more easily visible. God wants our representation of Him to be highly visible and unmistakably clear.

That's why we can't afford to hide our light under a basket (v. 15). It needs to be put up high so the beam can reach as far as possible. There is no room for "secret agent" Christians. We are not to be spiritual CIA covert operatives.

I'll never forget the time when the then-mayor of Dallas asked me to open a city council meeting in prayer. "Now, Dr. Evans," she said, "I would appreciate it if you would not use the name of Jesus, because we have a lot of different religions represented on the council and we don't want to offend anyone."

Now if you know me, you know we had a problem on our hands. I went to the council meeting and was introduced. Everyone bowed, and I started praying. "Father, the city council has asked that I open this meeting in prayer. You have already told me that there is only one mediator between God and men, the man Christ Jesus. So I can't accomplish what the council has asked me to accomplish without including Jesus.

"So, Father, first of all thank You for creating the people on this council, because if You had not created them, they would not be here today. And according to Your Word, everything that was made was made by Christ Jesus.

"And I thank You for creating government, which is an instrument of God according to Romans 13, a truth that was written by the apostle Paul, who met Jesus on the Damascus Road.

"Now, Father, if there are any council members here today who do not understand that Jesus was born of a virgin, lived a perfect life, died a substitutionary death, rose bodily from the dead, and is physically coming back again, would You please make that clear to them today? Bless them in their decision making. In Jesus' name. Amen."

No Apology Needed

Now please understand that I meant no disrespect to the mayor. But if homosexuals and others can openly flaunt their lifestyles without apologizing, then Christians should be willing to represent Jesus Christ without apology, regardless of the consequences.

Muslims aren't apologizing. They are handing out stuff on the street corners every week in our community. Everyone else is coming out of the closet. It's time for us to come out too.

What we need are people who are unapologetically Christian. Jesus said in Matthew 5:16, "Let your light shine before men in such a way that they may see your good works, and glorify your Father who is in heaven."

Making God Look Good

Glorify means "to show off." It means to make God look good, to display His perfections to the world.

I hate to do this, but God gives preachers wives for illustrations. If I say to Lois, "We have to go somewhere at 7:00 P.M.," at 6:00 she goes before the mirror of her glory. She sits down and brings out all her makeup and stuff, and she is transformed before my very eyes.

Now it's time to go. The car is in the garage and the garage is attached to the house, so Lois doesn't have to go outside and mess up her glory. But wouldn't you know it, as soon as we get in the car she pulls down the visor to check on her glory.

We finally get to where we are going, but Lord have mercy if there is a mirror in the elevator! Lois is checking on her glory. Then when we arrive, she runs into some people she knows. If they are women, they admire each others' glory and whisper to each other if that glory has become marred with a hair out of place.

Now I'd better stop right there. But you get the point. Glory means to show God off, to advertise Him and bring Him out in public, to make Him look good by the way we act.

Glorifying God Through Good Works

Jesus said the way we glorify God is by our good works. Sinners can do things like build hospitals and orphanages. They can feed the poor and on and on. But sinners cannot do good works in the biblical sense. What's the difference between good things and good works? Good works are God's goals achieved God's way for God's glory.

Paul says in Ephesians 2:10, "We are His workmanship, created in Christ Jesus for good works, which God prepared beforehand so that we would walk in them." Good works are God-created works. They aren't things we make up on our own.

So where do you find God-created works? In God's Word: "All Scripture is inspired by God and profitable for teaching, for reproof, for correction, for training in righteousness; so that the man of God may be adequate, equipped for every good work" (2 Timothy 3:16–17).

Paul was telling Timothy that scriptural good works are supposed to separate us from the world. We not only have biblical goals, but we also use biblical means to reach them because we use the Bible. When Christians try to do God's work the way the world does its work, we just confuse the world even more and dim the light of our witness.

When my younger son, Anthony, was small, we got him a bicycle for Christmas. I pulled out that thick assembly manual, looked at it, and said, "I'm not reading all this. I have an earned doctorate. I can put this bike together."

Hours later I had only the handlebars on, so my wife came to the door and said helpfully, "Honey, why don't you read the directions?"

She was really saying, "Maybe the bicycle manufacturer

knows more about this than you do." I swallowed my pride, pulled out the directions, and the bike was done in forty-five minutes.

See, you can save a lot of time if you will consult the manufacturer. Since God is the Manufacturer of life, the family, the church, and the government, how do we think we can put our puny Christian brains together and come up with something that's better than what the Manufacturer gave us?

My philosophy of ministry is simple. I believe there is a biblical answer for everything. So if you came to me and said, "I have a messed-up life. What should I do?" I would open my Bible to show you God's Word on how to put your messed-up life back together.

If you brought your family along and said, "We have a messed-up family. What should we do?" I would open my Bible and show you what God says about fixing your family.

I would do the same thing if the elders and deacons of our church came with a problem in the fellowship. And if the president called and said, "We've got a messed-up country. What should we do?" I would not jump to a new standard. I would do with him much like I did in my prayer before the Dallas city council.

I would point the president to Romans 13 and remind him that the Bible says government is a minister of God, and when government stops obeying God, it's chaos for society.

This is why the church has to get its act together. No one else is going to bring God's Word to bear in the public square. It doesn't do any good to have the answer if no one is asking you any questions.

But when the church is ready to glorify God, things happen like they did for a young man named Donald. Let me tell you about Donald. He stole $1,500 from his employer and got caught. The judge was going to lock Donald up for three years at a cost to the taxpayers of about $18,000 a year. Besides the cost, Donald would be going to prison where he would only learn how to become a better criminal. And his employer would never be repaid for his loss.

Well, we sent a group of men from our church to the judge and said, "Your Honor, if you will give Donald back to us, we will assign a man to be responsible for him, get him a job, and garnishee his wages to pay back his former employer.

"We will save taxpayers $18,000 a year and save the state of Texas a headache, because it doesn't have room for Donald in prison anyway. If you will give Donald back to us, we will bring you a brand-new kid in six months."

Well, the judge was happy to do that. So we put some men in Donald's life to influence him the right way, got him a job, garnisheed his wages, paid back the money he stole, saved the taxpayers money, and held him responsible. Six months later we took him back to the judge, who was astonished. Then we got a call from the judge: "Will you take twenty more like Donald?"

Donald is now a part of our church's ministry. He was my son's coach on the church baseball team. How did that happen? Because the church stepped in. And there's no reason we cannot duplicate that with other young people who have gone astray, because restitution is biblical (see Exodus 22:1–4).

Think of the people in the Bible who changed their cultures, people like Ezra, Nehemiah, Esther, and Daniel. Queen Esther "attained royalty for such a time as this" (Esther 4:14) and saved the lives of all the Jewish exiles in Persia simply because she decided to be God's salt and light in her world.

PRAYING FOR GOD'S GLORY

Glorifying our Father who is in heaven is what being salt and light is all about. It's interesting that in the same Sermon on the Mount, Jesus went on to teach us how to pray (Matthew 6:9–13). We call it the Lord's Prayer, but it's really the disciples' prayer. Let me show you what I mean.

Our Father. "I want to let You know that I know who You are. You are my Daddy."

Who is in heaven. "I want to let You know that I know where You live. You live in heaven, in the place of glory."

Hallowed be Your name. "Now that I know who You are and where You live, I want to let You know that I know I am supposed to honor Your name."

Your kingdom come. "Now in order for me to honor Your name, I'm going to have to redirect my whole life so that the result is the building of Your kingdom, not mine."

Your will be done, on earth as it is in heaven. "The only way I can help build Your kingdom is by making Your will, not mine, top priority in my life. Since Your will is already being accomplished in heaven, I'd better reflect that in what I do here on earth."

Give us this day our daily bread. "Now, Father, in order to hallow Your name, serve Your kingdom, and do Your will, You are going to give me the necessary carbohydrates, starches, fats, and proteins so I will have the energy to show You off today."

Forgive us our debts. "Forgive me for the sins I've done against You as I forgive those who have done sins against me, because I know that if I don't forgive those who have sinned against me, You won't forgive me of my sins against You.

"And if You don't forgive me of my sins against You, our fellowship is broken and You won't accept my hallowing of Your name, service for Your kingdom, or doing of Your will."

Do not lead us into temptation, but deliver us from evil. "Father, I know You won't lead me into anything I can't handle by Your power today, because if You lead me into something I can't handle, I'm going to embarrass Your name and Your kingdom and mess up Your will. So deliver me from the evil that surrounds me."

For Yours is the kingdom and the power and the glory forever. "Father, the reason I'm praying this way in the first place is that none of this has anything to do with making me look good. The kingdom, the power, and the glory belong to You and no one else forever. Amen."

The church needs to get on with the job of making God look good by being salt and light in society. We've tried the Democrats' way. We've tried the Republicans' way. It is high time that Christians tried it the kingdom way. When we do, the culture may either accept us or reject us. But one thing is certain: The culture will no longer ignore us.

CHAPTER 3

WHAT IN THE WORLD IS THE CHURCH?

D o you know why Jesus Christ didn't rapture us and take us to heaven the moment He saved us? He has an agenda on earth for us to fulfill on His behalf.

This agenda is called building His church and expanding His kingdom. And through the inspiration of the Holy Spirit, Christ has even given us a manual on how to build His church. This manual is called the book of Ephesians.

I want to take a survey of this incredible portion of Scripture as we seek to determine what the church is supposed to look and act like in the midst of a pagan society.

This is crucial for a number of reasons, not the least of which is that one of the primary things weakening America is the weakness of the church. Until we get our collective spiritual life in order, there isn't much use fussing about all the bad things going on out there in the world.

If the church that is designed to be the representative of Christ on earth is helping to destroy America by its weakness, the fault is not with its Founder. After his greeting, Paul tells us, "Blessed be the God and Father of our Lord Jesus Christ, who has blessed us with every spiritual blessing in the heavenly places in Christ" (Ephesians 1:3).

What a tremendous statement of power. Everything the church needs to do all that God expects of us has already been given to us. The verb *blessed* is in a tense that means it has already occurred. The church doesn't need anything new from God. We have already been blessed with everything we will ever need.

WHERE'S THE POWER?

Right away, that ought to raise a serious question in our minds. If the church is endowed by God with all we need to do our job, why does the church in America seem to be so weak? Why are we missing out on so much of God's power and doing so little to impact our nation for righteousness?

The Wrong Focus

I'd like to suggest two possibilities. The first is that we don't understand the underlying spiritual cause of the problems we face. Ephesians 6:12 is one of the key verses of the book: "For our struggle is not against flesh and blood, but against the rulers, against the powers, against the world forces of this darkness, against the spiritual forces of wickedness in the heavenly places."

One of the things Satan wants to do is get us flesh-and-blood oriented and cause us to focus on the wrong side of the equation. Let me give a very practical example of what I'm talking about.

I believe one reason crime is epidemic in America is that we are shedding innocent blood as a society through abortion. Crime is a spiritual issue. There's a cause-effect relationship between spiritual breakdown and crime.

Therefore, we need to ask the question, What are the spiritual issues behind the problems that are tearing our nation apart? That's the church's calling, to deal with the spiritual root of problems. If we only deal with their physical expression, we'd better keep on building more prisons.

The Wrong Realm

A second reason the church may not be benefiting from all of our spiritual blessings is that we have forgotten where they are located. Ephesians 1:3 says they are found "in the heavenly places." We read about them again in Ephesians 6:12. So the question is, Where are these heavenly places?

Well, if we are battling Satan and his forces in the heavenly places, then we can't be talking about the traditional understanding of heaven. Satan doesn't operate from the throne room of God. And it's not an earthly location, because Satan is the "prince of the power of the air" (Ephesians 2:2).

I think the heavenly places Paul is talking about are a realm more than a location. They are the sphere of spiritual influence and spiritual warfare, where the "spiritual control knobs" of the universe are found.

Let me illustrate it this way. Think about Capitol Hill in Washington, D.C. That's the place where Congress is located, the site of its deliberations.

But as we all know, Congress is much more than a place. It's not just a building or a body of men and women. Congress represents political power. It's a realm where power and influence are wielded, ideological battles are fought, and decisions are made.

The two political parties in Congress represent two philosophies of government that are basically opposed to each other. Each party seeks to gain control of Congress and get its candidate elected to the presidency. And the party that is out of power often seeks to undermine and thwart the ruling party's agenda.

That's exactly what is happening in heavenly places. The kingdom of light and the kingdom of darkness are at war with one another. But even though the opposition kingdom can cause some havoc, Jesus has already won control of the House of Representatives, the Senate, and the White House!

If our blessings are in the heavenly places and our warfare is there too, guess where the church is going to have to be successful in order to get those blessings? In the heavenly places. That means fighting earthly battles alone won't get the job done.

THE CHURCH'S TASK: TO COMPLETE CHRIST

Part of the church's calling is to bring spiritual answers and spiritual resources to bear on the issues of life. The goal toward which the church is moving is "the summing up of all things in

Christ, things in the heavens and things on the earth" (Ephesians 1:10).

God's goal is that Jesus Christ will be seen as the owner of all things and as Head of the church. So in Ephesians 1:22–23, Paul says: "And [God the Father] put all things in subjection under [Christ's] feet, and gave Him as head over all things to the church, which is His body, the fullness of Him who fills all in all."

Even though all things are in subjection under the feet of Jesus Christ, not all things have yet experienced His rule because He has not yet taken His kingdom. So we can say that although Christ's rule is undisputed, He has not yet been given to the "all things" over which He is Ruler. In this age, He has only been given to the church. Only the church has Christ.

Completing Christ's Person

So what is the church's function? To be the body of which Christ is the Head; to be the completion of Christ the way the head needs a body to complete it.

You say, "Now wait a minute. How can Jesus Christ be incomplete?" Well, He is certainly not incomplete in His essence. He is fully God. But He is incomplete in function. You have to distinguish between the two, and we'll do that as we go along.

The human body is Paul's favorite analogy for the church. What is the job of your body? It only has one job: to fulfill the dictates of your head. That's the only thing your body is supposed to do.

When your brain says move your arm, you move your arm. When your brain says walk, you walk. In fact, if your brain says one thing and your body does another, you need to see a doctor right away. Why? Because your body is supposed to obey your brain. The job of the church, which is the body of Christ, is to fulfill the dictates of our Head. That's it. That's all we are to be about.

But we have a problem, because we have more than one head in too many of our churches. We have two-headed monsters for churches. So when Jesus says, "Body, do this," some self-appointed extra head says, "Church, do that." And the body doesn't know which way to go.

The head is connected to the body by the neck. This is an

important link, because the head's ability to move the body is related to the quality of this connection. Christ's ability to function in history is related to His connection to His body. If there is a connection problem, then the Head will not achieve His goal because the body has redefined its reason for existence.

Notice the phrase with which Paul closes Ephesians 1. The body is "the fullness of Him who fills all in all" (v. 23). If the church is Christ's fullness, that means He's not full without the church.

Jesus is not complete in His function without the church because we are to carry out His program. That's why He could tell His disciples that, after He ascended, those who believed in Him would do even "greater works" than the works He did while on earth (John 14:12).

Greater in what way? Well, greater in that there was a lot of stuff Jesus did not pull off when He was in the flesh because He was only active in ministry for a few years. Even though Jesus is God and as such is omnipotent, He voluntarily limited the use of His divine attributes while on earth.

Jesus didn't travel to every corner of the earth with the gospel when He was here—but the members of His body can! And since His purpose is that we take the gospel to every person and reflect His sovereign rule in every aspect of society, we complete Christ's purpose when we carry out His orders in every sphere of life where we live, work, and play.

But how can the church be the fullness of Him who already "fills all in all"? Remember, we just said Christ has been made Ruler over everything. But how is He going to get to the everything over which He is Ruler? Through His body, the church.

Practically, what that means is that as the church grows and expands, the authority, lordship, presence, and power of Jesus Christ should be expanding with it. Christ should be seen in the culture as people take Him from the church back into their neighborhoods and onto their jobs. People within the sphere of our influence should see Christ when they see us.

I think Christ is unwilling to let some of our churches grow because that would just mean more people out there to embarrass Him. The church is the fullness of Christ. We are supposed to infiltrate our world and influence it for Him, like the "fifth column" did in the Spanish Civil War.

This term was applied to rebel sympathizers within Madrid as the four columns of the Spanish army advanced on their enemy city. The fifth columnists were people within the city who practiced sabotage and guerrilla warfare from within to undermine the enemy. The term "fifth column" became a description of those who infiltrate a society from within on behalf of their cause.

That's what the church is supposed to be in the world. When the benediction is pronounced on Sunday, that's a signal to get started, not to relax until next Sunday. The benediction doesn't end anything. It starts something.

So why isn't more happening out there in the world? One reason is the church's warped theology, particularly our warped eschatology. Let me explain this one.

I believe the Bible teaches the imminent return of Jesus Christ. He could come back at any time. But this doctrine was never meant to produce inertia in the church.

Throughout Scripture, the return of Christ is a motivation to work, not to sit back and do nothing. That is, the second coming of Christ should motivate us to move out into the culture as a "fifth column" so that when He comes, we have already invaded the enemy's territory.

Some would argue, "This world is going to be destroyed some day. Why polish the brass on a sinking ship?" For the same reason you jog and take medicine, even though you know you're going to die some day. You don't say, "Well, since I'm going to die eventually, why bother trying to get better?" That's warped thinking. The church completes Christ's person in the world by functioning as His body. But even more significant, we "polish the brass" so the *people* we know aren't among what is destroyed when the earth goes up in flame.

Completing Christ's Presence

Let's look at another important truth about the church, this time in Ephesians 2:19–22:

So then you are no longer strangers and aliens, but you are fellow citizens with the saints, and are of God's household, having been built on the foundation of the apostles and prophets, Christ Jesus Himself being the corner stone, in whom the whole building, being fitted together, is growing into a holy temple in the Lord, in whom you also are being built together into a dwelling of God in the Spirit.

Here Paul calls the church a holy temple established upon the cornerstone of Jesus Christ. This is a significant allusion, because in the Old Testament the temple was a very special building. It was the hangout for the Shekinah glory, the visible manifestation of God.

In his prayer at the dedication of the temple he built, Solomon made it plain that no house can contain the presence of God (1 Kings 8:27). But the temple in Jerusalem was where God chose to manifest His glory, in the inner room called the "holy of holies," containing a chest called the ark of the covenant.

This chest wasn't just a piece of wood. It had a lid called the mercy seat, where the presence of God came down among His people. At the dedication ceremony of the temple, the Bible says the glory cloud of the Lord came and filled the house so that the priests had to stop ministering (1 Kings 8:10–11). In other words, God was now hanging out there.

That changed everything. Back in the days of the Exodus, the cloud had led the people of Israel in the wilderness. Along with the pillar of fire at night, the cloud was the visible presence of God among His people. It was their guide and protection from their enemies as long as they followed it.

The glory cloud in the temple meant that God was in the midst of His people. As long as they did things His way, His presence would be in their midst in such a way that all the nations of the world would know that God was with them.

But many years later, something happened that caused the glory cloud to leave the temple in Jerusalem. The prophet Ezekiel describes the progressive departure of God's glory from the temple due to the gross wickedness of the people of Israel (see Ezekiel chapters 8–10, especially 10:18).

Once God's glory had departed, there was only one word that could be written across the temple: the Hebrew word *Ichabod*, meaning "the glory has departed" because God's presence was no longer in the midst of His people (see 1 Samuel 4:21).

The glory of the Lord departed when the temple stopped being the temple. See, you couldn't just strut into the temple talking about, "I think I'll just take in a little temple today." You had to get serious about God.

We know from extrabiblical material that when the high priest went into the holy of holies on the Day of Atonement to sprinkle the blood on the mercy seat of the ark, his robe had bells on it so they could tell if he was still moving around. And he had a rope tied around his ankle.

The reason for the rope was that if that boy did one thing wrong in there, he wasn't going to come out to talk about it—and nobody was allowed to go in there and get him. So if the bells stopped ringing and the rope went limp, that meant they had to drag the priest out of there.

In other words, in the temple everything had to be just right. Great pains were taken to make sure that the glory of the Lord was not offended. That's because they wanted God to hang out in their midst.

You say, "But that's Old Testament, where they had a place for God's glory cloud to come down and be seen." Well, Ephesians is New Testament, and Paul says the church is God's dwelling place. When God's people come together, His glory is supposed to be present.

In 1 Corinthians 3:16–17, Paul says the church is the temple of God ("you" is plural here), then in 1 Corinthians 6:19 he says the body of the individual believer is the temple of the Holy Spirit. No matter how you look at it, we are God's temple, the place where His glory hangs out on earth.

This means that the world ought to be so awed by the presence of God within us that they come to the church asking us what they should do. But when was the last time you heard of that happening? More often than not, it's the church going to the world to find out what they will allow us to do.

See, we have it backward. You never read in the Bible about God asking for man's advice. You never hear Him saying, "Look, I'm a little confused on this one. Do you have any ideas?" When was the last time you heard Jesus asking for suggestions? God is not into suggestions. He's into commandments.

But we have a church of "suggesters" today because we don't understand that we possess the presence and the glory of the Lord. That is a view of the church that most people will not address, so we have a church that, on the whole, is anemic.

Completing Christ's Purpose

In addition to being the completion of Christ's person and Christ's presence, the church is also the completion of Christ's purpose. "So that the manifold wisdom of God might now be made known through the church to the rulers and the authorities in the heavenly places" (Ephesians 3:10).

The wisdom of God made known through the church is "multi-colored." That's what the word *manifold* means. This is why racism is an affront to God. His wisdom comes in many shades!

The purpose for which God invests the church with His manifold wisdom is that this wisdom might be manifested or made known through us to "the rulers and the authorities in the heavenly places." There's that familiar phrase again.

God wants us to do His thing here on earth so that we can be the moon to His sun, reflecting His glory and wisdom back to the angelic world, to the ruling authorities in the spiritual realm.

Why does God want the church to reflect His wisdom to those in the heavenly places? Because that's where all the decisions are made. That's where the "spiritual control knobs" of the universe are located.

Decisions are not made down here. They're only acted out down here. So the church is either going to catch heaven or catch hell, if you will, based on whether the manifold wisdom of God is being reflected through us. That's why many of the things God tells the church to do don't seem to make sense from the perspective of earth.

The reason is that God isn't just operating on earth. He's trying to bounce His wisdom and His glory off the church back to the heavenly places where the decisions are made. That's why Paul prays this magnificent benediction:

Now to Him who is able to do exceeding abundantly beyond all that we ask or think, according to the power that works within us, to Him be the glory in the church and in Christ Jesus to all generations forever and ever. Amen. (Ephesians 3:20–21)

The glory of God is found in the church. The church is God's "ad agency" to show the world what He is like.

Because God is spirit, people can't see Him. So the church is called to dress God up, to make Him look good by the way we live. That's what glory means. That's what the church is about.

Our program is to be Christ's body. Our gathering is to reflect His presence. And our purpose is to give Him glory, to advertise Him. How well is Christ being advertised in your community by your church?

Completing Christ's Program

In Ephesians 4, beginning in verse 7, Paul turns to the subject of the gifts the risen Christ has given to His church in order to carry out His program in history. The apostle begins this section by saying:

To each one of us grace was given according to the measure of Christ's gift. Therefore it says, "When He ascended on high, He led captive a host of captives, and He gave gifts to men." (vv. 7–8)

This last phrase is a dynamic one, picturing Christ taking captives from the enemy and making them His, leading them in a triumphant procession like a victorious Roman general and distributing gifts to His people.

When the mighty Roman army conquered an enemy, whatever that enemy possessed, including the people, now belonged to Rome.

If you were a lawyer, you became a lawyer for Rome. If you were a businessman, your business was now at the disposal of the Roman Empire. You paid Roman taxes, and you got the whole treatment. Everything you owned was now available to Rome any time Rome had a need for it. The idea was that Rome would be better off because you were now its captive. The agenda of Rome had now become your agenda.

When Christ saved you, He captured you from Satan. That means everything you are and have is now to be made available to your new Captor. Before you were saved, what you had was available to the devil. And he probably got good use out of it.

But when Jesus Christ led you captive, you were supposed to bring all those goodies over to His kingdom. One of the major problems the church faces is that people who have been captured by Christ are not bringing what they have to Christ—especially their money.

GIFTS TO THE CHURCH

Ephesians 4:11 spells out the gifts the victorious Christ gave to His church. In this case, they are gifted people: "He gave some as apostles, and some as prophets, and some as evangelists, and some as pastors and teachers."

Then verse 12 gives the purpose these gifted people are to fulfill: "For the equipping of the saints for the work of service, to the building up of the body of Christ." Now stay tuned, because we have arrived at one of the greatest misconceptions ever to plague the church.

The misconception is this: The church hires professionals and pays them to do the ministry, therefore exonerating the members of their responsibility to do the ministry. This attitude is typified by the church member who, when asked to do visitation, responded, "Visitation? I thought that's what we hired the preacher for."

At our church in Dallas, a person can't be a member without agreeing to serve. When people come to our pre-membership class, we give them a list of one hundred ways they can fulfill their ministry responsibility.

If they don't want to serve, they will have to go to some other church to be a lazy saint. You can't say to the church, "Preach to me, sing to me, counsel me, visit me when I'm sick, take care of me when I'm in need, encourage me—but don't expect anything from me." That's ripping off the kingdom.

Does that mean an eighty-five-year-old woman who can barely make it to church on Sunday, but spends three hours a day praying for her fellow church members, is sinning for not teaching Sunday school? Or that a businessman who uses his gift of evangelism by visiting strangers in the hospital has misplaced his priorities because his church has no such official ministry? Of course not. Not all ministry is done under the church roof. But all believers have the obligation to use their gifts to build up the local body of believers and expand their church's impact.

My job as pastor is to equip the saints under my care to do the work of the ministry. If I'm not equipping them, then they won't know how to do the ministry. And if people don't know how to do the ministry, they'll go off and leave it to the few who do know.

That's why so many churches have 10 percent of the people doing 90 percent of the work. Then the 10 percent get burned out and want to quit.

But Christ has a better idea. He wants all believers to "attain to the unity of the faith, and of the knowledge of the Son of God, to a mature man" (Ephesians 4:13a). Notice that it's many people, but only one mature person; that is, all of our efforts are to be focused on one common purpose.

That's why the pastor must have a clear vision for the church. If you were to ask our church members to give you the vision for our church, I'm confident that 95 percent would be able to tell you, "Discipling the church to impact the world." Everywhere they go, they run into our mission statement which reflects our vision.

If the pastor is misty and vague on his vision for the church, the mist in the pulpit becomes a fog in the pew. So guess what happens? People go around creating their own visions for the church, and its impact is soon fragmented. Christ is only looking for one mature body, not ten.

A HEALTHY BODY

Paul continues in Ephesians 4 by saying:

As a result, we are no longer to be children . . . but speaking the truth in love, we are to grow up in all aspects into Him who is the head, even Christ, from whom the whole body, being fitted and held together by what every joint supplies, according to the proper working of each individual part, causes the growth of the body for the building up of itself in love. (vv. 14–16)

This certainly applies to the universal church, but remember that Paul is writing to the church at Ephesian. So he's speaking to a local church, saying that every member of the Ephesian church should be a supplier to the life of that ministry.

A healthy body heals itself. When your body is healthy and you scratch yourself, a scab is going to form as part of the body's process of healing itself. But when a body is unhealthy, instead of healing taking place, disease sets in. With cancer, for example, you get a rebel cell that says, "I don't want to go with the body's program anymore. I want to split off and do my own thing."

This cell decides to be independent and it splits off. That wouldn't be so bad, but that cell doesn't want to be by itself. So it reproduces after its own kind. And when it does that enough, a lump forms. Even that wouldn't be so bad if the lump would stay put.

But no, now it wants to investigate the rest of your body. So it metastasizes; it spreads and sets up shop elsewhere. By the time you discover the problem, the cancer may be all over your body. That's because cancer wants to run its own program in your body until it takes over.

The church today has been weakened by a cancer: too many members who want to do their program, not understanding that all the cells of the body need to follow the same "one mature man" program.

You always know a good church member from a bad church member because a good member is a supplying joint of the body, while a bad member is a "ripping off" joint, out for personal benefit and not the health of the body. But the church is meant to be the place where the people of God are active and vibrant and alive and growing together into a mature whole.

Completing Christ's Portrait

In Ephesians 5:22–33, Paul says that marriage is a picture of the relationship the church is to have to Christ. He is our Husband.

When Paul talks about the submission of the wife and the headship of the husband, he says this is how Christ and the church relate to one another (vv. 22–24). When he instructs husbands to love their wives (vv. 25–33), the comparison all the way through is to Christ and His church.

And just in case we might miss the point, Paul spells it out in verse 32: "This mystery is great; but I am speaking with reference to Christ and the church." He's saying that there's something bigger here than the marriage of two people.

Marriage is to be a picture of Christ and the church. Marriage was never merely an end in itself. It was created to be a picture of a bigger program.

But as long as two people keep focusing on each other's differences and personalities and don't get along, they play right into Satan's hands. He wants to get us focused just on ourselves so that we miss this bigger picture.

See, if a husband has never learned to love and lead like Christ and a wife has never learned to respond like the church is supposed to respond, they are not only failing to live up to God's expectations for them; they are failing to reflect Christ and His church properly.

The church is to respond to Christ the way a wife responds to a loving and self-giving husband. In this way the family functions as a "mini-church" in its community. Thus the world is never without a witness or without righteousness existing in its midst.

Completing Christ's Power

Finally, Ephesians 6 teaches us that the church is the recipient of Christ's power:

Be strong in the Lord and in the strength of His might. Put on the full armor of God, so that you will be able to stand firm against the schemes of the devil. For our struggle is not against flesh and blood, but against the rulers, against the powers, against the world forces of this darkness, against the spiritual forces of wickedness in the heavenly places. (vv. 10–12)

The church is to stand firm. That is, we are to hold our ground. Don't give up God's territory. Protect His turf.

The key verse in this section is verse 12. Unless the church understands that our ultimate battle is against spiritual forces and not against earthly foes, we will not have a biblically centered ministry.

As long as we believe that our real struggle is against "flesh and blood," the church is vulnerable to being corrupted by politics or social movements or unbiblical rhetoric. See, if you think the real enemy is in Washington, you'll be looking for political allies to help you take that enemy down.

I'm not saying Christians should not be involved in the political process. We need righteousness in the public square. I'm saying the church cannot afford to be co-opted by any other movement. Our warfare is spiritual, and so is our armor. And God has fully equipped us for spiritual battle (v. 11).

But when you look at the church today, you would not think we've been fully equipped for battle because we keep losing ground. What that must mean is that we're not wearing our armor.

The six pieces of God's armor that Paul describes in verses 14–17 are real spiritual equipment, not just some interesting metaphor. When you are engaged in battle, you need protection, not word pictures. This is the armor with which God has outfitted the church to stand firm and repel the attacks of the Evil One and his forces:

Belt of truth: The belt holds the rest of the armor together. For the Christian, it's the truth of Christ that holds it all together (see chapter 7, "Reclaiming Truth").

Breastplate of righteousness: Just as a Roman soldier's breastplate protected his heart, we are to guard our hearts with righteousness.

Feet shod with the gospel: A soldier had to have a good foothold when he was fighting, or he was an easy mark. The gospel gives us a firm place to stand.

Shield of faith: The soldier's shield was what he used to protect the rest of his body that might be exposed to the enemy's arrows. It was movable. Faith is a shield we can raise up on the spot to stop the enemy's missiles.

Helmet of salvation: The helmet protects the brain, the thinking apparatus. So how does God want us to think? Like people who have been saved from the penalty and power of sin!

Sword of the Spirit: This is the only offensive weapon in the whole arsenal. The Word of God is a weapon Satan has no defense against. Jesus used the Word to defeat Satan in the wilderness, and we need to wield it against him too.

That's an impressive lineup. But a church that has been weakened by fighting the wrong battles and is yielding ground to the enemy can't do much for a culture that is being devastated by the same enemy. Let's put on God's armor, draw a line in the sand with the sword of the Spirit, and take our stand.

A CONCLUDING WORD

Until the church functions as the continuation of the Incarnation in history, we will continue to see the deterioration of our families, communities, cities, states, and eventually our nation. The only way Jesus can be the answer for our culture is if He is demonstrated as the answer through the church.

An invisible church means an invisible Christ as far as the culture is concerned. That means there can be no spiritual solutions for the culture without the impact of the church. Satan has been so successful because he has kept us marginalized and confined to our holy huddles so as to render the church ineffective in the culture.

Therefore, when the church fails to complete Christ in the culture, we are inadvertently contributing to the destruction of the nation by our conspicuous absence. It's time for the church to be the church in the midst of a decaying world if America is to be preserved.

CHAPTER 4

BACKWARD, CHRISTIAN SOLDIERS

You may recognize the title of this chapter as a takeoff on the popular old gospel song, "Onward, Christian Soldiers." Obviously, soldiers are supposed to go forward. When an army is going backward, or retreating, something has gone wrong with the battle plan.

Christians in America are in widespread retreat today. We are losing ground in the face of the tremendous problems that are engulfing our society. And if we're supposed to be the troops on the front lines, trying to halt the advance of spiritual decay and deterioration in society, then America is in big trouble.

What kind of Christian soldier goes backward when he's supposed to be going forward? There's only one kind the Bible talks about.

THE CARNAL CHRISTIAN

In one sense, "carnal Christian" is an oxymoron, a contradiction in terms. The word *carnal* means "fleshly, of the flesh." A Christian is a spiritual being, not born of the flesh (see John 1:13; 3:6). So a carnal Christian is a "fleshly spiritual" person, which is like calling someone a "living dead" person or a "single married" woman. The terms don't go together.

A True Christian

But we know it's possible for Christians to be carnal, because Paul told the church at Corinth, "You are still fleshly . . . walking like mere men" (1 Corinthians 3:3). A carnal Christian is a genuine believer, but one who is still acting out fleshly, sinful patterns of behavior.

A Sick Christian

A fleshly or carnal Christian is caught between two worlds. He believes Christ is real and believes in His sacrifice on the cross. Even so, he clings intentionally to his worldly ways. Though he is saved, he is still swayed by the drives and desires of his old nature.

Like an overgrown infant, a carnal Christian who fails to move toward maturity is a sick Christian, attempting to keep one foot planted in each of two mutually exclusive worlds. This is more than just uncomfortable. It's impossible, for the flesh and the spirit are in mortal combat with each other (Galatians 5:17).

What happens when you round up a whole bunch of carnal Christians and bring them together inside the four walls of churches all across America? You get corporate carnality, a church that is too weak to fend off the attacks of the enemy and too fleshly to have much impact on a society that knows no other way to live but in the flesh.

The failure of the church to deal with carnality, both individual and corporate, is hurting our witness, causing conflicts within our own ranks, and ultimately contributing to the destruction of America.

A Christian in Need of Help

The church is like a hospital. If you're sick you are welcome, but expect your illness to be addressed. No hospital is going to allow you to take up a bed if you don't want to get better. And no authentic church should allow Christians to become comfortable in their sin.

We must understand that the job of the church is to perform spiritual surgery so that its healing power can be made visible to a sin-sick society.

The apostle Peter writes, "It is time for judgment to begin with the household of God" (1 Peter 4:17). That's where we need to begin in America today, with the church.

Why? Because the world knows nothing of the struggle we're talking about. As I said above, worldly people don't know any other way to live than in the flesh. They are what the Bible calls "natural," meaning unregenerate, dead in their trespasses and sins.

So if you called an unsaved person a natural man, he might take that as high praise. "After all," people like this contend, "we're only human." And in our society, the failings and foibles of sinful human beings are celebrated, not censored. Premarital sex is "natural." Divorce is "unavoidable." Abortion is "only reasonable."

Now make no mistake. I'm not trying to say we Christians are holier and better than everybody else. All of us sin. And if you say you don't, you have just committed the sin of lying (1 John 1:8, 10).

The difference is that whereas a spiritual Christian or church may fall into sin, a carnal Christian wallows in it. He has the mind-set, the motivation, and the methodology of sin. Let's look briefly at some characteristics of carnality so we can recognize the disease and deal with it. Until the church does this individually and corporately, we don't have much to offer America.

THE CHARACTERISTICS OF CARNALITY

If I had to describe carnality in one sentence, it would be this: Carnality is persistent, measurable regression in a Christian's or church's spiritual life.

By persistent I mean what I alluded to above. Even the most spiritually mature Christians sin. But the carnal Christian lives in failure and defeat, unwilling to address the sin in his life. Likewise, carnal churches allow sin to go unjudged in their midst.

By *measurable* regression I mean you can test yourself to see whether your Christian life is marked by carnality.

In fact, here's a biblical test you can take right now. Examine yourself and your church as we go to the book of Hebrews to consider four characteristics of carnality.

Spiritual Neglect

The first characteristic or trait that marks the carnal Christian is the neglect of spiritual matters:

For if the word spoken through angels proved unalterable, and every transgression and disobedience received a just penalty, how will we escape if we neglect so great a salvation? After it was at the first spoken through the Lord, it was confirmed to us by those who heard. (Hebrews 2:2–3)

The author of Hebrews was writing to a group of Jewish Christians who were being tempted to turn their backs on the faith. He raised a fundamental issue that is the first step down the road to carnality.

Neglect here simply means inattention, a lack of interest, or passive disobedience. In other words, you're not necessarily planning to do wrong, but you're not doing the right things that catapult you down the road to spiritual maturity either. It's like the second law of thermodynamics, which states that things left to themselves tend toward randomness and decay.

For example, a student doesn't have to curse his teacher or get caught cheating on a test to fail a class. All he has to do is neglect to study.

Some Christians end up in carnality because of neglect too. Satan lulls us into neglecting the Word of God, not getting on our knees in prayer, and staying away from fellowship with other believers. Why? What causes us to neglect "so great a salvation"?

The same blindness causes us to take people and things for granted: We forget what we have. It's like the wife who says, "My husband has gotten used to cooked meals and washed clothes and ironed shirts." Or the husband who says: "My wife has gotten used to the hard worker and sensitive husband and caring person." Both feel taken for granted. So does God.

He gives us His only begotten Son. He gives us eternal life. He gives us the enablement of the Holy Spirit. He answers our prayers. He heals our broken hearts. He gives us restoration for broken lives. Then we grieve and quench His Spirit (Ephesians 4:30; 1 Thessalonians 5:19), and He asks, "How can you neglect My great salvation?"

Churches can be guilty of corporate neglect as well. They can live for their traditions, going through the routines without any spiritual passion. Such churches are in danger of being rejected by Christ due to this lukewarmness (Revelation 3:14–16).

Spiritual Insensitivity

Next, the carnal Christian and church are characterized by increasing spiritual insensitivity:

Take care, brethren, that there not be in any one of you an evil, unbelieving heart that falls away from the living God. But encourage one another day after day, as long as it is still called "Today," so that none of you will be hardened by the deceitfulness of sin. (Hebrews 3:12–13)

Again, the use of "brethren" indicates the author is writing to Christians. He's also talking about people with hard hearts.

Many Christians grow insensitive and hard-hearted before they realize it, duped into complacency by "the deceitfulness of sin," which comes from a heart that doubts God. Some young people are in jail because they stopped believing their father and mother and started believing the wrong kind of peers.

That's when parents say to their children the words that God longs for us to hear and act upon: "If you had only listened to me and stopped listening to sin, you wouldn't be in this mess now."

How do you know if you or your church are growing insensitive? Sin bothers you less and less. Sin is like a woodpecker pecking away at your life. When you look at the individual pecks, it's not that big a deal. But when the pecking is over, you've got a hole in your tree.

Mature Christians and churches view sin like the dust in a room where the sun streams in through the window. You can see millions of particles of dust floating around in the air, and suddenly the air doesn't look so clean. When the light of Christ shines into your life, you grow more sensitive to the particles of sin floating around in your heart.

This is why regular communion is so important to church life. It calls believers to examine themselves before a holy God and judge themselves lest they be judged (1 Corinthians 11:31).

Refusal to Grow

The carnal Christian and church are also characterized by a willful refusal to grow:

Concerning [Christ] we have much to say, and it is hard to explain, since you have become dull of hearing. For though by this time you ought to be teachers, you have need again for someone to teach you the elementary principles of the oracles of God, and you have come to need milk and not solid food. For everyone who partakes only of milk is not accustomed to the word of righteousness, for he is an infant. But solid food is for the mature, who because of practice have their senses trained to discern good and evil. (Hebrews 5:11–14)

The writer wanted to talk about deeper spiritual matters with these Jewish Christians. But he realized that he was writing to the "Sesame Street" generation, the milk-and-cookies crowd. They simply had not grown because they were refusing their salvation.

Too many churches today are feeding this refusal by the overemphasis on the entertainment, "showtime" aspects of worship rather than the substantive spiritual aspects.

The people the biblical writer addressed had regressed. The word translated "dull" refers to slowness to perceive. At times it was used of a mule, a less-than-complimentary comparison! Here it refers to slowness to perceive due to moral laxness. Christians and entire churches can become "mule-minded" by choosing to become dull of hearing.

The test of whether you're a milk or a solid food Christian is simple. You ought to be able to lead someone else to Christ or explain an issue from Scripture. These Christians refused to go deeper into the things of God.

We make a similar choice, for instance, when we elect to watch television rather than study the Bible. The absence of evangelism and commitment to the study of the Word reflects the anemic nature of far too many contemporary American churches.

I'm reminded of the old bodybuilder's slogan, "If you don't use it, you lose it." In order to move from milk to solid food, you've got to learn, then use what you learn. It's up to you. Preachers and teachers can motivate you, but you must choose to move on toward maturity, seeking support from other members of the family of God along the way.

Withdrawal from Fellowship

Finally, the carnal Christian is marked by withdrawal from the fellowship of other Christians:

Let us hold fast the confession of our hope without wavering, for He who promised is faithful; and let us consider how to stimulate one another to love and good deeds, not forsaking our own assembling together, as is the habit of some, but encouraging one another; and all the more as you see the day drawing near. (Hebrews 10:23–25)

You can tell you're on the road to carnality when your involvement in the local church becomes marginal or nonexistent. God takes His church seriously, and when Christians withdraw from its fellowship, they withdraw from fellowship with Him.

When the church has to work around football schedules and other sports events, it is clear we are well down the road to carnality. God wants His children to receive the dynamic motivation, fellowship, correction, and teaching that comes uniquely through the context of a local body of believers.

Also, much of the value of the fellowship of believers has to do with what you bring to it, not just what you get out of it. It's like the father who asked his daughter to cook breakfast, only to have her reply, "I'm not hungry."

She failed to realize that she was not the only person in the family with an appetite. Part of her obligation as a member of that family was to help feed the others whether she was hungry or not.

As Christians, we are part of the family of faith. God wants us to gather together because He knows we need one another both to give and to receive. We all need to be held accountable. And we need to stimulate one another to faithfulness and good works. God saved us to be functioning parts of His body.

CARNALITY AND CONFLICT

One of the telltale signs that the church is going backward rather than forward is that instead of the world coming to the church for answers, the church is going to the world. One area where this is particularly visible is the way we deal with conflict and sin in the body.

We're talking about this in light of the thesis of this book, which is that Christians have a lot of spiritual "housekeeping" and rebuilding to do before we can talk about turning America around.

If we can't judge sin and solve our own problems biblically without resorting to fleshly methods, what do we have to offer the world to help it deal with its sin and social conflicts?

Take It to the Church

When disputes arise in the body of Christ, what do we do? Do we sue our brother or sister in secular court? Do we haul them downtown, or do we take it to the church?

Well, the Bible is clear. We are to take it to the church. Jesus Himself explained the process in Matthew 18:15–17:

If your brother sins, go and show him his fault in private; if he listens to you, you have won your brother. But if he does not listen to you, take one or two more with you, so that by the mouth of two or three witnesses every fact may be confirmed. If he refuses to listen to them, tell it to the church; and if he refuses to listen even to the church, let him be to you as a Gentile and a tax collector.

The first thing you do with a dispute between believers is attempt to handle it personally and privately. If a fellow believer or your mate has hurt you, you try to fix it privately. You never carry a problem beyond the circle of those who need to know about it.

Notice how Jesus widens the circle as it is appropriate. If the other party does not listen to you, is not open to correction, and is not repentant, then other witnesses can be brought in. The involvement of witnesses meant that there was a legality attached to the process, as we'll see below. It became official.

In the case of a married couple, for example, the offended

party is trying to fix this marriage, but the other partner won't have it. It's not a matter of one mate's word against the other's, because there are witnesses to corroborate the accusation. Where should the matter be taken? Jesus said, "Tell it to the church."

God's Courtroom

When it comes to conflict between believers, God has a court to decide the issue. This court is the church. You might wonder, "Where does God tell the church to serve as a court for disputes between believers?"

Well, we're going to go there right now. In 1 Corinthians 5, we see a specific problem in the church at Corinth that needed to be dealt with. A man was living with his stepmother, a shameful, sinful arrangement that even pagans would have been embarrassed to talk about.

We won't take the time to review all of this chapter. The bottom line for this case is verse 5, where Paul says he was turning the offending brother over to Satan for severe discipline, even to physical death if necessary.

This case gave Paul occasion to widen his discussion of the church as God's court. In 1 Corinthians 5:11, he instructed the church not to associate with "any so-called brother if he is an immoral person, or covetous, or an idolater, or a reviler, or a drunkard, or a swindler—not even to eat with such a one."

Therefore, relational fellowship can be broken for any number of reasons. The church's job in these cases is to judge those within its ranks (v. 12). In chapter 6, Paul explains how this process of judgment is to be carried out. He begins with a question: "Does any one of you, when he has a case against his neighbor, dare to go to law before the unrighteous and not before the saints?" (v. 1).

"How dare you," Paul says, "go to the unrighteous to decide matters that concern the righteous." This is strong language, implying that the idea of going to a civil court controlled by men who do not know God to render a judgment between people who know God is unthinkable.

Paul is saying to the saints, "You don't know who you are" (see v. 2). Well, who are we? We are those who are going to judge the world with Christ when He "sit[s] on His glorious throne" (Matthew 19:28). We will also judge fallen angels (1 Corinthians 6:3).

Judgment is a part of our role as God's people. If we are going to judge on that level, Paul says, certainly we can serve as a small claims court on matters such as business disputes or marital problems.

Notice that Paul confers on the church a legal status, making it a legal entity. Not legal in terms of the government, but legal in terms of the kingdom. Kingdom decisions are to be rendered by kingdom people, those who obligate themselves to kingdom rule. Therefore, kingdom decisions about kingdom people must be made by the kingdom's court.

Why? Because only the kingdom's court has the divine perspective and can render decisions based on the King's standards. That's why the Bible calls the church a court (1 Corinthians 6:2).

Most churches run from this because this is hard work. But the church was never intended to be simply a building where people go for two hours of services once a week. It was intended to be the expression of the kingdom, an extension of the King's rule.

Every Wednesday night at our church in Dallas, we have church court to deal with conflicts, disputes, and sin in the body. The decisions rendered there are final.

Some people try to get around our duty to judge by pointing to Matthew 7:1, where Jesus said, "Do not judge so that you will not be judged."

Jesus said that all right, but the problem comes when you stop there and close your Bible. Verse 2 explains what Jesus was talking about. He was not saying don't ever judge anyone. He was urging us to be careful when we judge, because the same judgment we use against another person will be the judgment God uses against us. The idea is to think twice before you make a judgment.

In other words, Jesus said we need to judge other people and situations carefully. We have just seen that Christians are commanded to judge. As people with access to the truth of God, we ought to be the best qualified to judge correctly.

The problem Jesus was dealing with was hypocritical judgment, people who need to deal with things in their own lives trying to judge others. That's why the church needs to be sure that when it sits to judge God's people, it does so with a clear heart and with God's perspective.

Jesus did not tell us to avoid judging others. He said to be careful how and when you judge. In fact, when Jesus prayed, "Your will be done on earth, as it is in heaven," He was saying there is a realm in which God's will is to be carried out in history. It is called His kingdom, and it is run by His church.

So, like it or not, judgment is a part of our ministry as the people of God.

When it comes to "matters of this life," Paul says the church should not be appointing judges who have no jurisdiction in the family of God. When a couple decides they want a divorce, for example, they shouldn't take their case to the unrighteous who have no kingdom view of marriage, who don't understand that God is the author of marriage, and who simply grant the couple a no-fault divorce.

Paul is not saying civil courts are wrong. You must have civil government, because the righteous aren't the only ones who live here. But matters of the kingdom are to be decided within the kingdom. Ideally, these decisions would then be confirmed by the government.

This issue of judgment is so important to the church's agenda that Paul said in 1 Corinthians 6:5 the Corinthians should be ashamed that they couldn't get their act together here. He chided them for not using the spiritual wisdom God gave them.

Paul went on to say in verse 7 that if two believers have to go to a secular law court to settle a matter, they have already lost for two reasons. First, because they have destroyed their testimony; and second, because God is against the process.

So the church is to act as God's judging agency. The absence of church courts reveals how truly carnal and inept the church has become and how unwilling it is to deal with sin in its ranks. How can we judge the world if we refuse to judge ourselves?

OLD TESTAMENT EXAMPLES

In the Old Testament, God also established His courts and granted them real authority. In Deuteronomy 17:8–10, Moses instructed the people of Israel:

If any case is too difficult for you to decide . . . you shall come to the Levitical priest or the judge who is in office in those days, and you shall inquire of them, and they will declare to you the verdict in the case. You shall do according to the terms of the verdict which they declare to you from that place which the Lord chooses; and you shall be careful to observe according to all that they teach you.

Read on through verse 12 and you'll see that the verdict was final! The man who did not listen was to be killed. The point is that God's court system was to be taken seriously because it had God's authority and His power behind it.

In Numbers 5:11–31, we read about the steps that were to be taken by the priest to determine if a wife had been unfaithful to her husband. Although the details of this process sound strange to our modern ears, don't miss the significance of what's going on here.

The priest acted as God's judge, and God Himself was directly involved in the process (v. 16) so that the truth was known and real justice was rendered.

This was called the "law of jealousy" (v. 29), but it was not just a petty jealousy thing. It was a serious accusation and a serious trial. Notice in verse 22 that the woman said "Amen. Amen" to the process.

Amen means, "So be it. I agree with what is being said or done." The woman was agreeing to accept the result of the Lord's judgment, whether blessing or cursing. She was saying that she understood what would come upon her as a result of the trial, and she was willing to accept God's verdict.

Obviously, this was a very serious statement for the woman to make. God's Old Testament courts were powerful entities with His authority not only to render decisions, but to execute people.

Paul says in 1 Corinthians 10:11 that these things in the Old Testament were written for our example as believers today. In other words, we can use the Old Testament not for its regulations, but for its revelation. The principle of God's people rendering His judgments still applies, even though the specifics of how that's carried out may not be the same today.

God still wants His people to render judgment on His behalf when there is a dispute. These kinds of cases come up constantly in the church, whether it is two Christian businesspeople who can't agree or a dispute concerning a contract or transaction made between two Christians.

THE PROCESS OF JUDGING

We saw earlier the steps Jesus outlined for dealing with a dispute between believers. The process begins with as small a circle as possible, the two parties involved. If that fails to resolve the issue, then the offended party brings in outside witnesses.

Rendering the Decision

But if that step fails, then the issue is to be brought before the church body. Why? Because the church is these believers' extended family. It's the environment where God's decisions are rendered. The church has been given the authority by her risen Lord of binding and loosing (Matthew 16:19), which is exercising authority on His behalf.

The church's leaders should be capable of judging whether the offense is genuine and—in our example of a marriage partner seeking a divorce—whether the possibility of forgiveness and reconciliation exists. If not, the church should be ready to render a judgment as to whether the offended mate has grounds for divorce. And of course, the couple should be willing to submit to the church's decision.

Dealing with the Unrepentant

But if the offender will not listen to the church, if he is unrepentant, then he is to be excommunicated from the fellowship and treated as a spiritually dead person, an unbeliever. Jesus said so in Matthew 18, which we read above, and Paul said exactly the same thing in 1 Corinthians 5:9–11.

Let's look at Matthew 18 again. To make His point, Jesus chose the two groups of people who were ostracized by the Jewish community of His day (v. 17).

Tax collectors were Jews, but they were barred from the temple and from much of Jewish society because they were basically traitors who collected taxes for the hated Roman occupiers and cheated their own people in the process. And no good Jew would have any fellowship with a Gentile.

The Church's Authority

In Matthew 18:18, Jesus tells us why God has given the church such authority. It's for the reason we have already talked about: The church is to act as God's earthly court, rendering His heavenly decisions valid on earth.

In fact, Jesus went on to give this promise, which is often used as a general promise of answered prayer: "If two of you agree on earth about anything that they may ask, it shall be done for them by My Father who is in heaven. For where two or three have gathered together in My name, I am there in their midst" (vv. 19–20).

Gathered for what? For prayer? To hear the Word of God? Is that what Jesus is talking about? Well, we need to gather together for both of those things, but neither is what Jesus has in mind here.

He's saying that when the church gathers together to render its decisions, He will be in the midst of His people. That process will certainly include the use of prayer and the Word, but for the specific purpose of rendering judgment on God's behalf.

So, since the church acts on God's behalf when it judges, this is the court a believer should go to if he or she wants to be blessed. As we saw above, Paul says that if we have to go to the secular courts to settle issues in the church, we have already lost.

That is where the rubber of our Christianity meets the road of real life. Being a Christian is more than just singing and praising God. Believers are also to render God's judgments because the church is a family court, if you will.

Just as you wouldn't want your children taking the family business out into the street, God does not want you and me taking His kingdom business out into the street, to people who don't have a kingdom mentality. When we avoid judging our own people, it hits the newspapers instead and gives God a bad name.

Here is why some people don't want to come to the church with marital disputes. They don't want to subject themselves to the rule of God, because His goal is always to preserve the marriage covenant. People want to go to somebody who is going to say, "You're OK."

Our kids are like that. If they can't get what they want from one parent, they go to the other. They don't want to be handed a righteous decision. They only want to hear the decision that gives them what they want.

But God says we can't do that as His people. We are to render His judgments, and we have His promise that He will be right there in the middle of the process with us if we will follow His instructions.

SPIRITUAL RESTORATION

Here is where God's system of judgment and the world's part company many times. The goal of God's court system is always to restore, to heal, to bring the offender back into fellowship with Him and with the church.

A Different Purpose

I'm not saying that secular courts never seek to restore people who have done wrong or to right an injustice. But take our illustration of divorce. When was the last time you heard of a divorce petition being denied because the judge said, "No, you two can work this out. Go back home, get help, and let's save this marriage"?

It doesn't happen. Our legal system takes the easy way out and grants the divorce, even though that's usually the most destructive decision that could be rendered. And because people know they have an easy out, all sorts of marriages are taking place in America that should never happen. Couples get married with the mentality that says, "If this doesn't work, we'll bail out."

Think of the witness and the impact the church would have if every Christian couple having marital trouble took God's Word seriously and submitted their marriage to the authority of the church.

A Tremendous Impact

You say, "But what if we all do this, and it doesn't change anyone's view of divorce out there in the culture?" Well, even if that happened, such a step would still have a tremendous restorative effect on America.

How? Because if the statistics are right, Christians are divorcing today at about the same ridiculous rate as unbelievers. So if the process described above only restored the marriages of a portion of the Christian couples who followed it, think of the families that would be spared the disaster of divorce.

The goal of Christian judgment through the church court is always spiritual restoration. You can see this principle at work in 2 Corinthians 7:8–9, where Paul wrote:

For though I caused you sorrow by my letter, I do not regret it; though I did regret it—for I see that that letter caused you sorrow, though only for a while—I now rejoice, not that you were made sorrowful, but that you were made sorrowful to the point of repentance; for you were made sorrowful according to the will of God, so that you might not suffer loss in anything through us.

The carnal Corinthians had improved by the time Paul addressed his second epistle to them. Why? Because he confronted them about the sin they were tolerating.

Sure, they were saddened. But they got over it. This passage demonstrates that sobs and apologies are fine, provided they are followed by a change of mind and action.

Bearing Each Other's Burdens

Another key passage is Galatians 6:1–5. Paul writes, "Brethren, even if anyone is caught in any trespass, you who are spiritual, restore such a one in a spirit of gentleness; each one looking to yourself, so that you too will not be tempted" (v. 1).

The word for *caught* means to be overtaken. The term suggests being stuck in the quicksand of sin. The word *restore* means to mend or put back together. So those who are spiritual aren't the ones who get on the phone and say, "Girl-l-l! Let me tell you what I just found out." Gossip makes you as carnal as the subject of your gossip.

Who are the spiritual believers who qualify for this ministry of restoration? They are the ones who possess the mind of Christ (1 Corinthians 2:15–16). So when a brother or sister is caught in a sin, spiritual believers and churches are going to come with a divine perspective, offering God's solution to the problem instead of their opinion.

A sinning believer is to be restored gently, because spiritual Christians realize that they may also fall into the same snare of the devil. Nothing is gained by stepping on a brother while he's down, especially if he wants to get up.

It has been well said that the Christian army is the only army that shoots its wounded. That's too close to the truth to be comfortable!

James 5:19–20 reminds us of the benefit of restoration: You save an erring brother from ruining his life, even from death, when you go to him and restore him. What a wonderful testimony for the world to see: a church that does not only judge its own, but restores them as well, reflecting the marvelous grace of God.

We might add that if enough Christian marriages are saved, if enough carnal believers are brought back, if enough disputing Christians are reconciled, God will honor our obedience and may even save our nation from an untimely death!

CHAPTER 5

NOT ENOUGH DISCIPLES

One recent poll stated that there are more than 50 million evangelical Christians in America. Now if that's true, it poses a great problem.

How can we have all these Christians in all these churches, led by all these pastors and supported by all these deacons, and still have all this mess? The answer is simple. We don't have enough disciples.

After He rose from the dead, the Lord Jesus Christ took steps to ensure that there would be disciples. He immediately called a meeting—but it was not any ordinary church committee confab. It was held on a hillside in Galilee, not in a boardroom.

This meeting was also different because of the people who were there. According to Matthew 28:16, Jesus' eleven remaining disciples showed up. Secondly, according to 1 Corinthians 15 more than 500 brethren showed up for the meeting.

But there was a third group of people included in that post-Resurrection meeting—and that group includes you and me! See, at the end of the meeting Jesus said, "I am with you always, even to the end of the age" (Matthew 28:20). Since the age Jesus was speaking of hasn't ended yet, and since you and I are living in that age, we are also part of that historic occasion.

Before we go any further, let's read the "minutes" of Jesus' meeting:

The eleven disciples proceeded to Galilee, to the mountain which Jesus had designated. When they saw Him, they worshiped Him; but some were doubtful. And Jesus came up and spoke to them, saying, "All authority has been given to Me in heaven and on earth. Go therefore and make disciples of all the nations, baptizing them in the name of the Father and the Son and the Holy Spirit, teaching them to observe all that I commanded you; and lo, I am with you always, even to the end of the age." (Matthew 28:16–20)

I'll bet you have never read any church committee minutes like those before! But despite the fact that this meeting includes all the saints in church history from Pentecost to today, I want to suggest that one of the problems in the church that is helping to weaken America is this: *We don't have enough disciples*.

We're going to unfold and examine this thesis as we go along, so I just want to plant it in your mind up front. Now if there is a disciple problem in the church, we can be sure it has nothing to do with the church's Head and the Leader of this meeting, Jesus Christ.

In fact, Jesus said that "all authority" had been given to Him in heaven and on earth. That announcement is loaded with significance. When Adam sinned in the Garden of Eden, he relinquished the rule of the earth to Satan, and a rumble ensued between God and Satan for control.

Now don't get me wrong. There was never any question about the ultimate outcome. God was never in danger of losing to Satan. But throughout history, Satan made every move possible to defeat God's plan and take over. He even tried to make Jesus worship him. When that failed, Satan tried to kill Jesus.

VICTORY ACHIEVED

He succeeded—for about three days. Hell must have had quite a party on the Friday evening of Jesus' crucifixion. It lasted all day Saturday too. But the Resurrection was God's way of saying to Satan, "Sorry. You lose. My Son is alive, and all authority is now in His hands. He's the right Person to rule."

That's what the word *authority* in Matthew 28:18 actually means. It's power in the right hands: the power of elected officials to govern, the power of a police officer to arrest a thief, the power of parents to discipline their children.

When Jesus said that all authority was His in heaven and on earth, He was saying that He is the right Person to wield that power. Now the idea of heaven and earth reminds us of the prayer Jesus taught His disciples to pray: "Your will be done, on earth as it is in heaven" (Matthew 6:10).

So according to Jesus, a disciple's first concern should be that God's will is done on earth just as it is done in heaven. So how is God's will done in heaven? Completely and perfectly, no questions, no objections, no debate. In fact, Satan was the only one to ever challenge God's will in heaven, and he was kicked out.

So Jesus' plan is that there be a group of people on earth, called His church, who reflect the nature of heaven. That way, no matter where people live, if they want to know what is going on in heaven, all they have to do is check out their local church. God's people are to be earthly models of heavenly reality.

VICTORY MAINTAINED

Since Jesus has already achieved victory and Satan is a defeated enemy, what is our role as the church Jesus has left behind here on earth?

Jesus answered that Himself in Matthew 28, but He also gave a very succinct answer on one occasion when He and the disciples were nearing Jerusalem just before His crucifixion.

His Occupying Force

The disciples thought that Jesus was going to Jerusalem to take over and set up His kingdom right then. Jesus knew what they were thinking, so He told them the parable of the nobleman who went on a long journey and left certain sums of money with his servants.

Then he told them, "Occupy till I come" (Luke 19:13 KJV). In other words, "Do business for me while I'm gone. I'll be back."

I like that word *occupy*. As Jesus' disciples, we're like the occupying army that a conquering general leaves behind in the conquered country to mop up after the battle and maintain the victory that has been won.

Even though Satan is a defeated enemy, he has still got a lot of fight left in him, and he wants to take as many people down with him as he can. So our task as Jesus' occupying force is more involved than just sitting back and keeping an eye on things. The risen Lord gave us our instructions in Matthew 28:19–20, known as the Great Commission.

We need a little grammar lesson here to break open this passage and find out what it takes to do what Jesus wants us to do. In the original language, there is only one command: "make disciples." Three participles explain how to make disciples: "going," "baptizing," "teaching."

So the purpose of the church is to make disciples, not just add names to the roll or increase Sunday school attendance. It's not enough for the church just to be open a certain number of hours a week or offer a variety of programs. We're to make disciples.

What Is a Disciple?

So we have to ask, What is a disciple? A disciple is a person who has decided that following Jesus Christ takes precedence over everything else in life.

Jesus did not say being a disciple would be easy. Disciples have to take up their crosses and follow Him (Mark 8:34). He emphasized that He would have to be first in their lives when He said, "If anyone comes to Me, and does not hate his own father and mother and wife and children and brothers and sisters, yes, and even his own life, he cannot be My disciple" (Luke 14:26).

Years ago when the military draft was still in operation, young men were often called into the service at very inopportune times. For example, it didn't matter if you had just gotten married. It was good-bye bride, hello Uncle Sam. The same was true if the guy just got a great job or whatever.

But this new draftee did more than just leave family and friends behind. He now became the property of the U.S. government. His new master dictated every detail of his life: when to get up or go to bed, what to eat—even how to dress, stand, and walk.

After boot camp, the military took a further step in controlling this soldier's life. It selected a new location for him, usually far from home, and a new occupation. If there was a war on, this soldier might be sent to the front lines where he might be killed, all in the line of duty.

If young men could be expected to sacrifice everything for their country, how much more should we as believers be willing to do whatever our Commander, Jesus Christ, asks of us? That's what is expected of disciples.

A Disciple Shortage

Of course, not everyone who heard Jesus speak became His disciple. Whenever He drew a large crowd, He eliminated most of them by talking about the requirements of discipleship. If Jesus were interested in just building a large following, He would have kept quiet about the cost of discipleship.

But Jesus wasn't playing the numbers game. He was making disciples. Unfortunately, most of the people who heard Him weren't interested in absolute commitment to His authority. Getting by was good enough for them.

Sadly, that's too often the case in the church today. Too many of us serve Christ as long as He doesn't start messing with our comfort. We're willing to follow Him as long as He keeps money in our pockets and smiles on our faces. But we don't want to be inconvenienced.

"Yes, I love the Lord, but I'm not really interested in teaching the kids." "I want to serve God, but my job keeps me too busy." "Wednesday prayer meeting is during my favorite TV show. But I'll give God two good hours on Sunday."

Few church members would ever say things like this out loud, but that's the message they convey. As a result, there are too few disciples around to enable the church to impact the world.

This helps to explain why so many people can go to church every Sunday in the city, but the cities don't change. It helps to explain why countless numbers of Christians go to the city every weekday to work, but the cities don't change.

The primary problem in our communities is not that we don't have enough money, not that we can't work through the sociological problems, and not that there are not enough government programs. The problem with our cities is not even that we don't have enough churches filled with Christians who know how to dress up and look holy. The problem is we don't have enough disciples.

What is missing in our urban centers are disciples. We have plenty of church buildings, members, and activities. But where are the disciples? Where are the men and women who understand that their purpose in life is to represent God's kingdom?

Where are the people whose lives are centered on God's Word, who live for His glory, and whose commitment is to carry out His program? Where are the people who are willing to surrender their existence to the will of God, no matter what the price, because they understand that this is why they are here?

This shortage of disciples explains why we have so many Christians and so little impact within our own churches, let alone in the community at large. What we need now are not more bodies in the pews. But we desperately need more disciples.

If we are going to see the cities change, if we are going to see the suburbs and small-town and rural America reclaimed for Christ, it will be because we make disciples in obedience to His command.

Until we become disciples ourselves and make disciples, we cannot hope to see change. The church in America will remain weak and ineffective, resulting in the continual deterioration of the culture. But there's still hope that the church can get its strength back.

VICTORY MULTIPLIED

Notice in Matthew 28:19 that Jesus told the people who were gathered at that meeting in Galilee to make disciples "of all the nations." That was a big job even when the known world was just the Roman Empire. In order for them to do that, those early disciples would have to be big dreamers and mighty doers.

Small Numbers, Big Impact

See, they were not just sent out to build a church. Christ sent them to take over! That is why the Jewish leaders got angry when the apostles came on the scene (see Acts 4).

They couldn't keep these guys quiet. They jailed them and whipped them, but Peter and his boys kept right on preaching Jesus. Later on, the Jews in Thessalonica said, "Uh-oh. Here come these men who have upset the whole world" (see Acts 17:6).

What was it that gave the apostles the boldness to stand in the temple and preach right under the noses of the religious leaders who had the authority to flog, imprison, and even execute them? What had happened to change their lives so radically?

The answer is back in Acts 2, in that upper room where Christ's followers were gathered together after His Ascension into heaven. There were only 120 of them, but they were serious about Christ, about paying the price, about enduring the pain and inconvenience of being His disciples.

God knew it, so He sent the Holy Spirit to indwell them just as He had promised. Those men and women, dedicated to Christ and filled with the Spirit, started making disciples in exactly the way Jesus told them to do.

Although 120 isn't a large number, there is a big lesson for us in that small figure. How often do we judge the importance of a church by the size of its membership? When we do that, we're missing the point. It's not how many members are in a church that matters; what counts is the number of disciples.

Big Numbers, Small Impact

I'm convinced some huge churches couldn't scare up five true disciples. And in some small churches every member is a disciple. Disciples aren't hard to spot. They're the ones paying the cost of the kingdom, the ones willing to be inconvenienced for Christ.

The difference between the church of the first century and the church today is that when those people showed up, folk either got real nervous or angry, or they got saved. But either way, when those early disciples showed up, people got shook up. When we show up, they relax and serve tea and cookies.

Can you imagine the city council of Ephesus asking Paul to do the invocation at the beginning of their meeting? But Christians are "safe" now. We can pray at all kinds of functions without upsetting anybody.

But Paul was always starting something. Whenever he came to town, a riot broke out. Right after Paul was saved, he had to leave Damascus hidden in a basket that friends lowered over the city wall late at night to keep his enemies from killing him (Acts 9:23–25). In Thessalonica, the enemies of Christ mistreated the man in whose house Paul was staying (Acts 17:5–9).

Paul was always starting something, but not because he was a troublemaker. Wherever Paul went, things started to happen because he preached Jesus. He lived and breathed Jesus and expected others to do the same. He was a disciple, and that's where the trouble started.

Do you realize that Christ has commanded His disciples to take over your community? He doesn't want your church to be just another church on the corner, not making any impact for the kingdom. When Jesus was on earth, no one was neutral toward Him. People either loved and revered Him or hated and tried to kill Him, but nobody ignored Him.

The world is ignoring the church to death these days. People are at best neutral about the church. And some members of the church aren't interested in Jesus either; they've grown cold toward Him. What we need are people who are on fire for Jesus, people with a burning desire to serve Him, people so excited about Him that they shake up the church and the community. That's what disciples do; they shake things up.

You can't be like Jesus on your job, in your neighborhood—and, possibly, even within your church—and not have opposition. Tribulation is a part of Christian experience.

If you're having an easy time of it, if Satan never bothers you, you'd better check the direction you're walking. You may not be walking hand in hand with Jesus. If that's the case, put your hand in His and start walking a disciple's walk.

VICTORY STRATEGIZED

Now that we know what a disciple is, let's take a closer look at Jesus' three-step plan in Matthew 28:19–20 for making disciples.

Step One: Going

The first step in disciple making is to go. That may seem pretty obvious, but it's a problem because we like staying better. We're told to leave the security of the church and go out into the world to represent Christ in the marketplace.

Did you know that nowhere in the Bible are we told to bring our non-Christian friends and co-workers into the church to win them to Christ? There's nothing wrong with doing that, but the biblical strategy is to go to them and be a witness where they are.

That means we've got to go out where the lost people are. Millions are all around us, and if they are going to be reached, we as believers have to do more than attend a two-hour meeting in a building each week. We've got to start applying God's truth to the world.

Step Two: Baptizing

Jesus' second instruction for disciple making is to baptize new believers "in the name of the Father and the Son and the Holy Spirit" (Matthew 28:19).

Water baptism is like a wedding ring, an external reminder of an internal reality. A man or woman can be married without a ring, but wearing it tells others that they are married and not available anymore. A wedding ring also reminds the married person that he or she is committed to another.

So although a gold wedding band is visible to all, its importance does not lie in itself but in the life-changing reality of which it is a symbol.

I don't believe Jesus was talking about the external reminder only when He commanded His disciples to baptize believers. The word *baptize* literally means to immerse; however, its theological usage throughout the New Testament is to identify with someone or something.

This sense of the word is employed in 1 Corinthians 10:2, where Paul says that Israel was "baptized into Moses." That is, Israel identified with Moses as their leader and accepted his leadership as they crossed the Red Sea. From that day until Moses' death, the Israelites identified with him as their leader.

In Romans 6:3, we see the same kind of usage. There Paul teaches that all of us who have been baptized into Christ Jesus were baptized into His death. When we placed our faith in Christ, we became identified with Him in His death on the cross and identified with Him through His Resurrection into newness of life.

So if baptism is used to mean identification, we can substitute "identify" in the commandment to baptize. Matthew 28:19 would then read: "Identify them with the name of the Father and the Son and the Holy Spirit." It is possible for a group to be identified with a name, as the Israelites were with Moses in the verse we talked about above.

But we have a grammatical problem, because "name" is singular, yet we have three names: Father, Son, and Holy Spirit. But the verse says name; there's no mistake about that. If we are to identify with this name that is three names, what are we supposed to be doing?

These three names, of course, represent the Godhead in its fullness. All three are equally God. If we identify with this "three-in-one" God, we become trinitarians in likeness to Him. When Jesus told all believers in the church to baptize "in the name of," He was telling us that when we become His disciples, we become trinitarians too.

This carries the identification aspect of baptism one step further. Not only are we to think like Christ, our behavior is to be Christlike. In everything we do, we are to remember that we represent the Trinity. If you are a disciple, you're more than simply a believer with a name and address. You are Christ's representative to the world, and everything you do reflects on God in His trinitarian fullness, whether for good or for evil.

That's why Paul said, "Whether, then, you eat or drink or whatever you do, do all to the glory of God" (1 Corinthians 10:31). Even our most common activities like eating and drinking should give God glory.

Do you eat and drink because you're hungry? Paul says that's not the real purpose of taking meals. Filling our stomachs satisfies our hunger, but that's a benefit, not the purpose.

The reason we eat and drink is to give our bodies the fuel necessary to bring more glory to God. We often enjoy eating a big meal and then taking a nap. But Paul tells us that instead, we should be eating for the strength we need to get up and give God glory.

That means that you are God's alternative to the world. So if you are a typist, you are not just a typist. You are God's representative to the typing pool so people can see what God looks like when He types a letter.

Do you know why many of us are miserable on Monday morning? Because we don't know why we are working. Many folk are working for a paycheck. But that should be a benefit of our jobs, not the purpose for them.

We work for the glory of God because we are identified with Him as His disciples. But because too many Christians don't understand this basic principle, our churches are filled with people who will do for a salary what they won't do in the church for the glory of God and the advance of His kingdom.

If our churches ever come alive with disciples who understand that they represent the Trinity, look out, America! The church will then become the most potent life-changing entity the world has ever seen.

Step Three: Teaching

The last of Christ's disciple-making instructions is to teach these disciples "to observe all that I commanded you" (Matthew 28:20). It's interesting that teaching comes after baptizing. Why not offer people instruction on what it means to follow Christ *before* baptizing them?

Well, there may well be instruction given on the meaning and importance of baptism. But the reason you don't try to teach new disciples all that Jesus commanded is that until they are identified with Him, they won't sit still long enough to hear that teaching.

What I mean is that until believers become identified with Christ, they will always have something else to do instead of learning about Him. But once they are identified with Him, they will want to learn how they're supposed to live as Christ's representatives.

I realize this progression is not automatic, but the order is important here. Jesus knew exactly what He was saying in this final command to His disciples.

Why do so many churches have middle-class people who come into the city for church but then go home, unwilling to leave any of their skills behind in the urban setting? Because they either don't understand, or are not willing to observe, all that Jesus commanded.

The teaching ministry of the church is a great thing, but if you're in a Bible-teaching church it's also a dangerous thing. Why? Because some people get the idea that the whole purpose of a Bible-teaching church is to teach the Bible.

Of course that's important, but it's only the first step in accomplishing our central purpose of making disciples. Bible-teaching churches encourage and lead their members to know the Bible, but the point of knowing the Scriptures is not just knowing the Scriptures. The point is the doing of the Scriptures that the knowing prompts.

In other words, God isn't excited about having us know the Bible unless it affects our lives. He wants to see what we are doing with the biblical truth we know. If all our reading and study doesn't lead us to obey what Christ taught, then all our reading and studying is worthless.

What we learn on Sunday is supposed to help us live more like Christ Monday through Saturday. A disciple is by definition a learner, a student.

But Jesus doesn't want us studying to pass a test of knowledge. He wants us studying to pass the test of life. Everything He has commanded us to do is designed to change our lives as disciples and to change the lives of those with whom we share it.

With such a dynamic mandate before us, how can there be so many people attending church regularly, but living ragged lives? How can there be so many churches making such a small impact on America? How can we explain the fact that the church is the number one institution in the community, yet the community is in such deep trouble?

There are only two possible answers. Either Christians are not being taught how to live, or they are refusing to live as they are being taught. Jesus said that being His disciple includes learning and applying what He taught.

VICTORY GUARANTEED

"And lo, I am with you always, even to the end of the age" (Matthew 28:20). Here is our guarantee that the victory Christ won over Satan will be a daily reality for His people. We are assured of victory because of Christ's never-failing presence.

Because this is such an impressive promise, people often quote it out of context. For example, when someone gets sick or loses his job, a fellow believer will remind the sufferer that the Lord is with him always.

But this verse isn't about being sick or losing a job. Of course, Jesus is with us in the tough times. But He is talking primarily about His making disciples. In other words, if you want to know where to find the presence of Jesus at work, find out where disciples are being made.

Do you want to know what church Jesus is attending this Sunday? Look for Him in a church where disciples are being made, not one where contacts are being made or religion is being practiced.

No matter how good a time is had by all at church, no matter how well the choir sings or sways or how loud the preacher shouts, rest assured that if that church is not making disciples, something critical is missing. What's missing is the empowering presence of Christ Jesus.

When Christ sees a disciple-making church, He gets involved there. When He sees disciples going out to make new disciples, then baptizing and teaching them, He gets excited.

According to Romans 8:29, God the Father wants His Son to be the first among many brethren. That is, God wants to see disciples who are conformed to the image of Christ, and He is willing to help us make disciples to accomplish that goal.

I like to think of disciples as God's previews of the coming attraction. You've probably seen enough previews on television to know that they all have one thing in common. The preview shows you the most exciting part of the upcoming program: the love scene, the fistfight, the car chase, whatever.

The program often turns out to be terrible. But the preview tries to make it look good, because its purpose is to make you tune in next week to see the whole show.

Well, the "whole show" is coming one day. Jesus Christ is

going to return and bring in His millennial kingdom. But in the meantime, He has left behind millions of previews of the coming attraction. These previews are called disciples.

The question we need to ask ourselves is, When the world looks at the preview of eternity we are portraying, do they want to see the whole show? Or do they decide that the real show will probably be just as disappointing as the preview?

Are you a good preview of things to come? Am I making Christ look so good that people can't wait to hear more? See, the major issues facing America today—urban and suburban— are spiritual, not social, political, or economic.

Government spending has addressed the latter issues, but it hasn't given us lasting solutions. The civil rights movement changed laws, not hearts. And the church has been far too busy counting members instead of making disciples.

It's past time to bring a divine frame of reference to the city by thrusting out into our communities a group of uncompromising, dedicated, biblically educated Christians who have one overriding goal in life: to do everything they do for the glory of God.

This kind of commitment won't just happen. It must be developed by dedicated Christians who have become disciples, men and women who have determined not to sell out to the secularism of this age.

My friend, the church isn't going to get much done until you and I decide to be disciples. This kind of commitment guarantees us some trials, suffering, and inconvenience, but it also promises us the power, presence, and provision of Christ that gives us something to offer a nation full of people who have run out of options.

There's a war on for America. Millions of souls are at stake. You can't be neutral when you're standing in the middle of the battleground. In this war, the church must decide whether it is going to fight the fight of faith or stand by and watch America be destroyed.

I'm choosing the former option, and I'm going for victory. It's ours in Christ if we will claim it by becoming His disciples. I urge you to fight the good fight in Christ's army by being His disciple. There are a lot of people depending on you. Satan can handle ordinary Christians, but he's no match for disciples!

CHAPTER 6

THE NEED TO TELL IT NOW

Did you know that of the four main areas of ministry the church is supposed to be doing on earth, we'll take three to heaven with us?

That's right, all but one of the church's four foundational ministries will be found in heaven. One of the ministries we'll perform in heaven is worship, in which we come together in the name of Christ to celebrate God for who He is and what He has done.

The second ministry we'll find in heaven is education, the ongoing growth in our understanding of God and His truth.

A third ministry we'll be doing in heaven is fellowship, in which believers love and encourage one another in Christ.

Think about it. Billions of years from now, we will still be worshiping God for who He is and what He has done. We will ever be learning more about His infinite perfections. And we will know uninterrupted fellowship with all the saints.

So what is the fourth area of the church's ministry that will cease with this life? Evangelism, making known the good news of Jesus Christ to a dying world. Evangelism is unique to the other three ministries in that it's our one ministry responsibility in history that will be unavailable in eternity, because in eternity men's destiny will be sealed.

So if we are going to be serious about being Christians, if the name of Jesus Christ means anything to us, if we care at all about the eternal destruction awaiting our families, friends, and neighbors, we must be willing to share Him with dying men and women so they will come to faith in Him and know what it is to have eternal life.

Otherwise, we Christians are guilty of helping to destroy America by our neglect, as people plunge headfirst into a Christless eternity.

If we want to see people in heaven tomorrow, we have to tell them about Christ today. That makes evangelism a priority for us. Romans 10 tells us four things that we need to know for witnessing to become a way of life.

THE MOTIVATION FOR EVANGELISM

You and I won't do evangelism unless we have a burden for lost people.

If our hearts don't bleed for people who don't know Christ, then we won't evangelize because it's not a burden. Paul said, "Brethren, my heart's desire and my prayer to God for [Israel] is for their salvation" (Romans 10:1).

A Heart for the Lost

We're picking up in the middle chapter of Paul's treatise on Israel (Romans 9–11), so if you want to know how badly his heart ached to see his fellow Jews saved, read Romans 9:1–5. Paul was even willing to be "accursed, separated from Christ" for them (v. 3). That's a burden.

A burden is a deep pain you carry for loved ones who don't know Christ. You hurt because people you care about don't care about God. Think about the people who matter the most to you. If they die in their sins without Christ, you will never see them again. Paul knew that, and he carried a burden for people.

But when it comes to this subject, I suspect a lot of Christians react like a lot of people do when they see starving children on TV. It tugs on our hearts to see those kids with their stomachs swollen from hunger and their starving mothers trying to nurse them. Our hearts go out to people in that condition, but it's easier to turn the channel because we don't want to be confronted with the awful reality of the pain and hunger and feel guilty because we're not doing something about it.

Cultivating a Burden

When God confronts us with the spiritual needs of men and women all around us, I'm afraid too often we Christians turn the spiritual channel to our entertainment, our agenda, to the things that matter most to us. As a result, we don't allow a burden for evangelism to grow within us.

See, if you keep watching that program about starving children long enough, you are going to wind up sponsoring a needy child overseas. And if you keep looking at non-Christian men and women through the eyes of Jesus Christ long enough, you are going to start telling someone about Him.

But if you keep turning the channel, then as soon as your burden comes, it's gone. Do you know the best way to develop a burden for non-Christians? Keep witnessing to them.

Understanding the Problem

Back in Romans 10, Paul went on to say, "For I testify about [the Jews] that they have a zeal for God, but not in accordance with knowledge" (v. 2).

The Jews of Paul's day were certainly religious. They went to the temple regularly. They offered sacrifices all the time. Their religion was regular. But they didn't understand that you don't get to heaven by virtue of religion or ritual attendance at religious meetings.

Let me remind you of something that I think Christians forget far too often when it comes to their unsaved family members and friends. A person can be born and raised in the church. He can bring in a table and chair, a stove, and a bed so he can eat and sleep in the church.

They can bring his desk from the office into the church so he can work out of the church. And when he dies, they can dig a hole under the pulpit and bury him in the church. But if that person dies without Jesus Christ, the church didn't help him at all!

If the Jews were so zealous, so on fire for God, what was the problem? They lacked "knowledge," a word that means "full understanding." They didn't get the whole picture:

For not knowing about God's righteousness and seeking to establish their own, they did not subject themselves to the righteousness of God. For Christ is the end of the law for righteousness to everyone who believes. For Moses writes that the man who practices the righteousness which is based on law shall live by that righteousness. (Romans 10:3–5)

Why must you and I be evangelists? Because people are confused about how to get right with God, and because of that they go about setting up their own systems for getting into heaven.

Most people think that by doing certain things or avoiding other things, they gain points with God because God grades on the curve. They figure, "Yeah, I'm bad, but John is worse. So I'm better off than John." People need your witness because they don't understand God.

My daughter once came home and told me she made a fifty on an exam. I was not happy.

She said, "Dad, don't worry about it. The teacher is going to grade us on the curve."

My reply was, "But I am not."

Let's set the record straight. God does not grade on the curve. He is a totally perfect and holy Being to whom one sin is as heinous as a billion sins.

Suppose you were going into surgery and the surgeon gave you a choice of three scalpels he had laid out to cut on you with. One scalpel had been dug in the mud. You would say, "No, don't use that one."

The second scalpel wasn't as dirty as the first one. It was sort of grimy. But it was still a big improvement over the first one. You would say, "No, doctor, that won't do."

Then suppose he said, "Well, OK, I have a third scalpel here. This one only has a little bit of dust on it."

You'd better say the same thing about the third scalpel that you said about the first two, because when it comes to cutting you open, a scalpel with dust on it could be just as deadly as a scalpel caked with mud.

It doesn't take a lot of dirt to contaminate your bloodstream. And it doesn't take a lot of sin to contaminate us in the sight of a holy God. People need to know the truth about sin and salvation because they're busy making up their own ways to get to heaven.

What do you often hear when you ask a person if he or she is a Christian? "Well, I'm trying to make it," "I'm doing the best I can," or "I'm trying to keep the Ten Commandments." Answers like that are your clue that the person doesn't have a clue how to attain the righteousness God requires.

Helping People See Their Need

I think one of the hardest things for unsaved people to grasp is the fact that no matter how good they are, their sin cancels their goodness and disqualifies them from heaven. Many people simply cannot conceive of a God who would reject their good because of their bad. This belief is especially widespread in America, but it will take people straight to hell. That's why we are helping to destroy America if we don't tell people the way of salvation.

Actually, though, it's not all that hard to understand. It happens every day. One of my favorite illustrations of this is the police officer sitting beside the highway with his radar gun. If you drive by him doing the speed limit, he's not going to pull you over and say, "Sir, I just want to let you know how wonderful it is to see a citizen like you obeying the law."

Has that ever happened to you? Me neither. Why? Because the law is not designed to pat you on the back for obeying it. But try going past that officer well over the speed limit and see what happens.

Not only will he pull you over, but it will do no good to say to him, "Now, officer, you need to know I've been driving the speed limit for the last ten miles. I just happened to go over the limit a few blocks before I passed you.

"I think you ought to credit me for what I did the last ten miles instead of giving me a ticket for what I did the last few blocks. I don't think it's fair for you to cancel out my ten miles of good driving because of my few blocks of bad driving."

I can tell you how far that line of argument will get you. That policeman will tell you that what you did over the ten miles before he caught you speeding is irrelevant. He will ticket you for those last few blocks regardless of how perfect you were over the first ten miles of your trip. The law is the law.

James wrote, "Whoever keeps the whole law and yet stumbles in one point, he has become guilty of all" (James 2:10). If lost people understood the perfection of God, they wouldn't want Him judging them on their supposed merit. God's law is all or nothing.

That's why the gospel is good news. Paul wrote in Romans 10:4 that "Christ is the end of the law for righteousness to everyone who believes." Christ fulfilled God's demand for perfection, so for every believer His death on the cross put an end to the law as the standard of judgment.

But what about the person who insists on trying to please God by his own works? Verse 5 answers that: "For Moses writes that the man who practices the righteousness which is based on law shall live by that righteousness."

Do you know why it is impossible to live up to God's standards? Because He judges not only our works, but our motives too. The rich young ruler of Luke 18:18–23 was doing fine until Jesus started dealing with what was in his heart.

When the man asked Jesus how to gain eternal life, Jesus went through the commandments and the guy said, "I'm OK there. What's next?"

Then Jesus looked into the man's heart and said, "Give all of your money to the poor and come with Me." The Bible says the young man walked away sad, because he had lots of money. But the fact that he had money wasn't the problem. The problem was his money had him. "Don't touch my money, honey."

You and I would have looked at that guy and said, "He's in." But Jesus knew his heart wasn't right. This man was trying to please God by his outward goodness, but it wasn't good enough.

That's why it's so important to understand that Christ is the end of the law. People don't have to try to satisfy God anymore. Christ has satisfied God's demands and God's anger against sin. All people have to do is put their faith in Him. This is another reason we need to share the gospel with lost people. Americans are raised to "keep the rules," and many are trusting in their rule-keeping to get them to heaven. We're helping to destroy them if we don't tell them any different.

THE MESSAGE OF EVANGELISM

A second principle is that evangelism is a message about the death and resurrection of Christ:

But the righteousness based on faith speaks as follows: "Do not say in your heart, 'Who will ascend into heaven?' (that is, to bring Christ down), or 'Who will descend into the abyss?' (that is, to bring Christ up from the dead)." But what does it say? "The word is near you, in your mouth and in your heart"—that is, the word of faith which we are preaching, that if you confess with your mouth Jesus as Lord, and believe in your heart that God raised Him from the dead, you will be saved; for with the heart a person believes, resulting in righteousness, and with the mouth he confesses, resulting in salvation. (Romans 10:6–10)

The issue in the gospel is the death and resurrection of Jesus Christ, which is already an accomplished fact. People are looking for something miraculous and supernatural, but the word about Jesus is already here. It's in your mouth—in your face, we might say.

It's Right There

What Paul is saying is that everything necessary for a person's salvation has already been done. The Scripture spells out in very clear terms why a person needs to be saved and how a person can be saved. You don't need an unusual, out-of-body experience to get saved. All you need is the Scripture.

Remember the story of the rich man and Lazarus? In hell, the rich man pleaded with Abraham to send Lazarus back to warn the rich man's five brothers, because they would surely repent if they saw someone rise from the dead (Luke 16:27–30).

But Abraham said, "They have Moses and the Prophets; let them hear them" (v. 29). In other words, "They have the Scripture. It's in their faces."

When it comes to believing the gospel, Paul says in Romans 10:9, "If you confess with your mouth Jesus as Lord, and believe in your heart that God raised Him from the dead, you will be saved."

He says the same thing in verse 10, but notice how he reverses the order. In verse 10, belief in the heart precedes confession with the mouth. Why the change in the order? Because verse 9 is salvation from the human side, but verse 10 is salvation from the divine side.

From the human side, our confession of Christ validates our salvation, since no one can see into our hearts to know whether we have believed. But from the divine side, belief precedes confession; that is, God doesn't accept our confession until we have believed.

When Paul says we must confess, he's talking about confessing to God: "For 'Whoever will call on the name of the Lord will be saved'" (v. 13). The word *confess* means to agree with. For a person to be saved, he must agree with God about his sin and about Christ and stop agreeing with everyone but God.

See, a lot of folk won't go to heaven because they have agreed with their friends and not with God. There are even some folk who won't go to heaven because they have agreed with their preacher and not with God. Others won't go to heaven because they have agreed with the wrong religion.

Believing That Jesus Is Lord

There are only two kinds of religion. Call them anything you want, but one kind of religion is the religion that you carry, and the other kind is the religion that carries you.

Christianity is all alone in the second category. Every other religion is predicated on what you do to get to God. But Christianity is unique because it starts with what God did for you.

So what is it that we must agree with God about in order to be saved? We must agree that "Jesus [is] Lord" (v. 9). That means it's not enough just to believe that Jesus is a good man or a prophet. It's an insult to Him to limit Him to those choices.

The only thing that will save you is believing that Jesus is Lord; that He is deity, God come in the flesh. That's why there can be no comparison between Jesus and anyone else.

Jesus can't be compared with Buddha, because Jesus is God. Jesus can't be compared with Mohammed, because Jesus is God. Jesus can't be compared with Confucius, because Jesus is God.

How important is it to insist on Jesus' deity? Well, He insisted on it even though it got Him killed. The Jews were offended by that claim. But as long as you tossed your pinch of incense into the pot and said, "Caesar is Lord," Romans didn't care what you believed.

That's why the Romans generally tolerated the Jews. But then Jesus came on the scene talking about, "I am the way, and the truth, and the life; no one comes to the Father but through Me" (John 14:6). Then Peter went around after Pentecost saying, "There is salvation in no one else" but Jesus (Acts 4:12). By this time even the Romans were upset!

This is what got Jesus crucified. The Jews could have tolerated Him except for this. But when He forgave a man his sins one day, the Jewish leaders got all upset. "Who can forgive sins but God alone?" (Mark 2:7). And they set out to kill Him as a blasphemer because He made Himself equal to God.

Most people in our culture don't believe that Jesus is the only way to heaven. They believe in Jesus and church, Jesus and living a good life, Jesus and doing the best you can, Jesus and whatever. But Jesus plus anything else equals nothing. Jesus plus nothing else, though, equals everything.

Jesus is Lord whether anyone agrees with it or not. The reason we need to witness to lost people is that Jesus is God whether they accept it or not, and someday they are going to have to bow and confess that Jesus is Lord. There are about as many belief systems in our culture as there are people, but only one works. Not to witness to the truth of Christ is destructive, because the truth is not up for debate.

See, witnessing is not debating. The issue is not whether Jesus is Lord, but what people do about that fact. Paul says in Philippians 2:10–11 that a time is coming when every knee will bow and every tongue will confess that "Jesus Christ is Lord, to the glory of God the Father."

So the only question on the floor in witnessing is when people are going to bow to Jesus, not whether they are going to bow. In fact, Philippians 2:10 says that "every knee" includes not only people on earth, but all the hosts of angels in heaven.

And it doesn't stop there. Paul also says every knee "under the earth" will bow and confess that Jesus is Lord. Throughout eternity, people in hell will be bowing and confessing Christ. There are no atheists in hell. People under the earth are saying, "Jesus is Lord."

Guess what Satan is going to say throughout eternity? "Jesus is Lord." And every man and woman who has rejected Him will have no question in eternity that "Jesus Christ is Lord."

But that confession will do them no good in eternity. So we need to be persuading them now to bow their knees before Jesus and agree with God that Jesus is Lord. A failure to witness is tantamount to saying, "I couldn't care less about the eternal destiny of my loved ones."

Believing the Resurrection

But Paul also says in Romans 10:9 that people must believe that God raised Jesus from the dead. The resurrection of Christ is not nice, it's necessary. If Jesus is still dead, He can't help you. If He's still dead, He's no different than Buddha or Mohammed or Confucius, because they're still dead too.

To believe means "to lay down on," to rest on something. We could say it means to put your full weight down. When you go to church, you probably sit down in the pew or chair without a second thought. You place your full weight on that pew because you believe it is stable enough to hold you up.

If you doubted that, you either would not sit in the pew or you would sit down very cautiously, only putting part of your weight on it. You don't sit on something until you believe it is all you need to hold you up.

The proof of your faith is that you sit in the pew and rest in its power to support you. Faith is not intellectualizing about the pew. It's not saying, "I believe this pew can hold me up. I'm not about to sit down, but I believe it." That's not faith. Faith is believing in the pew enough to sit down.

Most people will say, "I believe in Jesus." Many will even say, "I believe He's the Son of God." But most people are not Christians. Why? Because they won't rest their spiritual weight totally on Jesus Christ. They want Him and something else, because they don't think He can hold them.

But the beautiful thing about the gospel is that no matter how much your sins have weighed you down, Jesus can hold you up. No matter how circumstances have burdened you down, Jesus Christ can bear the weight. He can hold you up.

When Jesus was on the cross, He said, "It is finished." That is one word in Greek, an accounting term that means the transaction has been completed, the debt has been "paid in full."

On the cross, Jesus so satisfied the Father that He could say, "Father, I have paid You fully for all the sins of all people for all time. The sin debt is paid in full."

When you pay for something it's good to have a receipt, something you can go back to as proof that the bill has been paid. God has given every Christian a receipt of the transaction carried out on the cross. That receipt is called the Resurrection.

The Resurrection is our receipt that Jesus' payment for our sins was accepted by God and the debt cleared off our account. The Resurrection is central to the Christian faith because if Jesus hadn't paid our sin bill in full, He would never have gotten up from the grave. But it was paid, and He did get up.

Can you see why we Christians do lost people an eternal disservice when we don't tell them about Jesus? No one else in town is going to tell them that Jesus is Lord, that He is the only way to the Father. And no one else is giving out Resurrection receipts.

But look at what we have to offer people. "Whoever believes in [Jesus] will not be disappointed" (Romans 10:11). You can't say that about any other religious founder. A person who puts his faith in anyone else is going to be eternally disappointed because every so-called savior but Jesus is still in his grave.

When you have Jesus, though, you don't need any of those other guys, because He is "Lord of all, abounding in riches for all who call upon Him; for 'Whoever will call on the name of the Lord will be saved'" (vv. 12–13).

See, Jesus will save anybody who calls upon Him, even a dying thief hanging next to Him (Luke 23:39–43). Can you imagine someone telling that thief, "Just believe. It doesn't matter what you believe or who you believe in, just have faith"? He would have died in his sins and gone to hell.

But that thief knew better. He had better theology than a lot of church people. He realized Jesus was the only way, so he cried out to Jesus to save him—and it was done.

THE METHOD OF EVANGELISM

Here's the third truth about evangelism. The method is personal witness:

How then will they call on Him in whom they have not believed? How will they believe in Him whom they have not heard? And how will they hear without a preacher? How will they preach unless they are sent? Just as it is written, "How beautiful are the feet of those who bring good news of good things!" (Romans 10:14–15)

Paul says, "People can't confess until they believe. They can't believe until they hear. And they can't hear unless someone tells them."

We're All Messengers

He's not talking about professional pulpiteers here when he uses the word *preacher*. He's talking about anyone who proclaims and delivers the gospel message.

The church desperately needs people today who will deliver the gospel straight because we have all kinds of confusing gospels out there. Most people are pushing against a locked door when it comes to trying to get into heaven.

There's only one door to heaven, Jesus Christ (John 10:7), and we have the key. When you see someone pushing on a locked door for which you have the key—and you know that on the other side of that door is eternity—you're destroying that person not to stop and unlock the door for him.

How to Have Beautiful Feet

I love verse 15, which is a quote from Isaiah 52:7. Paul is saying the most beautiful thing we can do is to deliver good news (which also means the most ugly, destructive thing we can do is *not* to deliver good news). In Isaiah, the reference was to the deliverance of Israel from captivity. It was incredibly good news when the herald came with the announcement, "Free at last! We can go back home!"

"Beautiful feet" are the feet that bring good news of freedom. Paul says to the Christian, "Your feet are beautiful because you can tell the drug addict, 'Free at last!' You can tell the person who is weighed down with the burden of sin, 'Free at last!' " You've got good news; don't keep it to yourself.

In the mid-eighties, I found out how beautiful the feet of those bearing good news can be. I was in the hospital with a suspicious lump on my body that the doctor thought might be cancer. They put me under the knife. I remember waking up the next day and hearing the doctor's footsteps coming down the hall.

I didn't know what the news would be. He came in and uttered one line. "It's benign." Those were some pretty feet.

If you know Jesus, you know good news. So don't keep that news to yourself. If you really want something to talk about on the telephone, talk about Jesus. People have to get the message to believe, because "faith comes from hearing, and hearing by the word of Christ" (Romans 10:17). You've got to take the Word of God to people.

During the battle of Waterloo, in which the Duke of Wellington led a force from several nations against Napoleon, the message was sent out via code, "Wellington defeated." The people were stunned by the news, which was received through a heavy fog.

But when the fog lifted, they discovered there was more to the message than they could see at first. The full message was, "Wellington defeated Napoleon at Waterloo."

There's a lot of fog in the air when it comes to the gospel. People get confused as to what the truth really is. But we have the true message. Therefore, we are responsible to deliver it and not be ashamed of the gospel.

THE SCOPE OF EVANGELISM

Fourth and finally, I want you to see that the scope of evangelism is the whole world:

But I say, surely they have never heard, have they? Indeed they have: "Their voice has gone out into all the earth, and their words to the ends of the world. . . . I was found by those who did not seek Me, I became manifest to those who did not ask for Me." But as for Israel He says, "All the day long I have stretched out my hands to a disobedient and obstinate people." (Romans 10:18, 20–21)

No Distinction

Paul says the gospel has gone out to all the world. We saw back in verse 12 that there is no distinction between Jew and

Gentile when it comes to salvation.

That's good news. God doesn't play favorites. There are no black favorites or white favorites or Hispanic favorites or Asian favorites. There are no upper-class or under-class favorites. There are no educated or uneducated favorites.

People divide the world up into groups, but that's not what God does. See, when some people call Christianity a white man's religion, what they are objecting to is not the gospel, but the way some of God's myopic children propagate it. That issue has nothing to do with the true message, because God makes no distinctions.

Therefore, since there is no difference, it's our responsibility to make the message of God known to all people without distinction. It's our responsibility to press the truth home and urge people to receive Christ.

We have to do that with tact. We can't just bombard people with the gospel. I heard about a barber who was a committed Christian. He was shaving a man when he decided he needed to witness to him. So as he was pressing his straight razor against the guy's neck, he asked him, "Are you ready to die?" That's not what I'm talking about.

No Dawdling

But I am talking about taking the gospel to everyone without embarrassment and with the urgency of someone who is telling a person his house is on fire and he needs to get out. You don't dawdle with a message like that.

A man once got his wife a special gift, a little matchbox that was supposed to glow in the dark. He gave it to his wife, but when night came, it failed to glow.

The man got angry because he thought he had been sold a piece of junk. However, his wife found a little inscription on the matchbox, written in French.

Since she knew French, she knew what was wrong. The inscription on the matchbox said, "In order for this matchbox to glow in the dark, it must absorb the light of the sun during the day." She put the thing in the sunlight, and at night it gave off a beautiful glow.

We live in a dark world that needs the light of Christ. But we can't glow in the dark until we've been saturated with the Son. When the Son saturates you, you can't help but glow.

Are you glowing on your job? Are you glowing in your neighborhood? Are you glowing in your family, or are you ashamed of the gospel? If you and I and a few million other Christians will answer these questions honestly, we'll have a big part of the answer to the question of whether Christians are destroying or blessing America.

CHAPTER 7

RECLAIMING TRUTH

On October 3, 1995, just over an hour before I was to speak to a group of pastors and other Christian leaders on the subject of truth, I joined most of America in watching one of the most debated, awaited, and attention-grabbing decisions ever rendered in this country. A judgment about truth was about to be made.

While a few of the brethren and I watched together, the cameras focused on O. J. as the foreman of the O. J. Simpson jury stood and declared the "Juice" not guilty of killing his ex-wife and her friend.

As you probably remember, the decision prompted two immediate reactions: joy and disbelief. As with all human decisions—and especially such a controversial one—there was then, still is, and always will be the lingering question, Did the verdict reflect the truth?

At the heart of the O. J. Simpson decision was the question, What is the truth? That question should sound familiar. It's the one Pilate asked Jesus at His trial (John 18:38). Pilate couldn't have been too concerned about the truth or he would have let Jesus go. His question was that of a cynic.

CONCERNED FOR TRUTH

But those of us who know Jesus Christ are very concerned

about truth. When we talk about truth, we're not talking about the best that twelve imperfect people can come up with after sifting through mounds of tainted evidence, conflicting testimony, and racially charged revelations.

A Fixed Standard

We're talking about a fixed standard, truth that is clear and unmoving. Christians do not have to cast about wondering, What is the real truth here? We do not speculate in the realm of uncertainty. If you and I are serious about our faith, we believe there is such a thing as truth that is knowable and absolute, a reliable body of evidence for what we believe.

This body of truth is the Bible, and it is that which binds us together as believers in Jesus Christ. Jesus Himself prayed for us, "Sanctify them in the truth; Your word is truth" (John 17:17). See, as Christians we are not out there with the world trying to guess at what is truth. We may not understand everything, but this jury is sure about truth.

You say, "OK, Tony, I understand. We have the truth in the Bible. So what's the problem?"

Confused About Truth

The problem is that many churches and pastors are as confused about the truth as the unbelieving world. They're like lighthouses with the light burned out, standing and pretending to give light while people crash on the rocks trying to find direction and certainty and someone who knows what's going on.

That's destructive, and it's one of the biggest problems with the church in America today. Think about it. You don't want to go to the pharmacist with your prescription and hear him say, "I think this medicine is what you're looking for. Try it and let me know what happens."

You don't want an uncertain pharmacist. You want a pharmacist who knows the truth about medication. The same is true of a pilot. I fly enough that I don't want any pilot who says, "Well, I think this is the stick you move to take off, and I'm almost sure of how to land this thing."

When it comes to the important things of life, we want reliability. We want something we can bank on, someone we can count on. We live in a world in desperate need of truth, not more talk shows. Every day there seems to be a new talk show, babble by the hour, as troubled people confront confused experts.

Things like talk shows proliferate because everybody has a problem and nobody has a final word. I'm still waiting for a secular "expert" on one of these programs to say, "The problem here is sin." That hasn't happened yet to my knowledge.

A Schizophrenic Society

Our society is schizophrenic because on one hand, people want certainty in the important everyday stuff, but on the other hand, nobody wants to admit that there is such a thing as a reliable body of truth. The academic world has abandoned the notion that it is even possible to know truth. Relativism reigns.

In his best-selling, ground-breaking book *The Closing of the American Mind*, the late professor Allan Bloom said there is virtually no student in an institution of higher learning in America who is not being taught that all truth is relative. In other words, there is no absolute body of truth that should govern our thinking and behavior.

That doesn't just affect the ivory tower academics in the university. It has resulted in a society that has no bottom line for anything. Everybody has an idea, everybody has an opinion, but nobody has the truth.

This lack of truth has led to a "conscienceless" society in which people can sin big time and feel no emotional or spiritual pain. God created pain, whether physical or spiritual, to tell us something is wrong and to keep us from going as far as we could go.

But when people do not have truth, they don't have anything to give them pain when they make wrong decisions. They become "seared in their own conscience as with a branding iron" (1 Timothy 4:2). They become anesthetized, losing their sense of right and wrong.

The process starts early these days. It used to be that people didn't try to anesthetize your conscience until college, where the professor in Philosophy 101 was at best an agnostic and at worst an atheist. He would announce, "There are no absolutes."

To which one student would always respond, "Professor, are you absolutely sure?"

But now kids in middle school and high school are learning that one person's answers and ideas are just as good as anyone else's. No wonder that in a recent poll of church kids about 85 percent of the students couldn't find anything wrong with the statement that what's true for one person may not necessarily be true for someone else.

The Loss of Truth

In a world where everybody's answers are right, nobody's answers wind up being right. When a society loses truth it loses meaning, because no one is ever really sure about anything.

Any pilot will tell you that when you fly, you need a control tower. You need somebody who can see what you can't see, who has the whole field in front of him on his radar screen, who is in touch with people you're not in touch with. No matter how sharp a pilot is, he can't see and know everything in his vicinity.

There could be another plane above or below him that he can't see, or a plane coming through the clouds that he can't see. So a pilot needs somebody who knows more truth than he knows to guide him safely.

That's the limitation of science. Science can only see what it can see; it can't see what can't be seen. So we need somebody who can look at the whole picture at once and tell us whether what we see is reality or our imagination. What we need is the truth, a standard that governs how we operate.

That is exactly what our culture lacks. In the middle of a mess like this, the church ought to stand out like a beacon by proclaiming the truth of Scripture without stuttering or apologizing.

But in too many cases, the church has been co-opted by the culture so that we end up sounding just as confused as everybody else. The result is that we inadvertently wind up aiding and abetting the deterioration of our society.

For example, it was the failure of both the black and the white church to deal with truth that assisted in the success of Louis Farrakhan's Million Man March. Because the white church has refused to comprehensively and conclusively deal with the sin of racism, the door has remained open for Farrakhan's message. And because the black church has not sufficiently taught its people, many Christians were unable to distinguish between Jesus and Mohammed, God and Allah, the Bible and the Koran. Thus theology became the servant of sociology, rather than the other way around.

Now again, someone might say, "Yeah, but can't we all get along?" Sure we can all get along in the sense of living together in peace, doing good for the community, and respecting each other. But when it comes to the issue of spiritual truth, there can be no fellowship of light with darkness. We can only get along *around truth*. You don't get along around heresy and false teaching. You get along around truth, but that means you have to believe there is such a thing as absolute, unchanging truth.

THE LOCATION OF TRUTH

So that's the mess we are in as a culture, but where do we go to find truth? I'm glad you asked. I want us to consider a little postcard of a Bible book, the epistle of 2 John. Verse 1 says: "The elder to the chosen lady and her children, whom I love in truth; and not only I, but also all who know the truth."

Truth Entrusted to the Church

The first thing I want you to see from 2 John is that God has a place, a location, where truth is to be found. He has entrusted His truth to the church, which Paul calls "the church of the living God, the pillar and support of the truth" (1 Timothy 3:15).

This means there ought to be at least one place in a community where truth still exists. There ought to be one place where there is a standard that's non-negotiable. There ought to be one place where right and wrong can be distinguished, where good and bad are clarified.

That one place ought to be the church. But when the church loses its grip on truth, there is no hope left for the society.

John called the church to which he was writing the "chosen lady" in 2 John 1. That shouldn't surprise us, because the church is always viewed as feminine in the New Testament.

For example, Peter refers to the church as "she who is in Babylon" (1 Peter 5:13). In Ephesians 5:22–33, the church is pictured as the bride of Christ. I believe the church is in view in 2 John because in verses 6, 8, and 10, the pronouns change to the plural, even though John is addressing the "chosen lady."

So the addressee in 2 John is the church, and the subject is "walking in truth" (v. 4). John talks about love, but it's not an open-ended love that embraces everyone and every idea. It's love within the boundaries of truth.

That's why the church needs to be teaching truth instead of telling stories. Have you ever tried to walk or drive through a heavy fog? It's almost impossible to see where you're going. If the pulpit is pumping out foggy teaching, God's people are going to get lost in that fog. If there is confusion at the top, there's chaos down below.

"If the bugle produces an indistinct sound, who will prepare himself for battle?" Paul asks (1 Corinthians 14:8). How can people follow when there is a lack of clarity about what's right and wrong, good and bad, up and down, yes and no? People who are confused are in no position to impact the culture.

Some churches want to build a skyscraper on the foundation of a chicken coop. They want to have awesome ministries with no truth, no standard to govern what they believe and teach.

I'm all for Christians coming together. But the question is, Whose agenda are we being asked to support? Who's in charge? Unless there is a standard of truth, attempts at unity will always break down into chaos.

One reason it's so vital that the church reclaim its rightful role as the depository of divine truth is that it's the only place around where people are going to find truth.

See, you used to find truth everywhere. You could find it at church, and it was reinforced in the school and, at times, even by television. You could find truth just about anywhere because our culture bought into a certain worldview. People could judge wrong because culture believed that there was such a thing as wrong. But today, truth is just "your way of looking at it."

Truth Expressed in Love

That's not for the "chosen lady," the bride of Christ. We are to stand for the truth as it is in Jesus (see Ephesians 4:21). This truth is not just some esoteric exercise, unrelated to the realities of life. One of the charges made against the church is that we love doctrinal statements instead of loving people.

The truth of Scripture is always tied to our actions. The way we demonstrate that we love truth is not by waving our Bibles in the air and calling people names, but by the way we love. John says that this church was full of people "whom I love in truth" (2 John 1).

Love is the active demonstration, the visible manifestation, of truth. If love is not inextricably tied to truth, it's mere sentimentalism. But if truth is not tied to love, it's mere orthodoxy that leaves people cold.

See, the church has always battled these two extremes: people with truth and no love, and people with love and no truth. If I just hammer you with truth but don't hug you with love, you don't want to hear my information. But if I hug you with love but don't tell you the truth, then I haven't helped you even though I've given you some warm fuzzies.

If we are going to be the true "chosen lady," the church, our commitment to truth must be demonstrated by love. That's how God has dealt with us. "But God demonstrates His own love toward us, in that while we were yet sinners, Christ died for us" (Romans 5:8).

See, God demonstrated His attitude toward sin by demanding payment for it. But He also demonstrated His heart of compassion and His commitment of grace by giving His own Son for our sins. He didn't compromise His truth to express His love.

Love always refers to my decision, never just to my affection. Love has not only to do with how I feel, but what I do. And if what I do does not reflect truth, it doesn't matter how I feel.

Emotions have their place, but they must be based on truth. It's easy to get that fuzzy feeling when you talk about love, but John says, "This is love, that we walk according to His commandments" (2 John 6).

The commandment he has in view is Jesus' statement, "Love one another, even as I have loved you" (John 13:34). What we have here is a seamless garment where love and truth and obedience to God are all so interwoven that you can't separate them without ruining the garment.

What I'm saying is that the church is a context and not only a content. It is a gathering of the people of God, and that is why John says the validity of our declaration about the truth is measured by our love of the brotherhood. In 1 John 4:20, the apostle wrote: "If someone says, 'I love God,' and hates his brother, he is a liar; for the one who does not love his brother whom he has seen, cannot love God whom he has not seen."

Since God is invisible, John says the way people know about invisible truth is by visible love. If there's no visible love among believers, then the world won't buy our declarations about the invisible God. It's for this reason that there will be no racial reconciliation in society until it is being modeled by the church.

Truth is demonstrable. It can be seen. That's what Jesus meant in John 13 when He went on to say, "By this all men will know that you are My disciples, if you have love for one another" (v. 35).

Measuring the Invisible

The elementary school in my old neighborhood in Baltimore had a boiler room down in the basement. The water was heated in big tanks and pumped to the classrooms through pipes that were coated with asbestos.

I got to go down to the boiler room one time, and I noticed something. On the side of the boiler was a little gauge with a water line about three-quarters of the way up the gauge. I asked the janitor, "What's that?"

"Oh," he said, "we can't see how much water is left in the boiler because it's too hot to be looking in there. So we have this gauge to let us know externally how much water we have internally."

If the gauge registers only half a tank of water, then the tank is only half full. And if the tank is full, the gauge will show it. The only way to know what's in the tank is by what registers on the gauge.

It's the same with the church. The only way you know what's in your heart for God is by what's in your actions toward your brother. If there's nothing there for your brother, there's nothing there for God.

Where there is no relational Christianity, there is no proper reflection of the truth. Suppose God had simply stayed in heaven and talked about how we were sinners and needed a Savior, and how much He loved us, without doing anything about our need. God's love is an eternal truth, but it became real to us when Jesus manifested God's love on the cross. God acted in accordance with His love.

Why hasn't America been able to solve its racial problems after 250 years of discussions and legal wrangling? Because not enough people want to deal with the truth. And the church has helped to prolong the process by its own reluctance to come to grips with the truth.

When you deal with truth it doesn't take a quarter of a millennium to decide what's right. When you deal with truth you save a lot of time. When you deal with truth you can get to the bottom line in a hurry.

A few years ago a man in our church came to me upset because so many white people were coming. He said, "We're getting a lot of whites at Oak Cliff Bible Fellowship. I'm afraid they're going to take over. What are you going to do about it, Pastor?"

I said, "I'm not going to do anything. But if you're that worried and you want more blacks in here, then you had better go do some black evangelism."

He said, "Well, I'm upset and I'm leaving."

I said, "Bye." It wasn't hard. It didn't require any long counseling sessions. Now you may be saying, "He was probably raised that way. He just needed time."

Well, he may have needed time to adjust his heart, but the issue was that he needed to correct his speech right away because he wasn't acting according to truth. It's OK to give people time for their emotions to catch up. But you can insist that they adjust their actions immediately. We need to be able to make these distinctions because there is such a thing as truth.

THE ACCESSIBILITY OF TRUTH

So there's a location for the truth, which is the church. There's a demonstration of the truth, which is love. But there's also an accessibility to the truth. John was writing to "all who know the truth" (2 John 1). The commandment was "from the

beginning" (v. 5). God's truth is knowable. It's there for everyone to read and understand.

No Secrets Here

Watch out for people who claim to have special, secret
knowledge. Watch out for secret societies. They want to ensnare
you in their secrets, but God wants His truth known. He's not
playing hide-and-seek with the truth.

Jesus said, "You will know the truth, and the truth will make
you free" (John 8:32). Freedom is living in light of the truth, not
just doing what you want to do.

Suppose a fish said, "I want to be free of this water. I'm tired
of being in water all day long. I want to be free to roam the for-
est like the lions and soar through the sky like the birds. Set me
free from this water."

So you say, "OK, fish, you've been cooped up too long in the
ocean. I'm going to set you free." All you've done is set the fish
free to die, because the truth is that a fish was never meant to
be free of the water. Simply to give people what they want
because they want it may be to kill them.

Making the Truth Known

Down here in Texas, we have a big holiday we observe every
year called "Juneteenth." It commemorates the time when
slaves in Texas finally got the word that Abraham Lincoln had
signed the Emancipation Proclamation. The trouble is that it
took two years for the word to get here, so when it arrived it
was a big deal.

In other words, black people had been free for two years,
but nobody told us. So we were still walking around like slaves,
acting like slaves, saying "Yessir" and "Master" like slaves. We
were doing all that even though we were as free as birds,
because nobody told us.

But once they told us, we haven't forgot since! We celebrate
it every year. What a feeling it is to see the parades and the parties all over the city of Dallas reminding us of our freedom.

See, this freedom was real because it wasn't just based on
wanting to be free, hoping to be free, or pretending to be free. It

was based on a standard, the Emancipation Proclamation, that was a public document, available for all to read. It just needed to be made known to those who were enslaved.

Our standard of truth and of freedom, the Bible, is open and accessible to all. It will free people from racism, from addictions, from marital discord, from sin of every kind. This Book will set you free. All you have to do is proclaim it.

That's why the church needs to preach the Book. Martin Luther said it best: "The Bible is so deep that theologians can't touch bottom. But at the same time, it's so shallow that babies can't drown."

The beauty of the Bible is that when you dive down deep into it, you wonder if you will ever hit bottom because there's so much there. But a brand-new baby Christian can read the Bible and say, "This is just right for me. I can wade in this water." That's because it is the truth.

The church needs to stick to the Bible. We preachers need to preach the truth of Scripture flavored with the application of love, and people will get set free. The best thing the church can do for America is to hold the standard of truth high. We in the church had better make sure that the truth we declare is that of King Jesus, or we'll lead people astray. We have got to reclaim and hold to the truth, because there is no other standard out there that anyone can depend on.

"There is no other name under heaven that has been given among men by which we must be saved" (Acts 4:12) but the name of Jesus. Let's lift Him up. He is the truth, the whole truth, and nothing but the truth.

CHAPTER 8

"IF MY PEOPLE..."

In case I haven't made it clear yet, let me say it right here: The future of American culture is squarely in the hands of Christians. Our problem is not so much the presence of unrighteousness as it is the loss of God's glory. Unrighteousness and evil have dominated our culture because God's glory has departed, and that departure is primarily the result of the removal of Christ's lampstand from the church (Revelation 2:5).

Make no mistake about it. America's future is not in the hands of the politicians or the social scientists. Most don't know what to do. They are "always learning and never able to come to the knowledge of the truth" (2 Timothy 3:7).

The reason the future of our culture is in the hands of Christians is that the cause of our cultural demise is spiritual. And if a problem is spiritual, its cure must be spiritual.

Based on the premise of this book, you might be saying, "Tony, I'm not sure I'm excited about that, since God's people don't seem to be doing the job spiritually." Well, in many cases that's true. But there's hope, and in this chapter I want to look at one of the greatest sources of hope we have: the promise that we can move God's heart and hand through prayer.

If we Christians are going to build rather than destroy America, we've got to fall on our knees and our faces before God and pray. Not talk about prayer, but *pray*. Not agree on the importance of prayer, but *pray*.

HOW TO FIX YOUR WORLD

We're going to base our study on a single verse, one which is familiar to most believers: 2 Chronicles 7:14. Whether you're talking about restoring a nation, a city, or a family, this incredible verse holds everything you've always wanted to know about fixing your world, but were afraid to ask.

The context of 2 Chronicles 7:14 is very important, because the verse actually begins in the middle of a sentence. So let's set the stage here.

The occasion is the dedication of Solomon's great temple. Solomon offers a dedicatory prayer in chapter 6 in which he says, in essence, "Lord, I want to lead this people in righteousness. I want to lead this people in honoring You. Lord, I want to do it the way You want it done."

Then in 2 Chronicles 7:1–10, God's glory came down and filled the temple, and the people offered sacrifices and held a feast. Then the text records:

Solomon finished the house of the Lord and the king's palace, and successfully completed all that he had planned on doing in the house of the Lord and in his palace. Then the Lord appeared to Solomon at night and said to him, "I have heard your prayer and have chosen this place for Myself as a house of sacrifice. If I shut up the heavens so that there is no rain, or if I command the locust to devour the land, or if I send pestilence among My people, and My people who are called by My name humble themselves and pray and seek My face and turn from their wicked ways, then I will hear from heaven, will forgive their sin and will heal their land." (vv. 11–14)

We know the context of verse 14. What God is saying is that if a people turn away from Him and reject His ways, then it doesn't matter who gets elected to the White House or how much money the government has for social programs. When God starts withholding His rain and sends the locusts to devour your land, you'd better start dealing with Him. You say, "But I thought He was a God of goodness and grace."

He is, but He will not be played for a fool. You cannot continue to dismiss God from your civilization and expect everything to work right. If a culture wants to be free of God, He will let it have that freedom. But freedom from God brings dire consequences.

Our culture doesn't understand that, so we have people running for help to everyone but the right Person. Pagans don't normally seek after God in prayer, but they're not the ones this verse is addressed to anyway. "My people" are the only ones qualified to claim this promise. We are the ones who are supposed to know where to turn for help. So let's find out what God wants from us.

Who Can Pray

The first thing God says in 2 Chronicles 7:14 about those whose prayers get through to Him is that they are "My people who are called by My name."

This tells us who can pray. Have you ever wondered why they start off each session of Congress with prayer, yet none of this stuff is getting fixed? Why are they always praying down at city hall and in the statehouse, and nothing happens?

It has to do with whose prayers God hears. When God says "My people" are to pray, He is talking about His covenant people. In the Old Testament, His covenant people was Israel. In the New Testament, it's the church, the true Christians.

God is not obligated to hear the prayers of sinners, unless they are asking for forgiveness. God has no obligation to sinners who pray because they are not His people and they have not been called by His name.

Only Christians get through to heaven. Only God's children have access to the throne of grace. If God has decided to destroy America, only Christians can make Him rethink that. If God has decided to allow our cities to continue to deteriorate, only Christians can reverse that.

The principle here is that of representation. That is, only God's appointed representatives get through to Him. His people can get through to Him because they bear His name, which means they are under His authority. When God calls us His people, He is saying, "You belong to Me. You are called to live under My authority."

That's who can pray. And that's why Satan's main goal today is to keep Christians from getting it together, especially on their knees, because he knows if we ever get it together, he's in bad shape.

Satan's big thing is rendering Christians inoperative. He's not worried about the sinners. He can handle any sinner, because the sinners already belong to him. They don't know they belong to him, but they do. But if he can lull Christians to sleep spiritually, he's ready to run the show.

The Attitude of Prayer

There's also a definite attitude of heart God is looking for when Christians pray. He's seeking those who will "humble themselves."

Humble Christians get through to God. Humility has the idea of dependency. It marks those who understand that without Him, we can do nothing (John 15:5). Too many of us are arrogant. The Bible calls it being "haughty," big-chested, because we don't really believe that we need God. God is for emergencies only.

We say, "God, don't call me, I'll call You." And so God allows us to go through trials that we can't fix to humble us and to put us flat on our backs, as if to say, "Now let's see you get up all by yourself."

The opposite of God putting you flat on your back is you putting yourself flat on your face before Him in humility. When we kneel, or when we lie prostrate before the Lord, we are demonstrating humility.

Saints in the Old Testament often expressed humility and remorse over sin by putting on rough sackcloth and covering themselves with ashes, or by tearing their robes. Those were acts of humiliation.

God says, "If you want to get My attention, humble yourself. Don't come before Me boastful, proud, and independent because I will let you know you need Me. I do not need you. Humble yourself." Humility is tied to prayer because prayer is by its nature an admission of our weakness and need. Many Christians don't pray because they are too proud.

You say, "But I'm not proud." If you don't pray you are, because prayer says to God, "I need You. I can't make this marriage work on my own. I can't solve this problem at work on my own. I am not sufficient in myself to do what needs to be done and to be what You want me to be."

Now if God were to stop the rain today or send locusts or pestilence, most of us would form a committee to study the lack of rain. We would get together a commission to do something about the locusts.

We try everything except the one thing that could change the whole scene: Come before God and pray. This is why the first challenge of the church is to get Christians to bring themselves and their problems before the face of God. To put prayer last means to put God last, and to put God last means everything else we do is a waste of time.

The Intensity of Prayer

Then the Lord goes on to tell His people in 2 Chronicles 7:14, "Seek My face." This doesn't mean the kind of prayers we usually pray over dinner: "Lord, bless this food to our bodies. In Jesus' name. Amen."

Seeking God's face has much more than that in mind. The context here is one of God turning His face away from His people in judgment. They now have to gain His attention once again before He will give attention to their prayers.

You know how hard it is to carry on a conversation with someone whose back is to you. Once a person turns away from you in disapproval, if the problem is yours, you are now obligated to win back that person's approval. In other words, you have to do the adjusting so you can look at the person's face again.

What has turned God's face away from His people is our sin, so we are the ones who have to come to Him on His terms. Prayer is not a process of negotiation. We don't come before God's face and say, "Now, God, let me tell You what I'm going to do. Let's make a deal."

We want God to adjust to our will. We want God to reverse Himself. But God says, "No, you seek My face. You come to Me willing to submit to My terms."

See, we are the ones without the rain. We are the ones with the locusts. We are the ones whose culture is crumbling because of sin and rebellion against God. So we had better be the ones who are seeking God's terms of reconciliation.

The good news is that God is inviting us to seek His face, to restore fellowship with Him. He is open to our prayers. We can't always be sure of that when we alienate another person. He or she might not be willing to reconcile. But God is always ready for His people to seek His face.

Repentance and Prayer

Notice here in 2 Chronicles 7:14 that the phrase "seek My face" is closely linked with "turn from their wicked ways." This is how we seek God's face, by turning from our sin. The idea here is repentance, turning away from something that displeases God and turning toward something else that pleases Him.

If you are living the way *you* want to live, then you are wasting your time on your knees.

Someone will say, "Well, I prayed about it." Maybe so, but unless that prayer is followed by a decision of your will to do a 180-degree turn from the way you are going, you have no confidence that God has heard your prayer.

If you want God to show His face to you, then you must turn toward Him. And that involves turning away from anything that is contrary to His will.

If God has turned His back on a Christian because of his sin, and that Christian is going away from God in his sin, then what you have is two people facing in opposite directions. Somebody had better turn around, and that's the Christian.

A lot of prayers go unanswered because the lifestyle of the person praying is unacceptable to the One being prayed to. You can't come to God with junk and ask Him to ignore the junk but change your family, change your job, or change your culture.

The reason our culture is crumbling is that Christians refuse to forsake their wicked ways. The reason marriages are falling apart is that Christian couples refuse to live by God's standard of righteousness. Christian men don't want to assume their leadership responsibilities. Christian women want to define the role of womanhood other than what God has said in the Scriptures.

God will not negotiate on His standards. He wants us to place ourselves under the authority of His Word and conform to it. Failure to conform is wickedness.

In many cases, the message to the church today needs to be,

Get up off your knees. God isn't ready to hear until men are ready to love and lead their families. He isn't listening until women are ready to submit themselves to their husbands and husbands are ready to sacrifically love their wives.

The church is bringing to God something other than what He demands of us. And when that happens, we are contributing to the demise of society because we are redefining things on our own terms.

In 2 Chronicles 7, God gives Solomon the essence of the "wicked ways" He is talking about. Speaking of what would happen if Israel ever turned away from Him, God said that if anyone wanted to know why Israel was uprooted from the land (which did happen later), the answer would be:

Because they forsook the Lord, the God of their fathers, who brought them from the land of Egypt, and they adopted other gods and worshiped them and served them, therefore He has brought all this adversity on them. (v. 22)

The problem is idolatry, paying homage to someone or something other than God. Unfortunately, we Christians have a real knack for paying homage to false gods these days. We don't carve idols out of wood and stone, but we carve out a big place in our lives for work and play and self and all this other stuff that crowds God out.

Whenever you pay homage to something or someone other than God, you have created another god. Then God says, "Since that's the god you want, let that god take care of you."

God's people have allowed themselves to be shaped and defined by the culture's standards instead of shaping and defining the culture by God's standards. So we wind up giving God what everybody else is giving Him, which is a polite nod.

But that won't do. Imagine finding out that your teenager is smoking marijuana because "everyone else I know is doing it." That would not be an acceptable reason. Most Christian parents would say, "So what? You are not everyone else. You are my child, and I didn't raise you that way!"

In the same way, God doesn't want His children conforming to what the rest of the world is doing, adopting their standards. He is saying, "You are called by My name. I'm your Daddy. The rest of the world didn't die on the cross for you.

The rest of the world didn't rise from the dead. So the rest of the world shouldn't be telling you what to do."

But the church is accommodating to the culture. Our culture has redefined morality, commitment, and priorities, and we seem powerless to do anything about it.

Just recently a young brother in our church told me that he and his wife had been praying about it, and that she was leaving work so she could be home with their little girl.

I asked him, "Is it going to be a financial strain?"

He said, "Yes, it's going to be tough, but we decided that since our daughter is young, we want to invest that time with her."

I don't have a problem with women who work, as long as they prioritize the home. But this couple decided that the demands of her job would cause her to neglect their daughter, so they pulled the plug on her job. What drove their decision was a biblical perspective on family and work.

A single young man told me, "Guys make fun of me because I've given up sex since I've come to Christ. They call me all kinds of names." But he has continued to take his stand. Why? Because he no longer belongs to the culture. He belongs to Jesus Christ. That means there is a whole different morality.

The problem is we've got the wrong people bossing us around. God says His people must turn from their wicked ways. We have to stop letting this world govern our decisions. Our job as Christians is not to be popular. It's to be biblical.

THE RESULT OF PRAYER

There's an important transitional word right in the middle of 2 Chronicles 7:14. "Then," God says, "I will hear from heaven." That means when we as God's people have fulfilled His conditions and come to Him on His terms, then He will hear us—and not until then.

Getting God's Attention

We know that God hears everything we say. The idea is that He will pay attention to our prayers when we come humbly, seeking His face, and turning from our wicked ways.

It's like when you say to someone, "Didn't you hear what I said?" Yes, that person heard the sounds, but he or she wasn't tuned in to what you were saying. You didn't have the listener's attention.

God says, "If you will come to Me the way that I prescribe, you will have My attention." And more than that, God promises to forgive sin and heal the land when we get His attention.

Forgiveness is essential because God is holy. The root meaning of that term is that He is separate from everyone and everything else. He is distinct from His creation.

We don't pray to some "New Age" god who is nothing but the sum total of our experiences and our ideas. The New Agers want to become one with God by becoming gods. But nobody can become one with God. God is in a class all by Himself.

Because of who God is, you can't get past the need for forgiveness. God is distinct from sin. You cannot get God's attention if you go unforgiven. That's why we have Communion. That's why we are told to confess our sins, because God will not listen unless sins are forgiven.

In order for sins to be forgiven, someone must pay the penalty. God does not skip sin. Many people have the idea that forgiveness means God just skips over our sins. No, it's just that someone else paid the price.

In the Old Testament, animals paid the price. The people had to slay lambs and goats because a holy God demanded that sin had to be paid for. No one gets away with sin. Someone has to pay.

People go to hell because they reject Jesus' payment for sin on the cross, so they have to pay themselves. The reason we can be forgiven is that Jesus Christ has already paid for our sins. And we can keep on being forgiven as believers because the blood of Jesus Christ keeps on forgiving us of our sins as we bring those sins before Him (see 1 John 1:9).

Healing Our Land

Once God's people are forgiven, then God is free to "heal their land." That is, the effects of their righteousness will spill over to the environment in which they live. This was the way it was supposed to work with Israel. Israel was a special people with a special covenant, and God was to bless all the nations through them.

When Israel was right with God, even the Gentiles in their midst were blessed because of their obedience. The healing effects of the promise of 2 Chronicles 7:14 reach beyond individual Christians and even the church to touch the entire society, as in the case of Nineveh (Jonah 3).

Our problem, though, is that the church is like the prophet Jonah, totally self-centered and going in the wrong direction.

If our culture is to be granted a stay of execution, it will be because God's people are a force for spiritual and emotional healing in our land. If the whole concept of marriage and family is to be salvaged, it will happen when Christians get their marriages and their families lined up with God's commands.

You may say, "My marriage is too far gone." For you maybe, but not for God. When He acts in power, He can change the environment of your marriage.

You may say, "America is too far gone. How are we going to change public education, government, the media?" Well, you change education and government and families by having new people in those places, people who are going to represent Jesus Christ and His frame of reference. That doesn't mean that only Christians are qualified to serve in government or that politics is the primary force of change Christians can work through— but it does mean the political realm is a legitimate sphere of influence for some believers.

By that I mean Christians who are in step with God can use their positions to help transform society. Systems are only bad because the people running the systems are bad. As we move out into society, some of us will be placed in leadership by God, just as Daniel was.

If enough Christians in places of responsibility in medicine, law, government, the media, and even the church begin to humble themselves and pray and seek God's face and turn from their wicked ways, we could invade this culture and make the presence of Christ felt from top to bottom.

That's what God is after. He wants people who will commit themselves to Him personally and in their families, and then move out to penetrate the culture for Him.

A BIBLICAL EXAMPLE

Let me show you a perfect example of what I'm talking about in the person of Nehemiah. In Nehemiah 1, we learn that this man was a Jewish exile serving in the court of Artaxerxes, king of Persia. Nehemiah heard about the broken-down condition of Jerusalem, and he mourned over the city where God's name dwelt.

But Nehemiah also knew how to pray, so in verses 4–11 he went before God in intense prayer. He called on God's name, coming humbly with fasting. He repented of his sins and the sins of his people, and he sought God's forgiveness and healing for the land of Israel. Notice how his prayer ended in verse 11:

O Lord, I beseech You, may Your ear be attentive to the prayer of Your servant and the prayer of Your servants who delight to revere Your name, and make Your servant successful today, and grant him compassion before this man.

"This man," of course, was King Artaxerxes. Nehemiah could pray for success because things were now in proper perspective. As soon as Nehemiah said amen, he realized that he was "cupbearer to the king" (v. 11). In other words, it suddenly dawned on Nehemiah that God had already positioned him to make a difference for his people. That was important because Nehemiah was about to go before the king and make an astounding request. He was getting ready to ask permission to go back and rebuild Jerusalem.

Up to this point, Nehemiah had not made the correlation between being the king's cupbearer and the plight of Jerusalem. But now he realized he was in the most strategic position possible. King Artaxerxes was an unsaved and unregenerate man, but he had the power in his hands to solve Jerusalem's problem.

A person in Nehemiah's position didn't normally ask for time off to go and take care of personal business. As the king's cupbearer, he was the one who tasted the king's wine and food before the king got it so no one would try to poison him.

Nehemiah was someone King Artaxerxes had learned to trust and rely on. The king wasn't going to let him just disappear for months or even years. But this wasn't a normal situation. Nehemiah had prayed and sought God for his land, and he was willing to put his career on the line to make an impact for God.

Here is a fundamental flaw that has characterized the church. We have separated our careers from our worship. Many of us have not seen the kingdom connection between the God we worship, the needs of our culture, and the skills He has given us that we may already be using in our jobs.

Nehemiah's question was how to get the power of Artaxerxes to the people who needed it in Jerusalem. God had already provided the answer by making Nehemiah the king's cupbearer.

I don't think it has occurred to many Christians that God has strategically positioned them to affect their culture for Him. One of the things we need to do to rebuild our culture is "kingdomize" our skills; that is, discover how God can use our so-called secular skills for sacred purposes.

God is not limited in the means He can use to heal our land once His people get lined up behind His purposes. Your position of influence may extend to your family, your community, or well beyond that.

But however wide your circle, the key is seeking God and getting right before Him. Nehemiah may not have had 2 Chronicles 7:14 in front of him as he prayed, but his prayer and his life are an example of this great verse in action.

Before we wrap up this issue of prayer, let me point out that God does not only use the positions of believers to influence culture. He can use the position of the unrighteous to fulfill His goal for the righteous.

We see this in the description of the Promised Land in Deuteronomy 6:10–11. The land God was going to give Israel contained "great and splendid cities which you did not build, and houses full of all good things which you did not fill, and hewn cisterns which you did not dig, vineyards and olive trees which you did not plant."

Do you know how Canaan became such a luxurious land? Do you know how the cisterns were dug? The Hittites and the Amorites and all the other sinners who lived in the land fixed it up for God's people. Then God got rid of the sinners and replaced them with the saints. Let me say it again. God is not limited in the methods He can use to heal our land.

SOME QUESTIONS TO ANSWER

So as Christians, we need to ask ourselves a couple of questions. Are we going to sit and watch our culture fall apart? Are we going to sit and watch our families disintegrate? Or are we going to do something to point America back to God?

A lot of Christian husbands think their problem is their wives. They're like Adam: "The reason I can't get it together is because of this woman You gave me, Lord." And a lot of wives feel the same way about their husbands.

I'm not denying that there can be all kinds of relationship problems in marriages and in families, but our real problem as God's people is with Him. Until we are willing to humble ourselves and seek His face, there's not much anyone else can do for us.

The promise of 2 Chronicles 7:14 is an awesome promise, but you can't enjoy this kind of divine intervention with just a little prayer tossed toward heaven now and then. The kind of prayer that will reclaim lives, families, and a nation for God has to take high priority in our schedules.

In fact, if you look back at Nehemiah 1:4 you will see that Nehemiah prayed and fasted for days when he heard about conditions in Jerusalem. When you want something from God badly enough, you will push other things aside to seek Him for it.

Nehemiah didn't sit down and write out a "Great Society" program for Jerusalem. He didn't propose a Jerusalem "New Deal." He fasted and prayed and sought God, and God revealed His strategy. God was able to reverse years of deterioration in just fifty-two days. Prayer saves time!

We know that God moved in response to Nehemiah's prayer, using his position of influence with the king to get Artaxerxes to support the rebuilding of Jerusalem. But Nehemiah didn't start with his position. He started with prayer, which provided the link between God, Nehemiah's problem, and his position.

So let me ask you this: If you see something in your life or in your world that is broken, is prayer the first thing you do, or the last thing you do? If it's the last thing you do, more than likely, as I said above, you will have wasted your time on anything else. If prayer comes last, then so will the solution to your problem.

Nehemiah fasted over his need. Fasting is when you are really serious. You can pray and not be all that serious, but you don't fast unless you are serious. The last thing we give up is our food.

Fasting is giving up a craving of the body because of a greater need of the spirit. That is, there is something going on that is so deep, so heavy, and for which you need God's intervention so badly, that you give up something considered important for it.

The most common form of fasting is giving up food, but in 1 Corinthians 7:5 Paul talks about sexual fasting between a husband and wife; a mutual decision to abstain from physical intimacy for the purpose of sustained prayer.

There are different kinds of fasting, but they boil down to the same issue. Fasting means I am willing to give up something that my body demands in order that something my spirit needs is granted.

Far too often, we allow other things to push prayer aside rather than allowing prayer to push other things aside. My TV show is coming on, so prayer gets pushed aside. I've had a long day and I need extra sleep, so prayer will have to wait. I have this major deal working, so I don't have time to pray.

Well, God does not like being pushed aside. And if the church is going to help rebuild America, we can't afford to keep pushing Him aside. Some other things are going to have to wait, including our bodily appetites, if we are going to turn our communities around.

Congregations are going to have to come together in solemn assembly (Joel 1:14) to repent and to throw themselves before the face of Almighty God. Nehemiah was determined that nothing was going to stop him from seeking God and pleading for His favor.

We could save a lot of time running around and worrying about stuff if we spent time praying first. You would have to say that in Nehemiah's case, the crumbled walls of Jerusalem were a major problem, something that cried out for immediate and decisive action.

But Nehemiah fasted and prayed first. So my question to you is, What wall is crumbling in your life? Is there anything falling apart in your life? Or better yet, is there anything you want to shore up *before* it crumbles? Push some other things aside and get in contact with God.

If you can't think of anything that's falling apart, let me give you one: America. The spiritual foundations of this nation are crumbling fast. Political action won't stop the erosion. More money won't stop it. Before we worry about the problems in the White House, we need to begin rebuilding the piece of America God has given us: the church.

We have a great God who is willing to forgive and heal our land . . . *if* He can find some people who are ready to fall on their faces to seek His face.

CHAPTER 9

RESTORING THE FATHER-LED HOME

Some months ago, an ugly crack appeared in my bedroom wall. I called a painter, who replaced the defective plaster and repainted the wall. It looked great. I was happy; he was happy. I paid him, and he left.

But about a month later the crack reappeared, uglier than ever. Preachers don't get mad, but I was somewhat "evangelically ticked off." I called the painter back and asked him to fix my problem. He apologized and expressed surprise that the problem had recurred so quickly. He redid the work and everything was fine—for about forty-five days.

But then that crack came back, only this time it brought its aunts, uncles, cousins, nieces, and nephews. At this point I concluded that I needed a new painter. I called another professional to come and fix my problem for good.

This man looked at my wall and shocked me by saying, "I'm sorry, sir. I can't help you with your problem, because you don't have a problem with cracks in your wall."

Well, I looked at the cracks in my wall, then I looked at the "crackpot" telling me my problem wasn't cracks in my wall. I said, "Excuse me, but I can see a crack, you can see a crack. In fact, all God's children can see a crack."

"Oh yes," he replied, "you have a crack, but that's not your problem. It just reflects a much deeper problem. Your problem is a shifting foundation. Until you stabilize your foundation, you will forever be repairing cracks on your wall."

A METAPHOR FOR AMERICA

What a perfect metaphor for the condition of American society today. We can see "cracks" everywhere: social cracks, political cracks, moral cracks, even crack cocaine cracks.

But until we stabilize the foundation, no number of programs, government grants, or elections will be able to repair the cracks in our cultural walls. There is no place where the foundation of America needs to be stabilized more than in the home. The breakdown of the family is the single greatest contributor to the deterioration of our country.

Strong families hold the key to a strong society, while, conversely, weak families lead to a weak society. This is so because every other institution in society is predicated on and dependent upon strong families. And you can't have strong families without God at their foundation.

No wonder Satan didn't bother Adam until he got married. Satan knew that in order to shut down God's program of expanding His kingdom on earth, he would have to destroy the institution at the foundation of that program; namely, the family.

We can't talk about the role of Christians in affecting society without talking about the family. As Christians, we need to make sure our families are built on the solid rock if we hope to help others. If our families are a mess, we don't need to be exporting that into the culture.

As a husband and father as well as a pastor, I am convinced that the responsibility of building godly homes lies at the feet of the man. This is not to discount a woman's importance and input, but God has placed men at the head of their families. And I don't know of any greater task or any more risky business than to be a man holding the responsibility of leading a home. Look at what we're up against.

What used to be considered rather unusual not too many years ago, a family without a father, is now a crisis of growing proportions. The reality in our culture today is that a staggering number of children are growing up in single-parent homes, the vast majority of which are fatherless.

In 1970, for example, only 13 percent of children grew up

without both parents at home. But today, that number is at least 30 percent in the culture at large. For African-American children, the percentage more than doubles to 63 percent.

We're talking about millions of children growing up in homes where in most cases they will know little or nothing of a father's influence. I know that mothers are deserting their families today too, but the numbers are still heavily weighted toward missing fathers.

In fact, we're told that half of all American children will go through at least some part of their lives without having a father at home. And the future doesn't look any brighter. By the year 2000, it is predicted that 70 percent of black children will be products of single-parent (mostly fatherless) homes.

The implications of this are staggering in terms of the world we have to live in and minister to. This is not theoretical for me. My church in Dallas is not immune to the problem. One Sunday morning I asked for single parents to raise their hands, and then asked for those who had been raised in single-parent homes to raise their hands. In each case a good number of people put their hands up.

So in this chapter I want to address primarily fathers and husbands as we look at how Christians can strengthen America by stabilizing their own homes on the foundation of God's Word.

It used to be a lot simpler than it is today. At one time our culture shared a basic understanding about what it meant to be a father and a husband. But the role of the man has been radically redefined, leaving behind a whole generation of boys and men who aren't clear about what it means to be a man, let alone how to go about leading a home.

PASSING ON THE FAITH

Let me give you my thesis right up front, so you can see how crucial the man's role in the home is to the survival of a culture. The Bible teaches that the man's primary role in a family is to oversee the generational expansion of the Christian faith.

A Heavy Responsibility

That is, a man is to supervise, manage, and oversee his

home in such a way that a vital faith is instilled in his children and they grow up to live as followers of Jesus Christ and establish vital Christian homes in their generation.

This is no small task in itself. But it is made even more important because the degree to which men succeed or fail in this task is the degree to which you can see the deterioration of the communities of which those men are a part.

When Christian men succeed in this role, the world in which they live becomes a better place. When Christian men fail in this role, the world in which they live becomes a much more traumatic place.

We see this principle underscored in Exodus 20:4–6, the second of the Ten Commandments:

You shall not make for yourself an idol, or any likeness of what is in heaven above or on the earth beneath or in the water under the earth. You shall not worship them or serve them; for I, the Lord your God, am a jealous God, visiting the iniquity of the fathers on the children, on the third and the fourth generations of those who hate Me, but showing lovingkindness to thousands, to those who love Me and keep My commandments.

God says that the decisions of a father have generational repercussions. What he does or does not do not only impacts his own life; it spills over to his children and his children's children and his children's children's children.

Now that's a sobering thought. It would not be so bad if my mess stopped with me. But my mess gets passed on and on and on. And with each succeeding generation, it gets passed on worse. Why? Because God is doing the passing on, not just the man. God is "visiting the iniquity of the fathers on the . . . third and the fourth generations."

Can you see why Satan targets men? It's not that he is not out to destroy women too, but he understands this generational relationship and principle between a father and his family. So Satan knows that if he can destroy dads, he can control the generations.

A Frightening Answer

This is exactly what we are seeing today in our country. We

are seeing what happens when men are extricated from their roles, responsibilities, and presence in the home. We're seeing what the devil can do if he can remove a man from the home—or even worse, keep him from ever entering the home.

Today we are seeing the frightful answer to the question, What would it be like to have a whole generation of children grow up never having known the love, the touch, or the blessing of a father? What would it be like to experience a generation of children who have had no father to input values and right principles into their lives?

It is not so much that this is a lost generation. It is more accurate to say this is the *product* of a lost generation. This is a fatherless generation, and I hate to imagine what their children will be like if things don't change.

The violence and destruction we are witnessing today are the negative operation of this generational principle. The good news from Exodus 20:6 is that this principle works in the positive too. Fathers can turn this thing around for their families and ultimately for their culture.

But there is only one way to start fixing the mess we are in. We must raise up a new generation of godly men who will accept the challenge of reversing the trend. God says it can only be done by "those who love [Him] and keep [His] commandments" (v. 6). My generation of fathers and husbands has the challenge of being this kind of men today.

To our forefathers faith was an experience. To our fathers faith was an inheritance. To us faith is a convenience. And if we are not careful in passing on a vital, firsthand faith, to our children faith may become a nuisance.

It is through God's faithful ones that His presence is seen and experienced in a culture. God has given the men of this culture a lead role in transferring the Christian faith.

A Positive Example

This is illustrated poignantly in Genesis 18. You'll recall from our study in chapter 2 that the setting here is the imminent judgment of Sodom and Gomorrah. I want to go back to that text, not to retell the story, but to contrast the two men at the heart of that drama.

The first man was Lot. You recall that God was willing to spare Sodom if just ten righteous people could be found. Lot had more than half that number in his family alone, but they couldn't get ten godly people together because Lot had failed to pass the faith to the next generation. Because he failed, the culture could not be salvaged.

Standing in brilliant contrast to Lot was Abraham. Look at what God said to Abraham in Genesis 18 in relation to His decision to judge Sodom:

The Lord said, "Shall I hide from Abraham what I am about to do, since Abraham will surely become a great and mighty nation, and in him all the nations of the earth will be blessed? For I have chosen him, in order that he may command his children and his household after him to keep the way of the Lord by doing righteousness and justice; in order that the Lord may bring upon Abraham what He has spoken about him." (vv. 17–19)

It was too late for Sodom and Gomorrah, but it was not too late for everybody else because one man—Abraham—was willing to transfer his faith to his posterity.

And this wasn't a private deal either. Through Abraham's faithfulness, "all the nations of the earth" would share in the blessing. What does it take to transfer the faith across the generations so that a nation is transformed? There are at least four things involved in this transfer.

A SENSE OF DESTINY

The first thing that is involved in faith transference is a sense of destiny. You can see Abraham's destiny in the verses we just quoted from Genesis 18. He was a man chosen of God to establish a godly heritage.

Some man will say, "Well, that was Abraham. God spoke to him and made several great nations out of him. That isn't going to happen to me." Maybe not, but God wants to use you to build a great family and help build a great church that shapes a great community. That ought to be destiny enough for any Christian man.

Going Somewhere

What's missing in so many men's lives today is a sense of destiny, this conviction that they're going somewhere and that they're part of something bigger than a career. If you are going nowhere, you are going to take those who are following you with you so that they go nowhere too.

As someone has said, a person who aims at nothing will hit it every time. Our culture doesn't know where it's going. It doesn't need Christians who don't know where they're going either.

What answer would you get if you asked the average Christian man, "Where are you going?" He might say heaven, but beyond that he would be basically clueless. He might talk about his job or something else by which men define themselves, but you're not likely to hear a clear, strong statement of spiritual destiny.

But if the only place a man is going is to work, he is really going nowhere in terms of what we're talking about. If all he can see in the future is the next promotion, the bigger house, or the nicer car, then he has little to pass on to the next generation.

Something to Offer

What we offer our children and grandchildren has to be made of something other than metal, paper, or bricks. It has to have the stuff that life is made of.

Our problem is we have aimed too low. In the black community, our ancestors looked forward to the day when their children and grandchildren would be able to live free and there would be equality for all. Many gave their lives for that day.

But many of their children now live for a credit card. They have no sense of destiny. The great families that helped to build America were those in which great-grandfather had a vision a century or more ago and passed it down so that today, his great-grandchildren are carrying it out in some fashion. The vision shaped the whole family.

The basic idea is that way back there, the great-granddaddy had a vision, and he never let his children get away from it. God said of Abraham, "I have chosen him and given him a destiny, to be a blessing to the nations."

A Big Destiny

God gave Adam a big destiny. He told Adam and Eve to be fruitful and multiply and fill the earth. They were to "subdue" the earth and have dominion over it (Genesis 1:28). Adam was also given the task of naming the animals. Whatever he called them, that was their name.

If there is no call of God on your life, there is no sense of destiny. Destiny always involves two things. First, there's a sense of calling, the conviction that God has you here for a special purpose. Second, there is a sense of vision, a dream big enough to get you where you believe God wants you to go.

A visionless father and husband has nothing to transfer. His wife is often confused and frustrated because she doesn't quite know where things are going, since the one she is looking to doesn't know where things are going. And the children who are following don't know where things are going either.

What Satan did to Adam was mess up his ability to perceive his destiny. He got Adam and Eve focused on a single fruit tree when they should have been running the whole show and managing the environment. Satan got them all shook up about a piece of fruit, and they lost their mandate to subdue and rule the culture.

When Christian men understand that God has called them to transfer the faith to the next generation, a lot of other things fall into place. Now that doesn't mean it will be easy. The culture will still try to set the agenda for our families. But if we can go out as men chosen and called of God and ready to fulfill His destiny for us, we can lead our families—and help to recapture our culture for Christ.

A COMMITMENT TO DISCIPLINE

The second thing a man must have is a commitment to discipline. See, the only way to get from where you are to the destiny ahead of you is to discipline yourself to go there. God chose Abraham "that he may command his children and his household after him to keep the way of the Lord" (Genesis 18:19). Abraham was to put in place a structure whereby God's commands would be known and obeyed in his family.

Instruction

Like destiny, discipline involves two things. The first is instruction. These are the biblical rules we are going to follow as a family, the things we need to know. For us as fathers, this means sitting down with our children and our mates and spending the time necessary to impart the data they need to know to carry out the destiny God has for this family.

That is why the Bible says to train up a child in the way he should go so that later on, the instruction will hold him and guide him (see Proverbs 22:6). It takes discipline to fulfill a destiny and reach a goal, and we as fathers and husbands must give our families the tools they need to be successful for God.

Correction

The second thing involved in discipline is correction. The priest Eli and his household were judged by God "because his sons brought a curse on themselves and he did not rebuke them" (1 Samuel 3:13). Eli and both of his sons died because the boys turned left and Eli only scolded them.

Kids will stray from the path because they're sinners too and because they're free moral agents who can make their own choices. The problem in our culture is not that the world's kids are all little demons while ours are all little angels. All kids are born in sin.

The problem that is helping to destroy America is that in too many homes, there is no correction when the kids go left. Either the parents don't really believe in correction, which is the modern secular mind-set, or more frequently there is no father around to correct the wrong and apply loving discipline. Even if he is in the home, he leaves the child-rearing to his wife. So mom gets to do double duty and is soon overwhelmed.

The result is a generation of children who have not been corrected at home. And if they are not corrected at home, that means society must try to correct them when it's late and they're too far gone.

If you have read any of my books, you have been introduced to my father, Arthur Evans. My father was big on correction. He was really into it! My times of correction at his hands were known as "sessions." Mama could correct me all day long, but I did not want a session.

I will never forget the day I got suspended from junior high school for fighting. A guy was messing with my lunch. Sticks and stones may break my bones, but don't mess with my food. (It was probably fried chicken.) Anyway, he and I got it on. I mean, tables were turning and chairs were flying.

I got called to the principal's office and was suspended. The principal said, "I am going to call your daddy." Lord have mercy, talk about prayer in school! I could stand anything except for that phrase, "I am going to call your daddy."

My daddy worked as a stevedore, a longshoreman, unloading and loading ships. He was paid by the hour, and he only worked when the ships came in. So for him to come to my school he had to punch out at work, which meant that money needed for the family was no longer available for the time he had to leave work.

You get the picture. My father was not happy when he got to school. He sat down in the principal's office while the principal explained what had happened and said I was being suspended for three days.

My father just sat there. After a few moments of silence, he looked at the principal and said, "Thank you. I promise you that Anthony will never be suspended from school again." I knew what that meant!

When I got home my mother said, "Your daddy said to go up to your bedroom and wait for him." My father had this thing where he made you wait and think about what you had done. He did not just burst into my room. He would go walking up and down the hall, messing with my mind.

But finally he came in with his barber's razor strap, one of those things with two layers, and we had a "session." He said to me, "Son, are you going to get suspended for fighting again?"

"No, Daddy! Jesus is my witness. No, never again!" Between licks he would ask me the same question, until he was convinced that I was never going to get suspended for fighting again. I never got suspended again because he loved me enough to correct me.

We have a generation of children who have never known what it is to have a man who loves them enough to correct them in love, to say to them, "You don't talk like that in this house. You don't do that in this family." Anything I ever did wrong, I had to sneak around because there was discipline.

A DESIGN FOR DISCIPLESHIP

My fellow Christian father, let me ask you, Who wakes the family up for worship on Sunday morning in your home? Who says, "It's time for us to go to church"? Who leads the way in prayers at home? Who is the first one to open the Word at your house? If it is not you, you need to start discipling your family.

Discipleship is the third thing a man needs to fulfill his role in the family and pass the faith to the next generation. Discipleship is the process of training your family to keep the way of the Lord.

Evangelizing

One way a man can do this is by evangelizing his family. You are responsible to introduce your family to the Lord. Look at Genesis 17:26–27: "In the very same day Abraham was circumcised, and Ishmael his son. All the men of his household, who were born in the house or bought with money from a foreigner, were circumcised with him."

In other words, if you were going to live in Abraham's house you were going to be circumcised. What was circumcision? It was a sign of the covenant. It was bringing the family into the faith. It was letting them know that in this house, we are committed to the Lord.

Developing

Discipleship not only means introducing your family to the faith, but developing them in the faith. That's what Ephesians 6:4 says: "Fathers . . . bring [your children] up in the discipline and instruction of the Lord."

Notice that Paul did not say mothers. Why? Because a mother's job is to help the father raise their children in the Lord, not to replace the father. A mother is to be in partnership with the father as dad provides spiritual leadership in the home.

When I was growing up, not going to church was unheard of. Sometimes, because my father had to work some Sundays, I had to walk the five miles. I could not say, "Dad, because you are not here to drive me today, I'm not going to church." It was understood, if you lived in the Evans house, you were going to church.

Dad, if you don't have a sense of destiny, a commitment to discipline, and a design for discipleship, you don't really know what it's about. You are going to get bored with the new toys you collect along the way.

Nurturing

Here's another ingredient of discipleship that I want to develop in some detail by taking you to Psalm 128:

How blessed is everyone who fears the Lord, who walks in His ways. When you shall eat of the fruit of your hands, you will be happy and it will be well with you. Your wife shall be like a fruitful vine within your house, your children like olive plants around your table. Behold, for thus shall the man be blessed who fears the Lord. The Lord bless you from Zion, and may you see the prosperity of Jerusalem all the days of your life. Indeed, may you see your children's children. Peace be upon Israel! (vv. 1–6)

The first thing the psalmist says in verses 1–2 is that nurturing the family begins with "everyone" being committed to the Lord. The place to start fixing the family is by fixing the people who live there. If the family is going to be right, then the members must have their lives centered in God. Otherwise, the mess in one member's life will rub off on the other family members.

"How blessed," how happy, is the person who fears the Lord, who takes Him seriously. It has to do with holding God in awe and reverence.

What happens when you fear God? He will take care of your fortune: "You shall eat of the fruit of your hands" (v. 2a). He will take care of your feelings: "You will be happy" (v. 2b). And He will take care of your future: "It will be well with you" (v. 2c). What a guarantee!

God is saying, "You must be rooted in Me." Show me two people in a marriage who are rooted in God, and they have no

reason for not making it. Show me two people who aren't rooted in God, and they're lucky if they *do* make it.

A second thing Psalm 128 tells us about nurturing is that a
Christian family needs the right atmosphere. You as the man
must create a healthy spiritual environment for your family.
When verse 3 refers to "your wife" and "your children," it's
obvious that God is focusing on the husband and father in the
home.

A man is responsible for setting the tone in his family. That's
why Satan is after men. He knows that if he can get men out of
the picture, if he can keep them from being responsible, if he
can turn them into "baby makers" rather than "children
lovers," he can destroy the family, which destroys the church,
and ultimately destroys the culture.

The writer pictures the wife as a "fruitful vine" (v. 3). There
are three things you need to know about vines. First, a vine
clings. It will take hold of whatever it is attached to and cling to
it. The atmosphere in a home should be such that a wife can
wrap her "branches" around her husband for stability, security,
and love.

Vines not only cling, but they climb. A healthy vine will
spread out and take over a whole wall of a house. In other
words, when a husband is providing the right kind of atmosphere, his wife can develop her strengths and abilities. She can
grow, becoming a better woman than she ever was.

If you have a stunted, non-growing wife, the problem could
be that she doesn't have what she needs to cling to. She may not
be getting the spiritual nurturing and nourishment she needs.
Your wife should be able to say, "When I cling to my husband,
things start growing out of my life that I didn't know were
there."

The third thing you need to know about vines is that they
produce clusters of grapes. Grapes start budding out everywhere. Grapes are used to make wine. A person who drinks
enough wine will start becoming intoxicated. He will act different because the wine makes him feel good.

Maybe you get the picture. If your wife is a clinging, climb-
ing, and fruitful vine, you are going to become an intoxicated
man! You are going to start feeling different. You are going to
become a happy and fulfilled man because your wife will intoxi-

cate you with her love. It will flow naturally.

But before any of that can happen, a vine has to have the right atmosphere to grow. Don't expect a summer wife if you bring home stormy winter weather. Don't expect a vineyard to grow if it's snowing and hailing when you come home.

You say, "How am I supposed to create this atmosphere for my wife?" I have one simple answer: You out-serve her. It comes down to that.

That means putting her needs, concerns, and desires ahead of your own. It means instead of coming home and sitting down, waiting to be waited on like King Tut, you get up and help. Whatever it takes, you communicate to your wife, "Honey, nothing is more important to me than making you happy."

When it comes to children, the psalmist changes the imagery from a vine to olive plants. Notice they are not trees yet, but plants. Olive plants take up to fifteen years to mature. They have to be nurtured. Olive oil was used for many things in that culture, but in order to get the good product there had to be a long process of nurturing.

The psalmist is saying that we must provide a nurturing environment for our children if they're going to grow up to be olive trees. The beauty of an olive tree was that when it matured, it would produce olives for many more years. That's the picture of children raised in a nurturing environment.

One of the great places to do family nurturing is "around the table" (v. 3b). Mealtimes provide many great teachable moments—but dad has to be there around the table with the kids if those moments are going to be seized for God. The man who provides this kind of climate in the home will be blessed of the Lord (v. 4).

Notice the third thing the psalmist says about families. The family is maintained in the community of believers. "The Lord bless you from Zion," he writes in verse 5.

Zion was the city of God, Jerusalem. It was the place where a father would take his family to worship God. The author of Hebrews picks this up when he says, "You have come to Mount Zion and to the city of the living God" (Hebrews 12:22). The very next verse in Hebrews tells us that for us, Mount Zion is the church.

Mount Zion is the place where you meet God. The family that has God at its center, and that gathers regularly with God's people to be affirmed and reaffirmed in the things of God, will be blessed.

Dad, if you are serious about having a long-term family, about passing on the faith to succeeding generations, then you had better be serious about leading your family in corporate worship. The reason we have so many failing families is that they're not involved in a spiritual maintenance program in the family of God, with the people of God.

Affecting

Fourth and finally, the writer of Psalm 128 says that the believing family when nurtured properly will be powerful in its impact on society (vv. 5b–6). Notice the last phrase of the psalm: "Peace be upon Israel."

That's *shalom*, well-being in the community, because this family was right with God, right with each other, and right with other believers. When you get all of that lined up properly, guess what happens? You see the prosperity of the community. You see peace take over. You see a nation recover its spiritual health.

Some of us in America won't get to see our children's children because there's no peace. There's violence, corruption, and corrosion. The psalmist says, "If you want to fix the culture, then start with the house you live in."

How are we as Christian men going to help influence the leaders of our society if we're not willing to lead and love and nurture our own wives and children? Nurturing starts with your walk with God, moves to your relationship to your family, then to your involvement in the church—and soon, your city is not the same! That's impact.

RECLAIMING OUR DOMINION

Here's the fourth and final ingredient in the making of Christian fathers and husbands who can win back their homes and their communities and pass on the faith to succeeding generations: We need to reclaim dominion in Christ's name.

Remember, Sodom and Gomorrah were destroyed because God could not find ten righteous people. There were not enough believers to take dominion in those cities. Lot had not transferred his faith, so there was nobody there to salvage the culture.

Throughout the Old Testament, you read this phrase: "The God of Abraham, Isaac, and Jacob." That is, three generations of men with whom God was happy to identify. Why did God use these three generations of names? Because it was expected that the sons would continue what their fathers started.

It happens all the time in business: Smith and Son. It was understood that the son would continue what the father started. In this case, what the father started was the passing on of the true faith.

Some of us fathers have not been all that we should be. The good news is that God can take lemons and make lemonade. He can hit a bull's-eye with a crooked arrow. You can't fix what was wrong yesterday, but you can repent, and you can do a lot about what happens today.

It may mean turning off the television thirty minutes early and spending time on your knees with your wife and your family. It may mean taking the Scriptures and sitting down with the family Sunday afternoon after church to ask, "How are we going to apply the truth we have heard to our home?"

Satan will try to thwart you and discourage you. Maybe the kids won't want to cooperate at first. You may feel like there's no use. But if you will trust God, sooner or later the family is going to start lining up because God will honor your leadership as His representative leader in the home.

One day my mother told me the story of the three little pigs. You know the story. The first two pigs built shaky houses, so the big, bad wolf was able to huff and puff and blow them down.

But the third little pig was together. He is my man. He built a sturdy house, so when his brothers came to him for protection, he invited them to sit down and enjoy the fire in his fireplace while the big, bad wolf huffed and puffed.

The wolf blew, but nothing happened. He blew again and nothing happened. He blew again and nothing happened. The difference was that the third pig built his house out of bricks.

The first pig built a house of straw. If you are trying to build your home on a good income, Satan is going to huff and puff and blow your house down.

The second pig's house was made of wood. If you are trying to build your home on success and fame, Satan is going to huff and puff and blow your house down.

But if you will build your house on Jesus Christ, on the solid rock of God's Word, Satan can huff and puff while you and your family sit around the fireplace enjoying the blessing of God. And if enough fathers build homes like this, Satan can huff and puff on America and she will not fall!

This is what God offers to husbands and fathers who will build their homes on Him.

CHAPTER 10

WHEN CHRISTIANS ROB GOD

The subject of this chapter shouldn't surprise you, because you knew we were going to have to deal biblically with the subject of money if we were going to take the title of this book seriously.

We as American Christians have a real hang-up with money because our culture has a hang-up with money. Because we have bought so deeply into our culture's views on money, the way Christians as a body are handling their money is helping to bring a curse and destruction on America.

Throughout the Bible, God uses our attitude toward money —and all the tangible and intangible things money can buy—to take our spiritual temperature. And it's an incredibly reliable gauge too.

The reason God uses money as a measure of spiritual health is very simple. Our money is usually the last thing that gets committed to God. Jesus had so much to say about a person's money in relation to his standing before God because He knew that if a person ever gets his wallet sanctified, God really has him.

Money is not only the last thing that usually gets committed to God. It's also normally the last thing a person will give up. Many people will give up their lives before giving up their money. How do I know that? Because folk will work themselves to death to make more money rather than trimming back their wants.

One of the brothers in our church in Dallas told me that

before he became a Christian, he had decided that he was going to be a millionaire by the age of forty or die trying, because his life was being lived for that.

So how we Christians handle our money is a powerful measure of our spiritual maturity or lack thereof. But money itself is not the problem, as we will see. That is, there is no magic power and nothing inherently sinful in those pieces of paper imprinted with black and green ink.

The root of the church's problem with money goes much deeper than figures on a balance sheet or numbers on a paycheck. The underlying problem is one of value. We have devalued God, and we are paying for it. God has been marginalized in American culture, and as a result the church has been marginalized.

DEVALUING GOD

I want to illustrate what I'm talking about from the little Old Testament book of Haggai, particularly Haggai 1:4–11. Haggai ministered in the days after the Jews returned from exile in Babylon.

The people were back in Israel, and they were supposed to be building the temple so God would have a house in which to dwell among His people. But the returning exiles had lost their energy for the things of God, and His house sat unfinished.

The temple of God represented something bigger than a building. It was where God hung out among His people, where He met with them for worship and blessing. The temple was where the glory of God lived.

Neglecting God's House

By the time Haggai spoke, the temple had already been sitting unfinished for fifteen years. That was an insult to God. Taking His house lightly meant they were taking God lightly. So God issued a complaint through the prophet: "This people says, 'The time has not come, even the time for the house of the Lord to be rebuilt'" (Haggai 1:2).

In other words, the people were saying, "It's not time yet to finish the temple. It has only been fifteen years. We'll get to it after we finish building our own houses."

So God sent Haggai to ask the people a question: "Is it time for you yourselves to dwell in your paneled houses while [My] house lies desolate?" (v. 4).

See, God was getting to the heart of the problem. He was saying, "If it's a time problem, why is it that you have time to build your houses and not Mine?"

The people had no good answer to God's question because there was no good answer. They didn't have a time problem; they had a value problem. By their actions they were saying, "God, we're building our houses instead of Your house because we value ourselves and our comfort more than we value You and Your glory."

Now don't misunderstand what was happening here. We are not talking about wretched, homeless former exiles trying desperately to throw together a few shacks to shield them from the elements. These folk were building paneled homes. We are talking about homes with trash compactors, garage door openers, and manicured lawns. We are talking about nice places to live.

So the people revealed how little they valued God by letting His house lie unfinished while they built their own homes. God's house didn't matter all that much to them because worshiping and honoring Him apparently didn't matter all that much. No wonder God warned His people through Haggai:

Consider your ways! You have sown much, but harvest little; you eat, but there is not enough to be satisfied; you drink, but there is not enough to become drunk; you put on clothing, but no one is warm enough; and he who earns, earns wages to put into a purse with holes. (Haggai 1:5–6)

In other words, God was saying, "You haven't thought this through. You haven't really looked at how you are treating Me and what it has brought upon you. Haven't you noticed that nothing you do satisfies your needs? Hasn't it occurred to you that your paycheck never seems to last through the week?"

See, one way you know you are devaluing God is that your life is empty of satisfaction. When your ways are pleasing to God, He gives satisfaction, that inner contentment with your life even though you may not be where you want to be by human standards.

But when people devalue God, it doesn't matter how high they go. It will never satisfy. They will never have enough stuff. We expect this kind of behavior out of unbelievers because they don't know any better.

But what is helping to destroy America is the countless numbers of Christians who are living the same way, chasing the same pot of gold at the end of the rainbow. When we marginalize God and neglect His glory and honor, we bring upon ourselves a curse, and the culture feels the effect. We'll talk more about this when we get to the book of Malachi.

No Satisfaction

The Israelites of Haggai's day were never satisfied because they never had enough. And they never had enough because they were devaluing God. It's not that they didn't try to find satisfaction. But they tried to find it in the places people are still trying today.

Let's get away on a cruise. Maybe we'll feel better. Maybe a new car for the kids will help me get along better with them. Time to redecorate the house. Maybe it will perk up the marriage.

But God says, "You don't understand. When you neglect My house, which represents Me, you have a problem you can't buy your way out of with money. As soon as you get your paycheck, I am going to cut a hole in your pocket."

Someone says, "I just got promoted. I'm getting a raise. Things are going to be better now." God says, "Is that so?" As soon as you get your raise, the washing machine breaks down. The car dies. The roof leaks. Things you did not expect to come up appear all of a sudden because if you never get around to satisfying God, He won't get around to satisfying you.

A woman went to her pastor and said, "I am so dissatisfied. When I was getting $50,000 a year, I was happy. Now I make $500,000 a year, but I'm miserable. What should I do?"

Her pastor said, "Sounds like you need to give away $450,000."

Accumulation does not satisfy. Some of us married believers were happier when we were poor. We have moved up the ladder and the house is nice, the clothes are sharp, the car is new. But we can't stand to be in our fine house with the person we married because houses alone don't satisfy.

Only God satisfies. He tells us that His people cannot let His house and His glory lie desolate; we cannot devalue Him and expect to find satisfaction anywhere else. No matter what we get, God will just "blow it away" (v. 9).

Rebuilding God's Glory

So what was the answer for the Israelites? " 'Go up to the mountains, bring wood and rebuild the temple, that I may be pleased with it and be glorified,' says the Lord" (Haggai 1:8). The purpose of the temple was to house the glory of God.

The New Testament counterpart to the temple is the church of Jesus Christ. Christians are, individually and collectively, the temple of God (1 Corinthians 3:17; 6:19). We are to reflect His glory. But when we get our spiritual priorities all messed up, not only do we suffer; the culture also suffers on account of us.

I say that because God went on to say through Haggai, "Because of you the sky has withheld its dew and the earth has withheld its produce" (v. 10). When God's people don't act right, even nature doesn't act right. When we assign little or no value to His glory, the sky closes up for everyone.

I believe God has more than rain and crops in mind here. Closing up the sky is a picture of God withholding spiritual blessings. There is no answered prayer and no power coming down from heaven, in other words. This is a spiritual issue, not a matter of good or bad weather.

After the indictment was delivered, the people got the message. Haggai 1:14 says the Lord stirred up the spirits of the leaders and the people, and they got busy building God's house. But it wasn't until they changed their spiritual value system that God did something about the holes in their pockets and their lack of satisfaction.

God was just waiting to act on their behalf (see Haggai 2:4–9), but they had to get their priorities straight. God even promised to bring the wealth of the nations into His house (2:7). After all, it all belonged to Him anyway (v. 8).

God was saying to His people, "You have been banking at the wrong bank. All of these other banks are 'mini-banks.' I am the major bank. If I close you down, no other bank can help you."

It's a matter of what you value. If you value money more than God, it doesn't matter how much you have. Why? Because if God is against you, more money will not help you. What good is having lots of money if you are putting it in a "purse" full of holes?

You may make less money with God than you could make without Him and still have more left at the end of the month. That's because God will sew up the hole on your purse if you will honor Him. But He'll cut holes in your purse if He is neglected.

ROBBING GOD

All of this is laying a foundation for the text from which the title of this chapter is taken. People who value God lightly will have little trouble stealing from Him, and that's the issue the prophet Malachi was called to address.

Malachi also ministered to Israel after the Exile. He came along about one hundred years after Haggai. The temple was now finished, but the people had backslid into such a terrible spiritual condition that God called them a bunch of thieves.

In Malachi 3:8, God asked the people of Israel this startling question: "Will a man rob God?" Can you hear the inflection in God's voice? "Are you telling me that a puny human being would dare try to rob Me, the King of the universe who made him and holds his very life in My hands?"

Asking God for Proof

But look at the coldness and impudence of the people. They dared to ask God for proof of His indictment. "How have we robbed You?" Answer: "In tithes and offerings" (v. 8b). Now notice verse 9: "You are cursed with a curse, for you are robbing Me, the whole nation of you!"

This is the same principle we saw in Haggai 1. God's people were neglecting Him and His glory, and the proof of it was in what they did with their money. They kept it for themselves. God couldn't even get a decent tip out of them.

Now let me pause right here and state my basic thesis for this chapter. Just as the people of Israel in Malachi's day were under a curse for robbing God, so the church today is under

God's curse because we are withholding His tithes and offerings in staggering proportions.

I'll deal with all this in detail below, and you'll see what I mean. Let me just say here that one proof we are under a curse is that God has closed up the windows of heaven, and therefore His people have to rely on the government to meet their needs.

If all true Christians in America were faithful tithers and generous givers, there would be no need in the church we could not meet because God would open the windows of heaven and pour out His blessings. We could take welfare back from the government and do a much more efficient job.

Think what a financial curse and a burden that would lift from the backs of the American people! Our entire culture is laboring under an intolerable weight because Christians won't get it together in our finances.

How bad is it? Estimates are that only 18 percent of American Christians tithe. The average evangelical Christian gives about 2 percent of his income to the Lord. Yet the government takes up to 31 percent! Something is terribly wrong. We are under a curse. If we want to build America instead of destroying her, faithful giving is a great place to start.

Giving God the Leftovers

In the Hebrew text of verse 9, the word *Me* is in the emphatic position. God is actually saying for emphasis, "It's *Me* you are robbing!" This is another way of underscoring the absurdity of what was going on here.

One of the evidences that God's people were robbing Him is found back in Malachi 1:6–9. They were bringing defective animals for sacrifice, the worst instead of the best of their flocks and herds. They were literally stealing the best animals for themselves, taking them right out of God's hands, as it were.

The people were offering God their leftovers: leftover sacrifices, leftover commitments, leftover money. He got only what they didn't want or need. The proof that it was worthless was God's challenge to them to offer that mess to their earthly leaders and see how grateful they were (Malachi 1:8).

Again, it was a priority issue, a matter of misplaced value. God said, "Try serving that to your governor." Next Monday, many Christians will give more conscientious service to their bosses than they will give to God on Sunday.

But wait a minute. When was the last time your governor answered your prayers? Where are all the people your boss died to save? When was the last time you prayed to your mayor to come through for you?

You get the idea. We need God more than we need anyone on earth, and yet He is the One we are trying to rob. That simply doesn't compute no matter how you add it up.

So the indictment in Malachi 3:8 is that God's people were robbing Him by withholding their tithes and offerings. These terms need a little clarification and explanation because of the confusion surrounding the concepts of tithing and giving.

Tithes and Offerings

The term *tithe* means "the tenth." That much is beyond dispute. A lot of Christians today dismiss the idea of tithing because they say that was the Law of Moses, and we are not under the Law anymore.

But tithing predates the Law by hundreds of years. Back in Genesis 14:20, Abraham gave "a tenth" of all his spoils to Melchizedek, who was a type of Christ. Christ validated the continuation of the tithe as long as it was accompanied by a righteous life (Matthew 23:23).

The author of Hebrews recognized that the tithe continued to be practiced in the New Testament church (Hebrews 7:8). Tithing is transdispensational and reaches across time since all believers are the spiritual seed of Abraham (Galatians 3:7).

It's true that tithing was commanded in the Law, but the principle was already firmly established long before Moses showed up. The tithe was to be a testimony to and a recognition of God's ownership of everything. The tithe was required of every Israelite, as a way of demonstrating their recognition of God as the originator and source of all they had (Leviticus 27:30). Every Israelite, no matter how poor or wealthy, could give in the same proportion and honor God.

It's like farming. When a farmer reaps his harvest, some of those seeds are going back into the ground because if he doesn't replant, he will have nothing to harvest next year. A farmer does not keep all the seeds he harvests, because he wants to make sure something is invested for the future. The more he sows, the larger his harvest.

Paul wrote to the church in Corinth, "He who sows sparingly will also reap sparingly, and he who sows bountifully will also reap bountifully" (2 Corinthians 9:6). No farmer worries about how many seeds he is having to sow if he wants a bountiful harvest next time around.

This is the principle that is to govern all of our giving. The tithe was required because God wanted the people of Israel to understand that He owned it all and to express their gratitude by giving back a tenth of what He gave them. Not to tithe was tantamount to embezzling from God.

But the tithe was also the minimum the people of Israel were expected to give. Over and above the tithe were the offerings, freewill gifts given to God out of a heart that overflowed with praise and gratitude.

The tithe was required, but offerings were optional. The amount of the tithe was fixed, but gifts were according to the giver's generosity. Offerings were a way of saying to God, "I don't want to be limited to the minimum I can give You. I don't want to just get by. I want to show You how much I value You."

It reminds me of the man whose wife had a cat that he despised. This cat drove him crazy, but his wife loved the cat so much he really couldn't do anything about it.

But one day the cat went too far. So while his wife was away, the man put the cat in a sack, tied the sack shut, weighted it down with rocks, and threw it in the river.

When the wife came home, she naturally became distressed when she couldn't find her beloved cat. To throw off any suspicion and look like a hero, the husband soothingly offered to put a reward notice in the newspaper.

He put up a reward of two thousand dollars for the cat, telling his wife, "I know the cat isn't worth that much, but it's worth that much to me to see you find your cat."

A friend of the man read the notice and was stunned by the size of the reward. "Are you crazy?" he asked. "How in the world can you offer two thousand dollars for a cat?"

The man just smiled and said, "When you know what I know, you can afford to be generous." That's the message we need to hear as Christians. Knowing what we know about the grace and goodness of God, we can afford to be generous!

Cheap Worship

The problem in Malachi's day wasn't that the people were skipping out on worship. The temple was open, the priests were offering sacrifices, and the people were coming. Everything looked normal. The people said their amens and hallelujahs. They looked spiritual. They looked like they were really one-on-one with God.

But God said, "Oh that there were one among you who would shut the [temple] gates" (Malachi 1:10). God was sick of the whole thing. Their worship was useless to Him, because their heart attitude was, "My, how tiresome it is!" (v. 13).

So God told them, "Someone close the door. Don't let anyone else in because you are playing games." It's the same issue again that we encountered in Haggai. The people had so little regard for God that they yawned in His face. Let me say it again. When you don't place any real value on God, robbing from Him in the matter of your money is no big deal.

The way the Israelites handled their finances was part of their overall, long-term disobedience. Look at Malachi 3:7: "From the days of your fathers you have turned aside from My statutes and have not kept them." That is, they had robbed God in every category possible.

So we're back to the issue of Malachi 3:8. People who are robbing God usually ask the kind of question the Israelites asked in this verse: "How have we robbed You?" In other words, "Not *me*, Lord. I'm Your main man!"

With so much disobedience to choose from, why did God pick tithes and offerings to illustrate how the people had robbed Him? For the reason we talked about at the beginning of the chapter. God uses money to gauge a person's or a church's spiritual temperature.

How Much to Give?

When the discussion is tithing, someone will always ask, "Do I tithe on my net pay or on my gross pay?" I like what Larry

Burkett says: "That depends. Do you want God to bless you on the net or on the gross?"

The question is not the amount, but how thankful are you? How much do you want to tell God you love Him? How much do you want to tell Him you need Him? How much blessing do you want from Him?

A farmer was known for his generous giving. But his friends couldn't understand how he could give so much away and yet remain so prosperous. One day, one of his friends asked him how he did it.

"Oh, that's easy to explain," the farmer replied. "I keep shoveling into God's bin and God keeps shoveling into mine, but God has the bigger shovel!"

Now answer the question for yourself: Should you tithe on your net income or on your gross income? The motivation for giving comes from within as your response to the faithfulness of God.

But the big problem today, as it was in Israel, is that God's people take His faithfulness for granted. We get used to the goodness of God. We yawn at His daily blessings. When that happens, robbing Him of what is rightfully His is easier to do.

The Christian who doesn't rob God says, "God, I realize I only woke this morning because You are faithful. It's not automatic. I only have a job and a car to get there because You are faithful. My family is healthy only because You are faithful. Help me never to take Your faithfulness for granted."

Cursed with a Curse

Now let's talk about the curse of Malachi 3:9. It came because the people tried to rob God. The point is, nobody robs God and gets away with it. Anyone who robs God gets robbed *by* God. You lose big-time when you rob God.

God will guarantee that we do not rob Him and get away scot-free. How will He guarantee it? He will allow needs to come into our personal lives, families, churches, and communities that He will not meet. It's the reverse of the promise of Philippians 4:19 that He will supply all of our needs—a promise, please note, that is set in the context of generous giving!

If we try to rob God, He will allow problems to surface that we cannot solve. He may allow sicknesses to come that He will not heal. He may allow division to come into your family that He will not repair.

We hear people asking today, "Why are so many Christians getting divorced? Why are so many of God's people depressed or in such terrible financial bondage?"

Now read me carefully here. I am not at all suggesting that every setback in a Christian's life is the result of him or her robbing God. But neither can I ignore the curse God pronounced on the "whole nation" in Malachi 3:9. Where there is collective robbery, there is collective cursing, and the church in America is operating under such a curse because of how we continue to devalue God. The result is that rather than bringing help and hope to society, we are contributing to its defeat. How else can we explain the billions of dollars that flow through evangelicalism while we are simultaneously experienceing a decrease in spiritual impact? Like Israel, we are planting seed on cursed soil.

God was saying, "You've been withholding from Me, so the time has come for Me to withhold from you. You are going to find out that no one does withholding like I do withholding!"

What was the curse Israel was experiencing? We get a hint in verse 11 that tells what will happen if they turn back to God: "Then I will rebuke the devourer for you, so that it may not destroy the fruits of the ground; nor will your vine in the field cast its grapes."

So they were having agricultural failure. "The fruits of the ground" was their food, their livelihood. The people were robbing God because they thought they had to keep all of their crops for themselves since the ground wasn't producing much.

It's like the person today who reasons, "Well, I don't make much, and I need every nickel of what I make. My 'ground' isn't producing much, so I can't afford to give."

God says, "No, you don't understand. Do you know why the ground isn't producing? It's under My curse because you have been robbing Me. And if you keep on robbing Me because you're short on food, guess what is going to happen to the ground?"

Remember the "purse with holes" from Haggai? Have you ever had any paychecks like that? By the time you get home, it's gone. Most Christians think if they get a raise, God must be blessing them. Not necessarily. He just may be cutting a bigger hole in the bottom of their pocketbook!

If a believer has a financial problem, the solution is giving. Why? Because that triggers the blessings of God on our behalf. I'm not espousing prosperity theology. But we can't allow those TV guys to scare us away from God's promises. See, our mathematics are messed up. We think we have saved by not giving. Or we say, "God gave me this house. He expects me to pay for it." Yes, but He doesn't expect you to rob Him to do it.

A Word of Promise

In the midst of all this bad news in Malachi 3, there is a challenge and a promise to be found:

"Bring the whole tithe into the storehouse, so that there may be food in My house, and test Me now in this," says the Lord of hosts, "if I will not open for you the windows of heaven and pour out for you a blessing until it overflows." (v. 10)

God invites His people to test Him. Our responsibility is to bring Him the whole tithe. In the Old Testament, the place to bring the tithe was the temple, which contained storehouses for the grain.

The storehouses were chambers in the temple where the grain was stored. These storehouses served three purposes: They provided food for the priests who oversaw the temple and were responsible for maintaining the spiritual lives of God's people (Numbers 18:24–29), they fed the widows and orphans (Deuteronomy 14:28–29, and they met the needs of the poor Gentiles who were living in their society (Deuteronomy 14:28–29). Thus the storehouse had a very social function tied to its spiritual foundation that not only benefited the Jews, but the broader community as well.

In other words, the tithes not only met the spiritual, physical, and social needs of God's people, but they had a spillover benefit to the larger culture. If Christians were tithing today, we would not only have enough to meet needs in the body of Christ, but we could meet needs in the culture that the government is trying to meet today. Because we are not tithing, we are failing on both of these fronts. The welfare debacle we are facing today has more to do with the theft of God's people than the failure of government. It is part of God's curse on the church.

We also are to bring our tithes to the place of ministry, which is the local church today. Since in Malachi the storehouse and God's house were the same, and since the local church is God's house in the New Testament (1 Timothy 3:15), then the tithe should go to the local church.

The local church, then, is to use these funds not only for traditional, "spiritual" ministry, but to take care of the physical and social needs of God's people who have no other means of support, as well as overflow to the larger community. The early church understood this to be part of its God-given agenda, with the result that all the needs of its members were addressed (Acts 4:32–35; Galatians 6:10). Today we complain about the waste of welfare, but if the president were to turn welfare over to the church, we would be ill-prepared to offer a solution because of our own robbery of God.

God invites His people to try Him, to see whether He is for real in this matter of your money. He wants to see if you really believe that He owns the cattle on a thousand hills. He wants to show us that He can make a way where there is no way.

We go around saying, "God can make a way out of no way," but many of us have never tried Him and discovered that for ourselves. How do we know what God can do when the first thing we do is run to the bank?

The only thing required to test God and prove Him faithful is to bring Him the whole tithe. The Israelites could have said, "But, God, don't You see our meager crops?"

God says, "Bring all of Mine to Me."

They said, "But don't You see that we don't have enough food because the ground isn't producing?"

Again God replies, "Bring all that's Mine to Me. Obey Me."

If you are operating under the absolute authority of God's Word, if you put God to the test not only in your giving but in every area of life, God will do two things. There is no material need you have that He will not meet (Philippians 4:19). And there is no spiritual need you desire that He will not address.

You say, "But wait a minute. I know some people who aren't Christians, and they are making plenty of money."

That's right. They may be. People can become billionaires without God. But that doesn't tell you anything about what may be going on in their lives, the stuff they're facing that money can't remedy.

The beauty of walking with God is that He not only supplies our needs, but He also deals with those intangible areas that money can't help: a broken home, a child who is wayward, an addiction that can't otherwise be broken, a church that is in disarray, and a culture that is going to pot.

I'm not suggesting that the church try to strike a business deal with God: "God, we'll give You 10 percent, and You return 15 percent to us." God is not offering to cut a business deal with us, but He is saying that the natural result of hearts that are thankful for His faithfulness is that He will demonstrate that faithfulness in return and will do so in a powerful and collective way.

The story is told of a circus strongman whose big thing was to squeeze an orange so dry no one else could get a drop out of it. He would challenge anyone in the audience to try.

One day, a weak-looking little man accepted the challenge. The crowd laughed, but that little guy took the orange rind and started to squeeze. Every eye was on him. After a moment or two, to everyone's amazement, a drop of juice fell from the orange and hit the floor. The crowd erupted in cheers.

As the cheers subsided, the strongman invited the little man to tell how he squeezed that drop from the orange. "Nothing to it," he replied. "I happen to be the treasurer of the local church!"

Will God have to squeeze us to get anything out of us? That's not the way giving is supposed to be done. But for Christians who are intent on robbing Him, He has a way of squeezing our resources until every drop is gone.

Taking God at His Word

So I invite you to examine your life. God may not be investing in some area of your life because you have no investment in Him. If we as the people of God in America do not begin prioritizing His Son, we are robbing God—and He doesn't like to be stolen from.

But Malachi has a word of encouragement for us. If we will bring God His tithe, He will make heaven available to us. Not only will He pour out a blessing on us, but He will get rid of our enemies. The "devourer" was the swarms of locusts that were eating the crops. The people didn't only need rain, they needed someone to get rid of the locusts. God said He would do it.

But it's Malachi 3:12 that holds special interest for our purposes as we talk about the blessing or destruction of America. If we as God's people will honor Him with our giving, He will make our land "delightful," a witness to all the nations of what He can do. When we stop robbing God, then Christians will truly have "a story to tell to the nations," beginning with our own.

CHAPTER 11

CAN'T WE ALL GET ALONG?

On August 2, 1990, the armies of Iraq's madman ruler, Saddam Hussein, overran and occupied the tiny neighboring nation of Kuwait, spreading death and destruction.

The leaders of Saudi Arabia, knowing their country would be next on Saddam's hit list, made a call to Washington to ask then-President George Bush for help. In one of the great diplomatic moves of his presidency, Bush put in a few calls to Canada, England, France, Italy, and other nations around the world to build a coalition that would stop Hussein's aggression.

This was an amazing coalition, made up of people of vastly different languages, cultures, and races. Ordinarily, many of these nations would have had nothing in common. But these were not ordinary times.

This coalition, part of Operation Desert Storm, came together for one purpose only: to draw a line in the sand and serve notice to Saddam Hussein that not only could he not take more territory in the Middle East, but he would have to give up the territory he had already taken.

GOD'S COALITION

Another "madman" has made a move similar to Saddam Hussein's move. That is, he moved in and occupied territory that was not his, spreading death and destruction. This mad-man is called Satan.

But God built a coalition against Satan—a coalition made up of people of every possible skin color, background, and culture. God called His coalition the church, and our job is to serve notice on Satan that not only can he not take any more territory, he must give up the territory to which he now lays claim.

The Possibilities of the Coalition

Imagine what would happen spiritually in America today if the church were functioning as well as the coalition forces functioned in the Gulf War. We blitzed Iraq from the air with high-tech aircraft and "smart" missiles that could go in the front door of buildings.

Then our ground forces moved in and swept the Iraqi army out of Kuwait in an offensive that lasted only one hundred hours. If the church moved out against Satan like that in our country today, we would see a reversal of America's spiritual decline beyond anything we could ask or think.

But because the church is not moving out in a unified advance against the forces of evil, Satan is wreaking havoc all across America. He's not only fortifying the ground he has already taken, he's grabbing new ground every day. The apostle Peter says that Satan is a roaring lion, seeking whom he may devour (1 Peter 5:8). The problem is that many Christians don't know when lions roar. Lions do not roar when they are getting ready to kill their prey; they roar after they kill their prey. Why? Because lions are terrified of jackals.

Jackals are scavengers that travel in packs, eating the carcasses of dead animals. Because the lion knows it cannot defeat a pack of jackals, it roars in order to intimidate them from advancing toward its prey. The jackals get so intimidated by the roars that they forget the power of their unity. Rather than advancing, they retreat.

Satan is like the lion. He has a big mouth, but if the church would just keep on coming, our collective power would easily drive him from his control of the carcasses of our decaying communities, cities, and nation.

The Split in the Coalition

If we as Christians have on our side the power of God, the Person of Christ, the presence of the Holy Spirit, and the authority of the Word, why aren't we winning the battle? Because we aren't truly the one people of God joined together in one line against our common enemy, Satan. The coalition has been split.

Saddam Hussein's mama didn't raise a dummy! He saw half a million troops and all that weaponry arrayed against him, and he knew he had to do something to fracture the coalition.

So he began attacking Israel with Scud missiles. If he could draw the Israelis into the war, maybe he could split the coalition along Arab/Israeli lines and weaken it. The plan didn't work, and Iraq was defeated and driven from Kuwait.

Satan has done a yeoman's job of splitting God's coalition, His church, along racial, class, and cultural lines. The enemy has done a magnificent job of keeping us from being the one people of God. As a result, we have not seen the revival in this country for which so many Christians are praying.

God will not revive just a part of His church. He's not interested in bringing a white revival, a black revival, a Hispanic revival, or an Asian revival. He is only going to bring a Holy Ghost revival to His one people.

But Satan has split the divine coalition. He gets us talking about unity on Sunday, but then we leave our segregated churches to go back to our segregated neighborhoods with our segregated mentalities, forgetting that we are only a part of the one body of Christ.

The Challenge for the Coalition

Unity within the church is crucial for the dynamic impact of God's people in the world. Unity does not mean sameness; it means oneness of purpose. It refers to pointing our uniquenesses in the same direction in order to achieve a common goal. One of our problems is that we are letting Satan set the agenda for the church. When you are in a war you don't care about the color, class, or culture of the man next to you, as long as he shoots in the same direction as you. That's the only issue in a war.

We're at spiritual war, and the only thing that should matter is whether the person next to you loves Jesus like you do. The other stuff like race and class shouldn't matter. We may have all come over here on different ships, but we're in the same boat now.

When a team like the Dallas Cowboys takes the field, differences of race, culture, and heritage are secondary to the common agenda of defeating the opponent as a unified team. The only colors that matter then for the Cowboys are the blue and gray on their uniforms.

In the same way, Christians must subject their race, class, and culture to the color that really matters, the precious red blood of Jesus Christ.

Until we become the unified people of God, until being Christian is more important than color or race or class, we can forget the revival and get ready to hand this nation over to Satan. God's Spirit will only work in an environment of unity. Until we become that kind of people, nothing else will work.

That means we must deal with racism and culturism and classism for what they are. They are sin. They are not just holdovers from the way you were raised! They are sin.

What would you do if people were living in adultery in your church? You wouldn't wait 250 years to get it right. The same thing is true if people in your church were practicing poor business ethics or living in homosexuality. You wouldn't say, "Let's give them a few hundred years to work it out. They were raised this way."

You would say, "These things are sin, and we'll never get anywhere by calling them something else." You can't help someone until he is willing to call sin for what it is.

A THEOLOGY OF RACE AND UNITY

The problem with too many of the discussions on racism and unity is that they are sociologically driven. Whenever your sociology controls your theology, you're in trouble. But when your theology controls your sociology, your sociology will start to make sense.

It is my contention that the absence of a biblical theology of race has led to a sociology of racial calamity and confusion. So, in the following pages, I want to lay out a biblical theology of the issues of race and class that often divide the church and the larger society.

Before the church can help rebuild America, we have to get our act together. And we can't do that without understanding what God's Word has to say about these things. If the church's theology is not right, we will be intimidated by the sociology of the culture.

But if our theology is right, we can defend ourselves against false accusations and start building the kind of unity that will trigger God's power and cause society to sit up and take notice. I want to make three basic statements, develop them biblically, and then talk about where we go from here.

God Resists Unity Without Him

The first thing is that God resists unity outside of the church. That may sound a little radical, but stay with me. God works against mankind's attempts to become unified apart from Him. Outside the church, God is for apartheid.

Let me show you what I mean, beginning in Acts 17, where Paul gives his sermon at the Areopagus:

The God who made the world and all things in it, since He is Lord of heaven and earth, does not dwell in temples made with hands; neither is He served by human hands, as though He needed anything, since He Himself gives to all people life and breath and all things; and He made from one man every nation of mankind to live on all the face of the earth, having determined their appointed times, and the boundaries of their habitation, that they would seek God, if perhaps they might grope for Him and find Him, though He is not far from each one of us. (vv. 24–27)

God created the nations, and He decided where each nation would live and how long that nation would exist. And He did so for a specific purpose: that we, with all of our national and ethnic and racial divisions, would realize our human limitations and seek Him.

See, it's when people are separated by all these boundaries and divisions that they recognize they cannot be all that they want to be. Usually, when people try to come together across racial, cultural, or class lines, they are driven by a humanistic viewpoint.

That viewpoint says that if we can just get together, we don't need God to pull off racial and ethnic harmony and world peace. The United Nations is the contemporary expression of this approach.

You hear this theme in so many of today's efforts to bring people together. Mankind wants to show what human beings can do on their own. But God will never let people come together so they can brag about their humanistic accomplishment. He keeps races and nations apart until people understand that He's the only One who can heal the divisions, and they turn to Him.

This mess goes all the way back to Genesis 11 and the tower of Babel. The whole earth was of one language (v. 1). So the people decided, "Let us build for ourselves a city . . . and let us make for ourselves a name" (v. 4). The people wanted to build a monument to the glory of man, something that would demonstrate their greatness.

Did God applaud and support their efforts? Absolutely not, for this was being done independently of Him. So He confused them:

"Come, let Us go down and there confuse their language, that they may not understand one another's speech." So the Lord scattered them abroad from there over the face of the whole earth; and they stopped building the city. Therefore its name was called Babel, because there the Lord confused the language of the whole earth; and from there the Lord scattered them abroad over the face of the whole earth. (vv. 7–9)

It can't be any clearer. God resisted this attempt to unify apart from Him. There's no way around it. God will always resist human attempts to achieve unity outside of Him. Why? Because human-motivated attempts at unity are actually attempts to glorify man—and God is not into glorifying us.

God says, "No Me, no unity." So the people of Genesis 11 lost their ability to communicate. Wherever you find disunity, you always find the loss of the ability to communicate. The people couldn't understand one another. See, God had said to Noah and his sons after the Flood, "Be fruitful and multiply, and fill the earth" (Genesis 9:1). Then in Genesis 10:32, we find this summary statement just before Babel: "These are the families of the sons of Noah, according to their genealogies, by their nations; and out of these the nations were separated on the earth after the flood."

That's the way it was because God wanted it that way. He situated the nations to fill the earth, and did so in such a way that unity could only be achieved through Him, not apart from Him. The reality is that God segregated humanity by race and ethnic group and nation, and He did it on purpose.

Now I'm not talking about the evils of segregation as we think of it in America. God did *not* separate the races because He didn't want them to have any contact with each other, or so that one race could dominate and oppress another. He separated them so that mankind would seek Him.

The bad news is that this means God will not allow people to come together outside of Him. So every attempt by people to find unity outside of God will be frustrated by Him.

See, God knew what the people of Genesis 11 were trying to do. "Behold, they are one people, and they all have the same language. And this is what they began to do, and now nothing which they purpose to do will be impossible for them" (v. 6).

God saw that the people were trying to be God. And since there's only room for one God, He said, "I will frustrate their attempts to be God." God frustrates any attempts at unity that exclude Him. Disunity was a form of judgment to keep human beings from deifying themselves.

The Spirit Established Unity Through the Church

A second point I want to show you is that the Holy Spirit establishes unity through the church. In 1 Corinthians 12:12–13, Paul writes:

For even as the body is one and yet has many members, and all the members of the body, though they are many, are one body, so also is Christ. For by one Spirit we were all baptized into one body, whether Jews or Greeks, whether slaves or free, and we were all made to drink of one Spirit.

It is the baptism of the Spirit at the moment of salvation, the act whereby God places you into the body of Christ, that establishes the unity God wants His people to have. Only the baptism of the Spirit places you under the rule of God.

The reason the church is the only authentic cross-racial, cross-cultural, and cross-gender basis for unity is that the church is the only institution on earth obligated to live under God's authority.

The Greek word for baptism is used in the Bible to mean identification. It was used of a cloth maker dipping cloth into the dye so that the cloth would take on the color of the dye. The cloth was then said to be baptized or identified with the dye.

When we got saved, we were baptized into the body of Christ. We are now identified with a new family. We have been placed into a new environment. No matter what your race or culture or class, when you came to Jesus Christ you entered into God's authorized unity because you came under His authority. True unity is created by the Holy Spirit through the church.

That is why Ephesians 4:3 talks about preserving "the unity of the Spirit." We don't create unity. The Spirit created unity when we were saved. Our job is to find out what the Spirit has done and keep it going.

The reason we haven't solved the race problem in America after hundreds of years is that people apart from God are trying to create unity, while people under God who already *have* unity are not living out the unity they possess. The result of both these conditions is disaster for America.

I believe America's failure to find cultural unity is directly related to the church's failure to preserve its spiritual unity. The church has already been given unity because we've been made part of the same family. You don't have to get your family to *be* family. They already are. But sometimes you do have to get family to act like family.

When God wanted to block the attempts of self-directed people to build the tower of Babel and "disunify" them by scattering them over the face of the earth, He did so by confusing their language, their means of communication.

But when God wanted to unify Spirit-directed people, He gave them new communication on the Day of Pentecost when they spoke with other tongues (Acts 2:4). In other words, Pentecost was the direct reversal of the tower of Babel.

At the tower of Babel, God saw that unregenerate men wanted to be unified apart from Him, so He scrambled their languages. On the Day of Pentecost, when the Holy Spirit showed up, people spoke with languages they didn't know so that people from all sorts of backgrounds could unite under the Cross of Jesus Christ.

The people who heard the apostles speak on the Day of Pentecost were from all over the world (Acts 2:8–11). At least sixteen different geographical areas, racial categories, or ethnic groups are mentioned in these verses. But in spite of the great diversity, they found true unity in the coming of the Holy Spirit.

The message is obvious. If we want real unity, it can only happen where there is the coming of the Spirit. That's why you and I are baptized by the Spirit into one body. Authentic unity always and only comes to those who are under God's authority. Everybody else can only take a stab at it. They can only have a semblance of unity, but it never lasts very long.

So God has "disunified" self-directed people to keep them limited and therefore seeking Him. But in the church, God has unified Spirit-baptized and Spirit-directed people so that we have unlimited potential in Christ.

If this is true, what is our problem? Why can't Christians in America solve their racial problem and start shaking some things loose in the rest of this country? Our problem is a faulty view of Christ.

Christ Determines Unity in the Church

God resists unity outside of the church. The Spirit establishes unity through the church. But Christ determines unity within the church. Look at Ephesians 2:14–16, 18, where Paul writes:

For [Christ] Himself is our peace, who made both groups into one, and broke down the barrier of the dividing wall, by abolishing in His flesh the enmity, which is the Law of commandments contained in ordinances, so that in Himself He might make the two into one new man, thus establishing peace, and might reconcile them both in one body to God through the cross, by it having put to death the enmity. . . . For through Him we both have our access in one Spirit to the Father.

Here's the whole Trinity—Father, Son, and Holy Spirit—at work in the process of reconciliation. Why? Because racial and cultural relationships are first and foremost a theological issue, not just a sociological one.

Notice that Christ Himself has ended the conflict. He is our peace. The conflict Paul has in mind here is that which existed between Jews and Gentiles. Christ ended the conflict by breaking down the dividing wall through His death on the cross. He has made all believers into one body.

Therefore, the extent to which we imitate Christ in our attitudes and actions is the extent to which we will live out the unity we have been given by the Spirit.

ACHIEVING RACIAL AND CULTURAL UNITY

Why did God take people from every nation and race and tongue and unite them into one body? Because He wanted to demonstrate something to the world. The apostle Peter put it this way:

You are a chosen race, a royal priesthood, a holy nation, a people for God's own possession, so that you may proclaim the excellencies of Him who has called you out of darkness into His marvelous light. (1 Peter 2:9)

God has made a new "nation" of the church so that the non-Christian world can see what a real nation looks like. The church is to show the world what it looks like when people from different cultures, races, genders, and backgrounds unite under the banner of Jesus Christ.

There's a lady in New York harbor who holds up a torch, welcoming people from all over the world. America has been called the "melting pot," where people from Europe and Asia and Africa and everywhere else can be melted together into one nation.

But the melting pot has had trouble ever since it hit the stove. We have had trouble making all these different people into one. The dream of the Puritans was to make America a city on a hill, a light to show the way to other nations.

But until the church in America fixes its problem of racial unity, the culture has nothing to look at to see what real unity looks like. So Satan's goal has been to keep the saints apart so that the saints don't witness to the unity that God had in mind.

Two concluding passages bring all of this home. The first is in the book of Colossians:

[You] have put on the new self who is being renewed to a true knowledge according to the image of the One who created him—a renewal in which there is no distinction between Greek and Jew, circumcised and uncircumcised, barbarian, Scythian, slave and freeman, but Christ is all, and in all. (3:10–11)

Paul says that when you bring human divisions into the church of Jesus Christ, you divide the church and turn it into something other than what it was meant to be.

The reason the church hasn't gotten it together is that we've taken the divisions of the world and tried to make them work in the church. We have taken what Paul calls in Colossians 3:9 the "old self," the way we were before we knew Christ, and we've tried to fit the square peg of the old life into the round hole called the church.

When you enter the church, you enter into a whole new family. Leave that other mess outside. There's a whole different program in here.

Now don't get me wrong. Paul is not saying you cease to be black or white or anything else once you become a Christian. What he is saying is that those things that used to divide us must be brought under the lordship of Jesus Christ when we come into the church.

In the family of God, all people are now on the same level. No one is disadvantaged or advantaged. In Christ, human distinctions become irrelevant. They are overruled and transformed. The problem is that we bring the old self into the new organism—the church—and try to use our physical heritage for spiritual advantage rather than subjecting it to the Cross.

When you walk through the door of the church, your skin color must come under the Cross. You don't stop being who you are, but you subject who you are to Christ. Your gender must also come under the Cross, as we will see below. The way you were is the old self. You're now under the Cross.

It is because people will not submit who they are to Christ that there are divisions in the church. Blacks can't worship with whites, and Afro-centrism takes over. Or vice versa. It doesn't matter which, because they won't come under the Cross.

I get criticized all the time by people who tell me I'm not black enough. What they mean is that I won't go along with the old self. I will not let the old ways dominate. Now I am proud of the racial and cultural heritage God has given me. I applaud the wonderful history that God has given me.

But as wonderful as it is, it has to come under the Cross. It has to be evaluated by and subjected to the Cross.

In this passage in Colossians 3, Paul calls the members of Christ's body renewed people. We have been made brand-new. Look at some of the things that means for us.

No Racial Distinctions

First, our renewal in Christ means there should be no ethnic or racial distinctions, no "Greek and Jew" (v. 11). But note that Paul wasn't telling these Christians to pretend they weren't Greek or Jewish. People's racial identities will be maintained in heaven, since the apostle John said he saw people there from every nation and tribe and people and tongue (Revelation 7:9). Paul's point in Colossians 3:11 is simply that race shouldn't make any difference among believers.

That means I don't look at an Anglo member of our church or an Anglo brother in Christ and make a difference because his skin is different than mine. It means an Anglo brother doesn't look down on me as an African-American. We have the right to be what God made us to be, but we have no right to make a difference. We must treat each other as equals in the body of Christ.

When we don't do that, we begin to lose Christ. This is one reason the church has no power today. Believers are making distinctions that God never intended us to make.

Let me give you an example where this gets real nitty-gritty: the issue of interracial marriage. If two Christians of different races get married, that's not really an interracial or mixed marriage. Why? Because they are two people from the same holy nation, since Peter says we are one holy race (1 Peter 2:9).

The only true mixed marriage is when a believer marries an unbeliever (2 Corinthians 6:14). This is not to suggest that we create artificial means of mixing people. What I'm saying is that the church cannot use a non-Christian, worldly standard to evaluate people and their relationships.

When two people want to marry, what I want to know is, Do

they believe in Christ? Do they love the Lord? And are they willing to live by the biblical standard? If so, they fit the criteria of God's Word for marriage.

Someone will always say, "Well, what about the children of an interracial marriage? Aren't they going to have it rough?" Yes, they probably will. But so will anybody who lives godly in Christ Jesus.

That's why when so-called interracial couples come into the family of God, they ought to find the acceptance and protection of God in the context of a biblically sound local church. And they ought to know that when their kids grow up in God's family, they won't have a rough time. My point is, it's a whole new ball game in the church, a different standard.

No Religious Distinctions

Notice the second couplet Paul lists in Colossians 3:11: the "circumcised and uncircumcised." There are to be no religious distinctions in the church. Now he's talking about those under Christ here, not just about religion in general. We are always to distinguish between that which is Christian and that which is non-Christian.

But the issue here is the external religious practices that the Jews were trying to force the Gentile believers to follow. While we may need to divide over truth, we cannot divide over external practices.

In other words, if people don't worship or perform certain church rituals just like you do, that is not a basis for division. Circumcision was an external ritual having nothing to do with the heart of the Christian faith.

See, the church is fighting over all kinds of external stuff. I came out of a church where they argued, "Do we use individual cups in Communion, or do we share one cup? Do we use crackers or bread? Do we sprinkle or immerse?" People divide over externals like that. But Paul says if the essentials are straight, the externals can vary.

No Cultural Distinctions

A third distinction Paul says has no place in the church is

the cultural distinction: "barbarian and Scythian." The Greeks thought anybody who wasn't Greek was barbarian. And the worst of the barbarians were the Scythians. They were at the bottom of the cultural heap. They were the most barbaric of the barbaric. They didn't even know which fork to use when.

The church has always been tempted to draw cultural lines. Culture includes those things that are unique about us. We have people from Africa in our church in Dallas. If these people want to wear African garb, as long as it's modest they are free to do it.

You and I can't say that because something is not from our culture, other people should adapt to us. Remember, we're talking about non-essentials here. Anyway, in Christ there is no culture. Why? Because we are one holy nation, as we just saw in 1 Peter 2:9.

People have the freedom to do things differently from the way you and I do them. And we are no better off spiritually for having imposed our culture on someone else's culture. God hasn't called most of my Anglo brothers to like soul music. And I can assure you that God has not called me to like country music!

We have the right to our cultural preferences, because in the church there is no distinction. God has given us the freedom and equality under the cross to be who we are.

No Class Distinctions

Fourth, there are to be no class distinctions in the church, no difference between "slave and freeman." The church has always been tempted to make class distinctions. Just read James 2:1–3.

You've heard it said many times before, but it needs to be said again. The ground is level at the foot of the cross. We're all sinners saved by grace. If God has given you the ability to move up the social ladder, don't get too excited about it. Most middle-class people are only one paycheck away from going downhill anyway!

But if God enables you to move up, you ought to move up the social ladder backward so you can see where you came from and not turn your back on the brothers and sisters still coming up behind you.

Class distinctions are usually based on wealth, intellect, or power. If you have any of those things, they're gifts of God anyway, so don't brag about them as if you earned them (see 1 Corinthians 4:7). Class distinctions are irrelevant in the body of Christ.

No Gender Distinctions

A fifth distinction that's prohibited in the body of Christ is gender distinctions. Paul doesn't include this one in Colossians 3, but he does in Galatians 3:28: "There is neither male nor female; for you are all one in Christ Jesus."

Now again, this doesn't mean we stop being men and women. It means we don't exalt or devalue anyone because of gender. In Jesus' day women were put down. In the Greek world, women were an oppressed class who were there to work, bear children, and fulfill the pleasure of men.

But Christianity overturned all of that by declaring that women were of equal value to men and were to be treated as equals in the family of God. Although there will always be functional differences between men and women, both are equally valued by God and equally significant to His kingdom program.

Women are never to be demeaned. The Bible tells husbands to treat their wives as equal spiritual heirs (1 Peter 3:7).

BRINGING IT HOME

When you lay Colossians 3:10–11 and Galatians 3:28 side by side, you see what it's supposed to be like in the body of Christ, the church.

But let me tell you right here, if this is the stand you take, you will get some heavy flak. If you say, "I'm black, but I'm biblical first," "I'm white, but I'm biblical first," "I'm a man (or a woman), but I'm biblical first," you are going to get criticized and rejected by some people even in the church.

But let me tell you something else. If we Christians don't get our act together and start living out a biblical model of racial and cultural unity, this country is in trouble.

All the experts tell us that unless we start turning this thing around, what we're seeing today in terms of violence and the widening of class distinctions in America is just the beginning of things to come.

We're starting to hear terms like "race warfare" and "class warfare" as our society deteriorates and unravels along racial and class lines. But the bad news gives Christians a shining opportunity to help rebuild America.

What I mean is that this is one area where America is looking for help, for a new way. If the church can model biblical, racial, and cultural unity, the world will sit up and take notice. People will start asking, "How do you do this?"

But it has to start with the believer's commitment to bring his prejudices and upbringing and old ideas to the Cross and let them die there.

We need believers who will say, "Lord, I'm sorry. I've been raising my kids to be racists, and I've accepted racists in my church. When my neighbors made racist jokes, I laughed instead of condemning the jokes as wrong. I have made myself comfortable with racism, but no more."

We need believers who will say, "I'm going to build bridges to people of other races and cultures, and if I lose some friends from my own race because of it, so be it. As long as I gain Christ, it's OK."

That's risky Christianity, for sure. But unless we stop running from our problems and stop perpetuating old divisions, we won't have much left in America to turn over to our kids, spiritually or materially. It's too late to stay in our safe huddles. It's time to reach out and build some bridges between believers of different colors. That's what it's going to take.

CHAPTER 12

SHARING CHRIST ACROSS THE BARRIERS

By now it should be obvious that Christians don't have to do a whole lot to help destroy America. In fact, in many cases it's what Christians *aren't* doing that is the problem. Nowhere is that more true than in evangelism.

Now you will say, "I know, Tony. You're going to tell us that Christians aren't witnessing enough." Well, that's certainly true. A lot of believers are not sharing their faith within their own culture, where it's pretty safe and comfortable.

But the challenge I want to leave with you in this chapter is the larger need to reach out beyond our cultural circle to reach people from other cultures. The fact is that America is a multicultural environment.

By the year 2000, the sum total of minorities will outnumber the Anglo population, so any serious effort at evangelism is going to bring you into contact with people from other cultures.

So if we as Christians simply stay within our own circles, a lot more damage will be done than simply perpetuating racism. A lot of people in America will be left out when it comes to hearing the gospel. With that in mind, let me look with you at three principles of cross-cultural evangelism.

THE PRINCIPLE OF IDENTIFICATION

The first principle in witnessing for Christ cross-culturally is identification, which simply says that the more you can become like the one you are trying to reach, the better the opportunity for clear communication. Without changing the essence of who you are, you identify with your hearers so that the gospel can be understood and received.

The ultimate example of this is Jesus Christ Himself, who came to live among us by taking on humanity (John 1:14). He did this so that we could clearly see what God is like and understand the good news of the salvation He came to bring. Then, in the ultimate act of identity, Jesus took our place on the cross and died for our sins.

Paul wrote, "You know the grace of our Lord Jesus Christ, that though He was rich, yet for your sake He became poor, so that you through His poverty might become rich" (2 Corinthians 8:9). The Lord Jesus went out of His way to identify with us so we could identify with Him and receive the benefits of that identification.

That's the way it needs to be in our efforts to reach people who are not like us. Just as Christ became like us so we could partake of who He is, so we should become like those we are trying to reach so that they can appreciate what we are offering and come to accept its benefit.

If you and I are not willing to rub shoulders with people, identify with their hurts, eat at their tables, walk by their sides, and care for their concerns, why should they think our gospel can help them? If Christ is the answer, we need to understand the questions people are asking so that we can clearly articulate Christ's answer to them.

Paul wasn't afraid to identify with the people he wanted to win to Christ:

For though I am free from all men, I have made myself a slave to all, so that I might win more. To the Jews I became as a Jew, so that I might win Jews; to those who are under the Law, as under the Law, though not being myself under the Law, so that I might win those who are under the Law; to those who are without law, as without law, though not being without the law of God but under the law of Christ, so that I might win those who are without law. To the weak I became weak, that I might win the weak; I have become all things to all men, so that I may by all means save some. (1 Corinthians 9:19–22)

Paul identified with the unsaved, whether they were part of his race or not. He realized that to be so tied to his culture or racial identity that he did not have the flexibility to identify with others outside of his "comfort zone" would have been a hindrance, not a help, to the gospel. Even though Paul was a Jew, he was first of all a committed Christian. Therefore, cross-cultural evangelism was no problem for him.

THE PRINCIPLE OF LOVE

A second principle of cross-cultural evangelism is love. The nature of biblical love is to seek the highest good of the other person, even at your own inconvenience or expense. Again, look at the cross for a picture of love in action. It was a terrible inconvenience and expense for God to send His Son to die on that cross.

But as the gospel song says, "He did it all for me"—and He did it all for you too! No wonder Paul says it's the love of God that compels us to carry the gospel to the lost (2 Corinthians 5:14).

Notice that Paul wrote this to the predominantly Gentile church at Corinth. The idea is that the same love that motivated God to be inconvenienced in the giving of His Son should motivate His children to be inconvenienced in reaching people who are different from them in culture, personality, or background.

Jesus tied our love for God to our love for others in His statement of the great commandment in Matthew 22:37–40, where He said in answer to a question:

"You shall love the Lord your God with all your heart, and with all your soul, and with all your mind." This is the great and foremost commandment. The second is like it, "You shall love your neighbor as yourself." On these two commandments depend the whole Law and the Prophets.

In case you might miss the point, John says later that anyone who says he loves God and hates his brother is a liar (1 John 4:20).

Now you may have noticed that Jesus didn't say anything about culture or race in Matthew 22. But He covered it nicely in the story of the Good Samaritan (Luke 10:25–37), where He taught us that our neighbor is anyone we see who needs what we have to offer, no matter what his race or cultural background.

So when we see people who need the gospel and we have the gospel to offer them, it's a spiritual crime to neglect that responsibility and walk by on the other side. Because the love of God is without social distinction, our love for others must not be influenced by the distinctions of secular society.

THE PRINCIPLE OF TESTIMONY

Here's a third principle that should operate in cross-cultural evangelism. That is, we must recognize that when we allow our social biases to keep us from touching those who need the good news, we are both hindering the gospel message and causing its truth to be looked down upon.

This hurts the church's testimony. The truth embodied in the good news of Jesus Christ is that racial distinctions are broken down and those who were once enemies are now united in one body. Paul said that Jews and Gentiles had been made one by the work of Christ (see Ephesians 2:11–21).

Before Christ died the Gentiles were excluded from the spiritual benefits of Israel. But because Christ has made both groups into one, the responsibility of the church is to preserve the unity the Holy Spirit has already given us (Ephesians 4:3).

So it's a real tragedy that racial distinctions are allowed to exist in God's church. When we reflect the spirit of the culture, what do we have to offer individuals within it? It's true that prejudice of believers does not excuse a person from his responsibility to trust in Christ. But it does hurt the credibility of the messenger.

What we say is not being backed up by how we live. The cultural division that exists in our country, epitomized by the black/white schism, blurs our message. The lack of fellowship and interaction makes it appear that even though we say the gospel makes a difference and changes lives, we really don't believe it.

If the church doesn't help to break down these cultural and racial barriers, we are helping to destroy America. The testimony of our God is at stake. When we don't live out the gospel, we make God look bad to the culture that needs so desperately to hear from Him.

This issue is critical. The church of Jesus Christ must not allow itself to be influenced by any culture. We must leave the safety of our evangelical circles and present Christ as Savior to all. But at the same time, we have to demonstrate the reality of that truth by the radically different way we live together as brothers and sisters in Christ.

A MODEL OF CROSS-CULTURAL EVANGELISM

I often get requests from concerned Christian whites who want me or one of my staff to minister to black non-Christians they have met. Usually, I'm happy to do so. But many times the request is really the believer's way of escaping his responsibility to share Christ cross-culturally.

Sometimes the situation is reversed. Many Christian blacks are also hesitant to talk about Christ with whites who are in spiritual need. Some people are just uncomfortable with members of another race. Others have preconceived notions that hinder their outreach. We can only imagine where we might be today if Paul had responded to his call to another culture the way many modern-day Christians respond.

The basic question is, How do you begin the process of reaching out to people who are different from you? Jesus' encounter with the Samaritan woman in John 4 is one of the clearest answers I know of, and I want to examine this passage in detail. Even though this story is well known, its cross-cultural implications are often bypassed.

If you know your Bible and Bible history, you know that the Samaritans of Jesus' day were a despised group. They were considered racial "half-breeds" by the Jews because they were descendants of the intermarriages between Jews and foreign captives brought into Samaria by the Assyrians when they conquered the northern kingdom of Israel in 722 B.C.

Because of this mixture centuries earlier, the "pure" Jews from the southern kingdom of Judah rejected the Samaritans. In fact, the Jews referred to the city of Samaria as a "city of fools." The hostility between these groups was still strong at the time of the encounter between Jesus and the Samaritan woman.

John 4 begins with Jesus leaving Judea rather than allow Himself to become embroiled in a controversy involving John the Baptist. The apostle John interjects an interesting statement in verse 4: "[Jesus] had to pass through Samaria."

This is interesting because Jews, especially rabbis like Jesus, would go out of their way to avoid passing through Samaria and risking any contact with these people—even though Samaria stood directly between Judea and Galilee.

Jews would cross the Jordan River and go around Samaria, much like the priest and Levite crossed the road to avoid the injured man in the story of the Good Samaritan.

The Jews' animosity toward the Samaritans wasn't just racial; it was also religious. The Samaritans only accepted the Pentateuch, the first five books of the Old Testament, and they had their own temple and their own worship on Mount Gerizim.

So with all of this cultural and racial and religious stuff in the air, why did Jesus *have* to go through Samaria? The answer is in the story itself. There was a spiritual need there. A woman was there who needed help, and Jesus was aware of her need. So He made a point of going through Samaria, and at Jacob's well He met this Samaritan woman (vv. 5–7).

This tells us that for Jesus, cultural or racial differences were always subservient to spiritual needs. How badly the church in America needs to learn that lesson.

If American Christians would start ranking the meeting of spiritual needs above cultural and racial distinctions, we would see successful cross-cultural evangelism taking place on a grand scale in our society, and this country would never be the same.

The Key of Common Ground

I want to give you several keys that Jesus used to unlock this cross-cultural encounter. You can use them too, since they transcend time and culture. The first of these is that Jesus found common ground with the woman.

It's not accidental that Jesus stopped at Jacob's well. We learn in verse 12 that the Samaritans also claimed Jacob as their ancestor, just as the Jews did. So right away Jesus bypassed all the current prejudices and found a point of common ground. He was sitting by Jacob's well, which must have meant that He approved of Jacob. She could agree with that.

In determining common ground, you have to look at what makes another person tick. When you think about it, that's not at all hard to do. Certain things make all of us tick just because we are human.

Food, for example, is a common human need, not a cultural need. So having a non-Christian over for dinner is not something that is limited to a particular experience or a certain culture. The problem is that most Christians never get close enough to non-Christians to seek out the common ground.

What we feel comfortable doing is remaining in our Christian subcultures and expecting the world to come to us. We do not understand that our job is to go to where the world is with the radical message of Jesus Christ.

Whatever it is, the activity should be carefully planned. There should be a strategy laid out in your mind that takes into account where the person is in his thinking and what the best way might be of finding the opportunity to share Christ. The crucial question is this: Where do you both agree?

The meeting at Jacob's well was not an accident; it was Jesus' well-planned strategy. It enabled Him to meet the woman of Samaria at a point of agreement.

The Key of Culture Shock

After He established common ground with the Samaritan woman, Jesus asked her for a drink from the well. According to verse 9, the woman was stupefied at Jesus' request: "How is it that You, being a Jew, ask me for a drink since I am a Samaritan woman?"

This woman was shocked that Jesus was actually asking her for the privilege of putting His Jewish lips to her Samaritan cup. And before it was washed, at that. This was an act of fellowship and acceptance that was culturally shocking.

How did this woman know that Jesus was a Jew? John doesn't tell us that Jesus ever told her He was a Jew. So how did she know? He must have looked like a Jew or spoken with a

Jewish accent, or had some trait that publicly identified His racial and cultural heritage.

In other words, when Jesus Christ went through Samaria He didn't give up His own culture. He didn't stop being a Jew. But He also didn't let His culture stop Him from meeting a spiritual need.

This counter-cultural move left the Samaritan woman stunned because it was contrary to everything she had been raised to expect. But Jesus cared so much for her that He was willing to drink out of the same cup. He understood that He could never get to her sin problem until He was first able to communicate with her cross-culturally.

But Jesus gave respect and acceptance to her as a person to be related to and not just a soul to be won. This gave Him a hearing for the gospel.

One of the great barriers in evangelism is the fact that Christians continue to let their backgrounds interfere with their communication with unsaved people from other cultures. It always seems easier to get someone of that other person's race or color to do the job, even though we see the one in need every day at work, around the neighborhood, or in some other setting. And even when we do witness, it is often done without the sense that we are concerned for the person.

Jesus does not ask whites to become blacks, blacks to become whites, or any other exchange in culture or nationality. He simply demands that whatever our culture, we not let it interfere with sharing the good news in a caring way that accepts the person as we seek to win his or her soul.

The fact that our backgrounds have oriented us to certain likes and dislikes is all part of God's variety. But God never meant for His variety to stand in the way of the task that confronts every Christian—getting the good news to everyone. When the gospel is hindered by our background or race, we have elevated culture to a higher position than our commitment to God.

Jesus Christ left His culture for this brief moment by Jacob's well. He stopped acting like a typical Jew would act, even though He maintained an obviously Jewish appearance. He stepped out of His world and into the woman's Samaritan world. He cared, and that's why she responded in utter surprise.

Here's one way our own society fails to take a caring

approach to cross-cultural evangelism. When many Anglo Christians talk about Africa, for example, they always talk in terms of Africa's great spiritual need. But when they talk about black Americans, they are somehow blinded to the same spiritual needs.

That's why many Christians would rather go across the ocean to do evangelism than go across the street. They know very little about the spiritual needs of their black neighbors, and they often don't make any effort to know.

This is also true of the way blacks tend to look at Hispanics. Blacks often caricature them in a way that mimics the cultural bigotry of whites toward blacks. But Christian blacks ought to see non-Christian Hispanics as an opportunity for getting the gospel out in spite of the cultural differences.

If being black or white means ignoring someone of a different race because we prefer not to explain the gospel to him, at that point we have become too black or too white. In that situation, black is no longer beautiful and white is no longer right.

What I'm saying is, if you want to understand a community, look deeper than the color of the flesh. Get down to where it's hurting.

The Key of Spiritual Truth

Jesus did not only show us that cultural differences must be subservient to spiritual needs. He also taught that cultural differences must be subservient to spiritual truth.

Read Jesus' exchange with the Samaritan woman in John 4:10–18 and you'll see that He soon got down to the truth: He was there to offer her the water of eternal life, and she was a sinner who needed it. This was a spiritual truth that had nothing at all to do with her culture.

Then when Jesus invited her to go back and get her husband, the truth that she was living promiscuously also came out. At this point she was probably thinking, as a lot of people would: *This guy has stopped preaching and gone to meddling*.

Jesus was beginning to get personal, and she didn't like that. So she backed off the subject, as we'll see below. But remember that Jesus had gotten this far because He was willing to drink from her cup.

In verses 19–20, the woman changed the subject to a hot cultural/religious controversy between the Jews and Samaritans: where people should worship. The Samaritans had their own temple, but the Jews believed you had to go to the temple in Jerusalem to worship God properly.

Note especially that the woman's argument rested on what had been handed down to her by her ancestors. "Our fathers worshiped in this mountain" (v. 20). In other words, she was arguing from the standpoint of her cultural heritage, what her daddy and granddaddy had taught her.

This is important, because when the woman had mentioned culture earlier in relation to drinking water, Jesus ignored the subject of culture altogether. But when she tried to turn the truth into a cultural issue, Jesus didn't let it pass.

When the woman made God subservient to what her ancestors had taught her about worship, Jesus quickly corrected her in four powerful verses about the nature of worship, the nature of God, and the nature of spiritual truth.

The bottom line is, when my culture or yours comes into conflict with what God has said in His Word, then culture is wrong and must be rejected. Culture is not valid when it gives out wrong information about God.

But Christians are not rejecting culture today. In fact, we are pushing God out the door to make sure that everyone in our culture loves us. When the culture tells us to dress a certain way, live in a certain location, and associate with certain people, and we reject people who do not follow those standards or fit that mold, we are accepting cultural standards instead of biblical ones.

But Jesus didn't let the Samaritan woman get away with appealing to her upbringing to justify faulty doctrine and practice. We can never appeal to our upbringing to justify our actions if our upbringing has given us bad information about God.

What our ancestors taught is acceptable only to the degree that it conforms to divine truth. If they taught us to dislike people on the basis of racial, class, or cultural differences, then we must reject that teaching. If they taught us to value possessions over people, entertainment over worship, or our own desires over God's truth, we must choose God's way and reject our culture's ideas. A believer's obligation to God must be greater than his commitment to his cultural heritage. Culture must be dumped when it conflicts with Scripture.

Jesus was telling this woman that *where* people worship is irrelevant to God. What matters is *how* an individual worships Him. God is looking for people who will worship Him with the right heart, based on the right information—"spirit and truth" (vv. 23–24). God does not look at the cultural barriers that separate folk. He looks at the heart.

A white seminary student will sometimes ask me, "Should I accept the pastorate of a church that does not accept black people who are spiritually qualified to join?" I usually like to turn the question around to show how absurd it is. "Should you accept a church that won't accept white people who are spiritually qualified to join?"

See, that question is not valid today because God has already answered it. Believers should be able to worship Him in any place they choose, irrespective of culture. Rejecting any believer because of secular biases is unacceptable. I will never forget the day my wife and I were rejected by a white church because of the color of our skin, especially since the sermon for the day was on love.

Why? Because God is interested in truth. Once you know the truth that in Christ, God has broken down the wall of partition between the races (Ephesians 2:14), then all you need to do is act on that truth.

When black members of our church in Dallas ask me about people worshiping with us who are not part of our culture, I tell them that cultural differences are irrelevant because God has spoken. It's amazing how many evangelicals believe God has spoken until it gets to the issue of race or culture. Then the congregation feels it has to speak. But God has already spoken!

What that means is that for believers to refer to themselves as black Christians, white Christians, Hispanic Christians, or Asian Christians is theologically incorrect. The word *Christian* becomes a noun being defined by the adjectives *black*, *white*, *Hispanic*, or *Asian*. Yet our Christianity should never be modified by our culture.

It needs to be just the opposite. We must see ourselves as Christian blacks, Christian whites, Christian Hispanics, or

Christian Asians. When we do, our culture is being modified by the nature of our Christian commitment.

Culture must always be controlled by our commitment to Christ. Once you come to Christ, you belong to a higher order than the temporary, earthly culture you are in. Everything is to be brought into conformity to your new life in Jesus Christ. Christianity must always inform, explain, and change our culture, never the reverse.

What we desperately need today is Christians of all cultures who are committed to the Scriptures without negating their cultural background. This opens the door for every believer to evangelize every nonbeliever, because cultural barriers are no longer an issue.

We are not obligated to the world anymore. We do not work for the god of this world. We are under a new contract. Thus, all cultural decisions must be biblically informed.

The Key of Spiritual Outreach

Finally, Jesus' encounter with the Samaritan woman in John 4 demonstrates that cultural differences must be subservient to spiritual outreach. The question at this point is, How far do we go in trying to meet the spiritual needs of another culture when we have our own culture to contend with?

That is a valid question, and in verses 27–35, Jesus answered it with something that is astounding and unparalleled in the history of cross-cultural evangelism.

According to verse 27, the disciples came back from town at this point. They were shocked out of their sandals when they saw Jesus talking to the Samaritan woman. Although it was true that many rabbis didn't talk to women, we know that Jesus didn't always follow that practice.

The disciples were offended that Jesus would talk with this *Samaritan* woman, which explains why Jesus let them go to town to get food (v. 8). He knew their attitude would have been cultural baggage as He witnessed to this woman. Jesus knew these guys were not ready to "integrate," so He got them out of the way while He dealt with her soul need.

See, getting criticism is part of the cost of cross-cultural evangelism. Whenever Christians make the commitment that they are going to act biblically even if it contradicts their tradition, the culture will resist.

Culture is not accustomed to being contradicted. It expects to be accepted. Whenever the Christian acts or speaks biblically, he runs the risk of being rejected by others, even other Christians, who don't accept that kind of antithesis to the status quo.

In my opinion, one reason that revival has not broken out in America is that it is more popular to be American than to be Christian. While being an American is a privilege, it also gives us the awesome responsibility to use our freedom to accomplish spiritual ends, not just personal ends.

From the human perspective, there will be many people in hell because we let our culture stand in the way of being a witness to them.

The disciples needed a lesson in cross-cultural evangelism, and they were about to get it. According to John 4:28–29, the woman went back to her town to invite the men to come out and meet Someone she believed might be the Messiah.

Picture the scene. Here was a crowd of Samaritan men coming out to Jesus (v. 30). The encounter had all the makings of a racial catastrophe. Jews didn't like the Samaritans, and these Samaritans didn't know they were on their way to meet a band of Jewish bigots along with Jesus. This was a potentially volatile situation, particularly with Peter there, sword at his side.

But as the Samaritans approached, look what Jesus said to the disciples: "Do you not say, 'There are yet four months, and then comes the harvest'? Behold, I say to you, lift up your eyes and look on the fields, that they are white for harvest" (v. 35).

Here was the disciples' evangelism lesson. When they looked up, they saw a crowd of people who were very different from them. In other words, one of the strongest evangelistic passages in all of the New Testament dealt with cross-cultural evangelism, not just Jewish evangelism. Jesus was saying, "These people from another culture are the harvest field."

In essence, Jesus said to the disciples, "Gentlemen, it's time to go to work." Then He led many of those Samaritans to faith in Himself that day (vv. 39–42). Jesus Christ had just taught His disciples that the will of God, which in this case was winning people from another culture to the Savior, was more important than eating (vv. 31–32).

Do we as Christians in America today think about evangelism like that? Do we want our neighbors to go to heaven more than we want to eat breakfast, lunch, or dinner? Are we so full of the will of God that our concern for the souls of men—be they black, white, brown, or yellow—burns inside of us as strongly as does our hunger at mealtime?

Jesus was saying that what is important is doing the will of God, which includes evangelism. It's important even when the person you are witnessing to is someone you may not hang out with ordinarily, someone whose skin color or cultural tastes are different from yours.

See, the problem throughout history has always been in finding laborers, not ripe fields. There is a sense in which men and women are hungry to come to Christ, even though the flip side of that coin is that they are rejecting Him.

People are hungry for life, and Christ is that life. They are hungry for meaning, and Christ provides that meaning. They need to be confronted with that reality.

But until Christians in America get so hungry to see people of all cultures come to Christ that we quit worrying about mealtime, nothing much is going to happen. Unless we see people as Jesus saw them, we may wind up like Nero, fiddling while Rome burned—except that we will be feeding our faces while America falls under God's judgment.

A CONCLUDING WORD

Cross-cultural evangelism is neither convenient nor easy. You have to be willing to set aside your preferences, and perhaps even your friends, to do it. But the reward is well worth the sacrifice and effort.

One of the cries we hear today is that the church of Jesus Christ needs to be unified. But how can this happen when we let culture tell us with whom we can be unified? The quickest way to develop unity is to tear down the barriers between those who are not unified. And the best way to start that process is by pointing them to Christ.

New believers can be instructed in the attitude they should have toward those who are unlike them. The oneness of the body of Christ can be taught immediately.

The problem, however, is that we in the church have perpetuated cultural standards and not biblical truth. If new Christians were taught the truth about their responsibilities while they were still excited about their newfound faith, that excitement would help to reinforce the truth before it got blurred by the cultural norms and standards of the day.

So how do you start doing cross-cultural evangelism? Identify a non-Christian near you and develop a strategy for his or her conversion. First, seek the common ground. Where can you and this person agree?

Second, demonstrate concern for the person as well as for his soul. Then reach out to him in ways he might not naturally expect. Communicate the gospel in a manner he can clearly understand. But most of all, depend on the Holy Spirit to bridge the barriers that cultural bias may have raised.

When you begin to win those unlike yourself to Christ, I can assure you that your confidence level in the faith will grow rapidly. You and I are to be involved in cross-cultural evangelism, not because it is convenient or easy, but because it is commanded. The only way to reach all nations for Christ is to cross cultural barriers, and the only way to cross barriers is to decide to do so, not to wait until the other side invites you over.

Until we begin to do that, the church in America will continue to deteriorate and miss a golden opportunity to reach the world right here in our backyard—and that will only contribute to America's demise.

Let's attack this world with the good news of Jesus Christ. Let's shock it with the fact that Christians are willing to march into enemy territory in spite of rejection, conflict, or national distinctives. Let's declare that *anyone* who believes on Jesus Christ and His work on the cross will be saved!

CHAPTER 13

BECOMING GOD'S ALTERNATIVE

I n chapters 11 and 12, we talked about some specific issues of race and culture. Now I want to deal with the broader issue of the role Christians should play as God's representatives in our secular culture. Whenever God's people function as His representatives in this world, they do so cross-culturally because they are part of an order that is heavenly in origin.

Our identification with Christ automatically brings us into conflict with the accepted values of the day. The reality of this conflict has become increasingly clear as we have watched the values of our society corrode in front of us.

Our society is deteriorating spiritually, ethically, and morally. As Christians, therefore, we must ask ourselves whether we are contributing to the destruction of America or bringing the righteousness of Christ to bear on society.

We are living in a nation that has thrown the so-called Protestant work ethic out the window—along with the theology that sustained it. People no longer feel obligated to buy into a Christian framework of thinking.

This is a deteriorating culture, whether we're talking nationally or locally. The local papers show us in miniature what is happening nationally. People are doing and saying things, and espousing ungodly causes, that shock us when we stop to think about them.

The problem is compounded when we realize that more is

being done in the name of Christ today than ever before. There are more outreach programs and Christian broadcasts and other forms of ministry than ever, yet America is not getting turned around spiritually.

There are reasons for that, and we have been addressing some of them in this book. Here I want to consider in broad strokes the approach or stance we as Christians need to take toward this decaying culture if we are going to help stop America's spiritual decay.

HOW TO LIVE ON A SINKING SHIP

Let me illustrate where I'm going by likening our secular culture to a ship. The inhabitants of this ship are the people of America, including Christians like you and me.

We know from the Bible that this ship is going down someday. In 2 Timothy 3:1–5, Paul says this world will get worse, not better. This cosmos is going to come under God's judgment and be done away with.

But in the meantime, God has put us here, and He has called us to live for Him and display His love and character. So how should we relate to the other people on this ship of culture? Most believers are divided into two primary groups.

The Isolationists

The first group of Christians are those I call the isolationists. This group knows the ship is going down. They've read their Bibles. They have their theology straight. They know the ship is going to sink. The others on the ship don't know it, but the isolationists do.

So they have decided not to waste time doing anything about this doomed vessel. Instead, they want to lower the lifeboat, get into it, and sail off singing the songs of Zion and talking to each other about the impending doom the ship faces.

The isolationists won't have anything to do with the ship. They won't interact with its people, they won't sleep in its cabins, they won't swim in its pool, and they won't play shuffleboard on its deck. They simply leave the ship because they know it's going down.

To a large degree, this group represents one major segment of evangelicalism today. These believers ignore the realities of living in a secular world due to a misguided and misapplied understanding of dispensational theology.

Apart from a few select issues they have chosen to identify with, they ignore the glaring, flagrant unrighteousness in areas such as social oppression, racism, and economic injustice.

The isolationists meet regularly and smugly in their churches, insisting upon correct doctrine but having little or no contact with the ungodliness of this age. Their message is to repent and believe. But because isolationists have so little involvement with the secular culture, very few sinners hear their message.

The Conformists

But there's a second group of Christians who like the ship. I call them the conformists. They enjoy the swimming pool, the plush cabins, and the excellent cuisine. They get along with all of the crew members and enjoy the benefits of the ship to such an extent that they cannot be distinguished from anyone else on board that sinking vessel. They may not even realize the ship is going down, and if they do realize it, they keep the bad news to themselves.

This group, in the words of Paul, has become "conformed to this world" (Romans 12:2). They have become comfortable in Satan's territory. They have been lulled to sleep by America's pseudo-Christian atmosphere of "baseball, hot dogs, and apple pie." Personal peace and affluence have become their national pastime.

So while the isolationists are heralding truth but removed from the world, the conformists are heralding nothing in the midst of it. The results, however, are about the same for each: God's people making little or no difference in the cosmos.

The problem is that both isolationist and conformist Christians have missed the biblical mandate. What we need today in America is a group of Christians who are neither isolationists nor conformists, but God's *alternatives*.

What do alternatives look like? They are on the ship of culture, but they are not *of* the ship. They understand that the ship is eventually going to sink.

But they also understand that their job is to offer the people an alternative to the options of religious legalism or carnal conformity, a way of escape from the judgment coming on the ship, as well as a new way of living while they're on the ship. God's alternatives show this sinking world system what God looks like in its midst.

Alternatives understand that this present age is under God's judgment and will be destroyed someday. But an alternative does not stand by and watch while society self-destructs. As God's alternatives called the church, we are called to show the world what this ship would look like if it sailed under divine direction.

THE PORTRAIT OF AN ALTERNATIVE

Let me paint a portrait of an alternative by turning to a real-life biblical example, the prophet and statesman Daniel. The book of Daniel contains both his own story as a Jewish captive and a section of prophecy. We are going to spend most of our time looking at three incidents in the early chapters of Daniel, but the key verse comes in the prophecy section.

It's the last half of Daniel 11:32. Daniel was prophesying about the persecution Israel would endure several hundred years later under Antiochus Epiphanes (11:21–35). In the midst of a badly deteriorating situation, Daniel writes, "But the people who know their God will display strength and take action."

Basically, that's what it means to be God's alternative as a believer. In the midst of a society collapsing socially and religiously, those who remain faithful to God and stand for Him will be given internal strength so they can do great things for Him externally, in the culture.

Daniel's life and the lives of his three Hebrew "homeboys," Hananiah, Mishael, and Azariah (aka Shadrach, Meshach, and Abednego), illustrate this principle. They show us what the people of God should look like in a decaying society. Their lives are a portrait of an alternative.

Alternatives Don't Eat the King's Meat

The book of Daniel opens with the historical setting. Daniel and other young men of nobility and ability have been taken captive from Jerusalem to Babylon by King Nebuchadnezzar. There the king ordered that they be educated in "the literature and language of the Chaldeans" (Daniel 1:4).

That wasn't the problem. The problem was in verse 5: "The king appointed for them a daily ration from the king's choice food and from the wine which he drank."

Nebuchadnezzar's goal was to "Babylonize" Daniel and his Israelite buddies so they would forget their past and adjust to their new cultural environment. His plan was for them to become Babylonian men reflecting a Babylonian worldview through a Babylonian education and Babylonian names based on the names of Babylonian gods.

But according to verse 8, "Daniel made up his mind that he would not defile himself with the king's choice food or with the wine which he drank; so he sought permission from the commander of the officials that he might not defile himself."

Nebuchadnezzar was offering Daniel the world. Daniel could have had the best. He could have lived in the king's house, become the king's top administrator, and eaten at the king's table—things he never could have expected as a captured slave.

But Daniel determined that he was not going to eat the king's meat. Why did he decide that? Because God had commanded the Jews not to eat meat offered to idols (Exodus 34:15). And there was some meat they were not permitted to eat anyway. To do so would be to disobey the Law of God.

See, Daniel had a divine perspective. He knew God had spoken about this. He had gone to the king's dining room that first day, where they had the best slab of pork chops he had ever seen. And if they had a little Babylonian "soul," there might also have been some hogmogs, chitterlings, and pigs' feet. They set all that in front of Daniel.

But he chose God's alternative. No matter how hungry he may have been, no matter how much his future—and maybe even his *life*—depended upon it, no matter how much the king demanded it, Daniel could not eat because God had already addressed the issue.

This suggests that God expects His people to live in a secular society without being conformed to that society. When

God's Word and the world's perspective collide, God's people need to decide that He has spoken, and that what He has said is right and everybody else is wrong.

What America needs desperately today is a group of Christians who will not eat the king's meat or buy into the king's system at work; people who will not go along with the immorality of the day or do what everybody else is doing just because it's the popular thing to do.

Daniel knew that when God said don't eat that meat, he couldn't eat it. If it cost him his future, he couldn't eat it. If it cost him his new status in Babylonian society, he couldn't eat that meat—simply because God had said so.

We usually focus so much on what Daniel didn't do that we forget what he did do. He did submit himself to a Babylonian education. He did serve in the Babylonian court. He did take his new Babylonian name.

Why didn't Daniel just refuse the whole mess? He could have said to Nebuchadnezzar, "Look, I don't want any part of your ungodly system. God is going to judge you, and I don't want to be around when He does. So not only will I not eat your meat, I am not going to wear your clothes, answer to the name you have given me, or accept a job in your court. I'm separating myself completely."

The reason Daniel didn't do this is that God only spoke concerning the defilement of the meat. So Daniel went to Babylon State U. and graduated magna cum laude. He took the job in the king's court and was voted "Employee of the Year."

God doesn't ask us to withdraw completely from the world. He just wants us to make sure that we are influencing our world for Him and not being influenced by the world. What Daniel did was let Nebuchadnezzar and his whole ungodly society see what God looks like by providing an alternative.

This means that a Christian secretary is not like all the other secretaries around her. She may type the same way and file the same way, but here is a woman who does not do the same things for the same reason.

She is not only in her job to get a salary, she's there in that office to show people what God looks like. When the other secretaries talk about the boss and other employees, she does not participate. Why? Because God has said something about gossiping and she doesn't eat the "meat" of gossip. Yet she does her job to the best of her ability.

The same is true for believing lawyers, doctors, and bus drivers. They are operating by a different set of instructions, because they understand that God has said not to eat the "meat" of dishonesty or sloth or compromise.

One reason thc church is having so little impact in America today is that we don't have enough Christian alternatives out there. We have churches that are full on Sunday mornings, but that is not where Christianity is lived out. Christianity is lived out in the marketplace of the world.

To the degree that a believer lives for Christ in the world, he is offering the world something it can't find anywhere else. And to paraphrase a famous line from a popular film, "If we live it, they will come." People will be attracted to Christ within us and want to know about this alternative.

This story does not end with Daniel's refusal to eat the king's meat in Daniel 1:8. In verses 9–14, we read that Daniel offered Ashpenaz, his Babylonian baby-sitter, an alternative when it came to the food. Daniel requested that he and his three friends be tested by going on a vegetable diet for ten days.

The point of Daniel's request was to show what God could do through His people's obedience. Daniel's obedience would produce far more good than any benefits he might attain by conforming to the ungodly requirements of Babylon.

According to verses 15–16, the results of this experiment on Daniel, Hananiah, Mishael, and Azariah were spectacular:

At the end of ten days their appearance seemed better and they were fatter than all the youths who had been eating the king's choice food. So the overseer continued to withhold their choice food and the wine they were to drink, and kept giving them vegetables.

God rewarded Daniel's obedience by giving him and the other boys "knowledge and intelligence in every branch of literature and wisdom; Daniel even understood all kinds of visions and dreams" (Daniel 1:17). And when King "Nebby" interviewed these guys, he was so impressed that "they entered the king's personal service" (v. 19).

In other words, being God's alternative made God look good, made His people look good, and began the process of establishing a divine testimony before the king. It even made Ashpenaz look good for being associated with God's people.

This principle is illustrated in the game of football, where having an alternative is very important. A quarterback may call a pass play to his wide receiver downfield, only to have the defense call a blitz where the defenders rush the quarterback.

When this happens, the quarterback often doesn't have time to wait for the wide receiver to complete his pattern. But this play includes an alternative, a secondary receiver. The running back has peeled off to the outside in case the quarterback gets in trouble.

So now the quarterback looks to the sideline and passes the ball to his running back, his alternative receiver. This player's job is to be there when the defense charges the quarterback so he can take the pass and continue the play.

God's original program was to bring in the kingdom through Israel. But according to Matthew 12, Satan "blitzed" the play and got Israel to reject Jesus, her Messiah. The people said in essence, "We don't want Christ's kind of kingdom."

The illustration doesn't fit at every point, because God was not caught off guard by Israel's rejection. The kingdom was delayed because of Satan's blitz, and God turned to His alternative "receiver," the church.

God has passed the ball to the church, as it were, and our job is to advance His agenda in history and score touchdowns for the kingdom of God, showing that "greater is He who is in you than he who is in the world" (1 John 4:4).

Christians are God's alternatives. Because Daniel was willing to be an alternative, all Babylon began to know of his God. He was internally strong and externally powerful before the king.

If we expect to dramatically affect our culture for Christ, it will be because God's people have taken the ball of the gospel and have begun to run with it in spite of the opposition and confrontation of an opposing culture; to run with it in love, but with the determination to make a difference.

Alternatives Don't Bow to the King's God

The second story is told in Daniel 3, where the focus is on the three Hebrew young men we know as Shadrach, Meshach, and Abednego. They were now rulers in the province of Babylon (3:1–2).

How did they get those positions? The answer is given in the last verse of chapter 2: "Daniel made request of the king, and he appointed Shadrach, Meshach and Abednego over the administration of the province of Babylon, while Daniel was at the king's court" (v. 49).

Daniel didn't forget his godly pals. Daniel was already employed in the king's court. He could have said, "I've got mine, you get yours. I struggled, I interpreted dreams, and you should do the same thing."

But Daniel was not satisfied with just being a godly alternative. He wanted to multiply the influence for God in high places. So he requested high positions for these three men who also had refused to bow to the pressure of a godless culture. It's called discipleship, believers assisting one another in developing their full potential for Christ.

So impressed was Nebuchadnezzar with Daniel as God's alternative that promoting three more young men like him was, shall we say, a welcome addition to the company. There's nothing wrong with getting to the top—as long as you are still God's representative when you get there.

Then in Daniel 3, the king began to develop a "theo-ego," a god complex. He had a huge monument built to himself and ordered that the moment his leaders heard loud music, they were to bow down and worship the image. Anyone who didn't would become a French fry (vv. 2–6).

There was a lot at stake here. These leaders' livelihoods and even their lives depended on their bowing down. Nebuchadnezzar was CEO of the Babylonian corporate structure. He did the hiring and the firing. And when he fired you, you stayed fired! Nebby ran the show, and if you liked your job and your head, you obeyed him.

But when the music sounded, three men wouldn't go down before this idol (vv. 7–12). There were plenty of jealous Babylonian leaders eager to report these disobedient Hebrews to the king, and when Nebuchadnezzar heard about it he was enraged. He called Shadrach, Meshach, and Abednego on the carpet (vv. 8–13).

Even though the king was hot, he gave the men one more

chance to change their minds (vv. 14–15). He was saying, "Listen, boys, let's solve this problem right now. Bow down to my statue and I won't hold it against you. We give a man another chance. We're not a hard company to work for. I'll give you a second shot at it.

"But let me explain something, gentlemen. If you will not bow down and worship my image, there will be no review board or appeal. You will be cast into my furnace. And let me ask you, what god can deliver you out of my hand? This is my company; this is Babylon the great that I have built all by myself. So if I decide to kill you, who is going to stop me?"

Nebuchadnezzar was calling for the total submission of these Hebrews to an alien authority. He held their future in his hands in every sense of the word.

They had no doubt been able to enjoy some of the privileges of being at the top. Were they going to give up the "Babylonian dream" to offer an alternative witness? Everyone else was bowing. Maybe they could have just bowed on the outside while standing up on the inside. Like many American Christians, they could have argued that they needed to keep religion and politics separate. After all, how could they serve God if they were dead?

But these men were too well informed biblically to remain neutral. They knew the First Commandment: "You shall have no other gods before Me" (Exodus 20:3). They knew that God's Word took precedence over Nebuchadnezzar's threats.

Babylonian culture and religion would have to be judged by the divine standard. This should be the case with any believer living in a foreign culture. And there is a sense in which all cultures are foreign to believers, in that cultures are under the control of Satan and Christians are citizens of God's kingdom.

Note the answer Shadrach, Meshach, and Abednego gave to Nebuchadnezzar's threat:

O Nebuchadnezzar, we do not need to give you an answer concerning this matter. If it be so, our God whom we serve is able to deliver us from the furnace of blazing fire; and He will deliver us out of your hand, O king. But even if He does not, let it be known to you, O king, that we are not going to serve your gods or worship the golden image that you have set up. (Daniel 3:16–18)

What a powerful statement! First of all, it's powerful

because of who said it. Whether they spoke in unison or one spoke for all three, the answer from these men was the same.

They didn't have to confer and take a vote on whether they would obey God. They didn't have to rehearse their answer or change it because one of them objected. They didn't worry about trying to word it just right so Nebuchadnezzar wouldn't get the wrong idea.

To Nebby's question, "What god can deliver you from my hand?" their answer in effect was, "our God is able to deliver us from your corporate system." No hesitation there at all.

See, when you become an alternative for Jesus Christ in the secular world, you often become an enemy of that system. If a culture does not run on Christianity, then the Word of God declares that it is in the hands of the Evil One. It is run by Satan himself.

And when Satan sees believers becoming alternative witnesses, he tries to bring all the worst of that system down on them to threaten their comfort and even their lives. When we stand up for Christ, when we condemn immorality, when we refuse to participate in sin, we become an enemy of the world.

But that wasn't all there was to the issue. These three Hebrews understood that God is after our obedience more than He is after our comfort. So they acknowledged that even if God did not deliver them from the furnace, they still would not bow.

How could they make such a statement? Because they had a history with God. Their parents had told them about the Red Sea, the Jordan River, the manna from heaven, and the rock that gushed water. Therefore, when they were under fire they remembered what their God could do.

That's why it's important for us as believers in the secular culture to walk with God day by day and watch Him accomplish the little things. Then, when the fiery furnace is threatening us, we'll remember what God did yesterday. That will strengthen our faith in the same God who is operating today.

We are witnessing the rapid demise of the Christian ethic in this country. These Hebrew men had absolutes; they were not going to bow. That's the testimony America needs to see from us. America doesn't need to see Christians bowing to the world. It needs to see believers who won't bow, in spite of all that might happen.

America needs to see a group of Christians who may have gone up the ladder of success, but who are willing to come back down the ladder rather than surrender their principles, because they realize they have been put there to be God's alternatives.

When Nebuchadnezzar saw the God of the Hebrews in action in that furnace, the name of God was proclaimed throughout Babylon. Sometimes God joins His people in the fire rather than keeping them out of the fire, so the world can see what He can do and come to recognize Him as the only true God.

Alternatives Don't Stop Praying

The third story is in Daniel 6. It's another illustration of what it means to become God's alternative.

The amazing thing about this account is that Daniel was probably in his eighties by now. Babylon was gone, conquered by the Medes and Persians. But Daniel was still around. Nebuchadnezzar was long dead, but Daniel was still there.

Cultures come and go, corporations come and go, jobs come and go, but God's people are still around because He will always keep a witness in the world. God destroyed Babylon, just leveled the whole culture. He raised up a new one and gave Daniel a top job in it as well. The problem remained, however. Even though there was a different culture, the same sins were still being committed.

A new scheme had been devised to give King Darius a "theo-ego." Every secular structure wants to be God. Its basic philosophy is that man asserts his independence from God so that he might be his own god. This is called humanism. I firmly believe, however, that no culture should be allowed to proclaim its humanism without Christians asserting their theism.

In Daniel 6, jealous officials in the Persian government set out to bring Daniel down (v. 4). They went through his file drawers. Yet they couldn't find anything wrong with this man, because he lived like an alternative.

Daniel served a different God. He did not buy into their ungodly system. He was in the system, he worked for the system, and he was paid by the system. But Daniel was not going to bow down before the system. It was then that they attacked his faith.

A law was passed that for a period of thirty days, no one could pray to any god except Darius (vv. 7–9). When Daniel heard of it, his biblically trained mind began working. God had commanded that His people worship no other god but Him. That took care of that as far as Daniel was concerned.

But now Daniel was confronted by this Persian law. Doesn't the Bible command us to obey the law of the land? Yes, but only until man's law conflicts with the higher law of God. In this case the law of God said no other god, so according to verse 10:

When Daniel knew that the document was signed, he entered his house (now in his roof chamber he had windows open toward Jerusalem); and he continued kneeling on his knees three times a day, praying and giving thanks before his God, as he had been doing previously.

When this new law was signed, the memo came across Daniel's desk informing him of the new rule. As soon as Daniel heard of this ridiculous law, he went straight home and immediately began to pray.

One of the major issues in this generation was the Supreme Court's decision to ban prayer in public schools. It was amazing to see how upset Christians became at this attack on our religious freedom, as though the secular culture is obligated to recognize our faith.

I'm for prayer anywhere, anytime, but my point is this: We should expect such attacks and not be surprised by them. When laws like this are passed, they provide believers with an opportunity to model the divine alternative while they're working to overturn them.

Daniel did not go out of his way to provoke the wrath of his enemies. Rather, they went out of their way to indict him, since they followed him home. It's ironic that Daniel's testimony was so well known to these men that they knew exactly what he would do—and he didn't disappoint them.

Daniel knelt down and gave thanks to God just as he had been doing for years, with his windows open. None of that "secret agent" believer stuff here!

The change in the culture didn't make him change his habits. He was still committed to his spiritual priorities. For him, a night in the lions' den simply became another opportunity to display God's power to a pagan culture.

ARE YOU AN ALTERNATIVE?

Becoming God's alternative, then, is not so much a matter of what you do on Sunday, but how you live on Monday when you're among the ungodly.

When you go to your job, do the other people know you're different? I don't mean different as in odd or unusual, but different in that you have something to offer that no one else in the office or in the shop is offering—and an alternative to the ways and the gods of this world.

That's what God is after, people who will let the world see that there's something better. When America sees that we Christians are not cut from the same old cloth, when it becomes obvious that we have a relationship with God, then we will begin to see Christians helping to rebuild America.

It's interesting to note Darius's response the morning after Daniel had spent the night in the lions' den: "Daniel, servant of the living God, has your God, whom you constantly serve, been able to deliver you from the lions?" (Daniel 6:20).

That question is full of implications. Darius was asking whether serving God really did make a difference for Daniel. No doubt Daniel had previously testified to the king and his cabinet about the glories of being a servant of the Most High God. Now Darius wanted to know whether Daniel was just talking or whether God could really make a difference.

Daniel's response from the lions' den was as expected. God had come through. This reality led to Darius's decree for all to fear and tremble before Daniel's God (v. 26). While this doesn't mean that the king and everyone in the country became believers, it does mean that Daniel's alternative way of living brought God glory in Persia and caused Him to be recognized by the unsaved.

Likewise, when we Christians begin living as God's alternatives, our generation will tremble because of our testimony to the greatness of God and to the grace of Christ.

Although we cannot bring in the kingdom by our witness alone, we can provide such an exciting preview of what it will be like that the ungodly will wonder how they can get in on the deal.

But if we are no different from the American culture of which we are a part, the people around us will figure they haven't missed anything.

Like other aspects of the Christian life, offering God's alternative to the world won't always be easy. Some people will reject us, even try to bring us down. But like Daniel, we too will make an impact by conforming to divine standards in a secular society. Nothing less than this will have any preserving effect on a decaying American culture.

CHAPTER 14

RENEWING THE CHURCH

The church in America is desperately in need of surgery. It's going to take some pretty heavy cutting and stitching to put God's people back in shape, but we need to go under the knife now before God puts us—and America—under a bigger knife later on.

In the previous chapter, we suggested an alternative to the way most Christians are living, an alternative that will result in new power in our lives and new impact on our culture. Now I want to take a more focused look at the church, zeroing in on ten areas in need of renewal.

We have covered several of these areas in detail in previous chapters, but I want to include them here in a summary way as we talk about how the church can regain its impact, authority, and leadership in society, and how we can be the salt and light that God has called us to be. Then in the closing chapter, we'll talk about regaining some of the ground we have lost in the culture itself.

EMPHASIZE SOUND BIBLE TEACHING

The first area where the church in America needs renewal today is that of the teaching and preaching of God's Word. Paul admonished Timothy:

Preach the word; be ready in season and out of season; reprove, rebuke, exhort, with great patience and instruction. For the time will come when they will not endure sound doctrine; but wanting to have their ears tickled, they will accumulate for themselves teachers in accordance to their own desires. (2 Timothy 4:2–3)

Teaching involves more than imparting information from the Bible. It requires the relevant explanation and application of biblical truth to the hearer's world. And that requires the expository teaching of God's Word.

Exposition is the careful explanation and relevant application of Scripture, taking into account its grammatical, historical, and theological contexts. Proper exposition helps the hearers to understand a passage's historical meaning and learn how to apply its truths to their current lives.

In short, exposition is teaching that is faithful to the original meaning and intent of the biblical authors and relevant to the lives of believers today. Because the church needs to be taught rather than entertained, expository preaching and teaching is critical to the development of churches that will be able to affect our culture for God.

Passionate preaching void of solid biblical content leads to emotional fanaticism, whereas solid content void of contemporary relevance leads to dead orthodoxy. Our culture needs a clear, strong word from God that is both biblically sound and relevantly communicated. Unfortunately, far too much preaching today gravitates to one extreme or the other rather than holding these two aspects of exposition in balance.

The explosion of religious TV programming in particular has had the inevitable effect of giving the modern-day church a "show biz" mentality that deals in sound bites and spectacular testimonies. In such settings, the Bible is often used to verify the experiences being promoted.

At the other end of the spectrum are those who approach the Bible as a storehouse of information to be dissected, debated, and digested. But the Bible was not written to teach propositional truths only. It was written to teach us how to live. Jesus' final commission to His church included "teaching them to observe all that I commanded you" (Matthew 28:20).

Now "observe" here doesn't mean sit by and watch. It means to keep, to obey. The goal of Bible teaching is application. Truth can't be taught as though it were unrelated to life. When that happens you leave church knowing what Paul said, for example, but not knowing how to put the truth into practice.

We will not change our culture with correct grammar and definitions. Those are important in understanding the Bible, but we have to demonstrate that God's Word has answers to today's questions. We must preach and teach for life-changing results.

When the pastor opens the Bible, it is God who needs to speak from the pages of His Word. Churches need to insist that their pastors know and teach only what God has said. If the preacher teaches something that God hasn't said, and if the people don't know the Bible for themselves, they are going to be led astray. Nothing can replace the relevant, clear teaching of Scripture.

MOVE BEYOND TRADITION

Faced with a deteriorating culture and its own declining influence, the church in America cannot afford to cling to manmade traditions. The Bible, not tradition, must sit in judgment over us. Paul wrote, "See to it that no one takes you captive through . . . the tradition of men" (Colossians 2:8).

The traditions of men aren't necessarily God's traditions. When the Pharisees and scribes asked Jesus why His disciples transgressed the tradition of the elders by failing to do the ceremonial hand washing (Matthew 15:1–2), Jesus answered them with another question: "Why do you yourselves transgress the commandment of God for the sake of your tradition?" (v. 3).

Religious traditions may or may not be good. But what God wants is for us to obey Him—and that's always good.

It's amazing that we will get mad at people if they don't follow our religious traditions, but we don't get upset if they disobey the Word. In some churches it's acceptable to live in sin, but you'd better not leave your choir robe at home. Raising money through chicken dinners, choir sings, and special days because "that's the way we've always done it" is not good enough.

Colossians 2:8 warns us to beware of human traditions.

That means if what your grandmother taught you is in line with God's Word, that's fine. But if it isn't, then follow Paul's warning and change that tradition. It's that simple, but you have to know what the Bible says in order to make that decision.

We need to ask two questions about every church activity. First, is it biblical? Second, is it effective for ministry? If the answer to the first question is no, the activity may need to be eliminated no matter how popular it might be—and no matter how effective it may seem to be.

All churches have forms that are not expressly commanded in Scripture in the sense that you won't find them in the New Testament. Children's church is a good example. But if a ministry is being done for the biblical goals of teaching kids about God and bringing them to faith in Him, then it's a biblically sound activity. The forms can vary, but the spiritual and biblical foundations must be constant.

What I'm talking about are the things many churches do just because they have always done them or because somebody thought they were a good idea. When "Bingo Night" or "Las Vegas Night" comes to the church, someone had better start asking some hard questions.

If an activity has a biblical basis, we then need to ask how effective it is. If the answer to this second question is "Not very" or "Not at all," then it's time to reevaluate it and find out how to make it effective.

One reason today's middle class is not as involved in the church as their parents were is that they feel church is not relevant for them. These urban professionals have had broader exposure and more access to information and are not as tied to tradition as their parents.

Yet this is a group that must be reached if the church is to impact culture. They provide a vital resource and skills base to support the programs and ministry of the church.

In the black community, professionals also provide access to masses of black people. And because they have achieved the goals and aspirations of the black underclass, they are potential role models. But to reach and keep this group, the church must have more going for it than tradition.

Let me hasten to add, however, that many of the "old-time ways" are important because they give us a sense of heritage and historical continuity. The gospel spirituals are a prime example of something extremely valuable from the past that should be retained. But note that they adhere to the first guideline as well, because they have a biblical basis. Those things, new or old, which give us a better understanding of who God is should never be compromised.

USE THE GIFTS OF THE BODY

According to 1 Corinthians 12:12–31, God has constructed the spiritual body, the church, like the human body. It is made up of many parts, and every part has a function to fulfill in order for the whole body to operate properly. Every member of the body is gifted for service in some way.

When a part of my physical body is injured or sick, I go to a doctor, because the breakdown of one part impairs the working of all the others. When one member of the spiritual body stops functioning, it makes it more difficult for the body to achieve its goals. If many members of the spiritual body fail to do the work they were designed for, the body might not function at all.

Believers need to be held accountable to serve the rest of the church family so that the gifts of the body can be enhanced and leaders developed. Non-participating members must be held accountable for their inactivity.

Maybe they just need help getting started. Or maybe no one has ever asked them to serve anywhere. But if they are simply trying to take advantage of church membership without taking on responsibility for the growth and development of the church, they need to be lovingly corrected or removed from the rolls. The crisis we now face leaves no room for "church leeches"—people who enjoy the benefits but do none of the work.

When I was playing high school football, we used to do killer practices they call "two-a-days." We'd have morning practice, a lunch break, and then afternoon practice. It was tiring.

I'd go home with my gear slung over my shoulder, yawn, and say to my mother, who was hard at work in the hot kitchen, "Wow, am I tired! I think I'll go upstairs and rest."

I was really saying, "Don't ask me to give you a hand with the work." Well, Mom read me loud and clear every time. She'd say, "Boy, you better get in here and help me."

"But I'm tired," I'd wail.

"Tired? If tired was good reason for quitting, there'd be no breakfast on this table, no lunch for you to take to school, no dinner when you came home, no clean clothes, and no beds made up."

She went on to say, "Boy, if tiredness were a reason, I'd have gotten rid of you the day after you were born."

In other words, if you're a member of a family, you have a responsibility to fulfill for the family's benefit as well as yours. Every disciple serves in the family of God.

The idea of striking members from the church rolls is frightening to many pastors and churches, because numbers are important to them. Numbers give a sense of accomplishment, but it can be a false sense if the ministry is faltering spiritually.

Whenever the church is tempted to be impressed by numbers, we need to go back and read John 6 again. One day, Jesus drew a crowd of 5,000 men—with the total crowd probably closer to 20,000 counting the women and children.

But by the next day, He had emptied the place out. When He started talking about ministry and the cost of being His disciple, the people melted away until He was left alone with His twelve disciples. So the numbers didn't mean much.

Read Revelation 2–3 and notice that nowhere does the risen Lord Jesus discuss the size of the churches He addressed. His concern was not how many members the churches had, but how many members *He* had.

For a family to function properly, every member must bear his or her share of the load. If a person were to tell our church that he would give money but wouldn't serve, membership would not be extended to him. Membership in the church can't be bought, and people can't enjoy the benefits of the church without accepting the attendant responsibilities.

Please note that if we are going to challenge people to get involved in ministry and use their gifts, there must be opportunities for them to serve that go beyond ushering or singing in the choir. Social services, prison ministry, and counseling are just a few of the possibilities.

In most churches, finding places for people to serve is not the problem. When ministry is your goal, the list is usually endless.

Some people try to get out of serving by saying that they don't yet know what their spiritual gift is. But that's a weak excuse. The Holy Spirit is not going to write it on the wall for us or whisper it in our ears. He only hits moving targets.

But when we get busy serving, He shows us what we're best qualified to do. The first thing to do is get started. If everybody does a little, a few people won't have to do it all. No one should have to be at the church every night of the week, sit on every committee, and teach Sunday school too. Burning people out at church is not the way to light a fire in the culture!

DISCIPLE MEMBERS

This is one of the areas we have already devoted an entire chapter to (see chapter 5). But I want to make a couple of points in this context that I didn't deal with earlier.

One is the relationship between salvation and discipleship, and there *is* a relationship. Discipleship is the ongoing application of one's salvation. Salvation is free, but discipleship is costly.

Being a disciple means denying yourself and bearing a cross (Mark 8:34). It means removing anything and everything that would hinder you from obeying, serving, and living absolutely for Christ.

There's a brief but instructive picture of what a disciple does in John 2:1–11, the wedding at Cana where Jesus' mother asked Him to provide more wine for the guests. Mary told the servants, "Whatever He says to you, do it" (v. 5).

That pretty well sums up what it means to be a disciple. Those servants probably wondered what filling waterpots had to do with the wine shortage at the wedding, but they obeyed. You don't have to understand Christ's command to follow it.

Do you explain to your children every motive and reason for telling them to do something, or do you sometimes tell them to obey simply because you said so? Children don't need to know every nuance of every decision you make to obey you. They don't even need to agree with what you're asking them to do. All they need to do is obey and let you handle the consequences.

Our relationship with God is like the one we have with our children—only He never misses a call! We are His children, and

He is our Father. When He commands, we must obey whether we understand what He is doing or not. "Trust and obey" really is the essence of discipleship.

The church needs to remember that discipleship is not the same as church membership. Obviously, church membership hasn't changed America. The church is having little impact on our culture despite all the polls that show that the "baby boomers" are going back to church.

In order to disciple someone, you must know the Word and know how to apply it to daily living. In 2 Timothy 2:2, Paul instructed Timothy: "The things which you have heard from me in the presence of many witnesses, entrust these to faithful men who will be able to teach others also."

Paul was calling on this young pastor to make sure he discipled other believers he could depend on so that they could disciple others with a multiplying effect. In this way a pastor disciples his elders, for example, who then disciple the deacons, who in turn disciple other believers, and so on.

You say, "Tony, that just isn't happening in most churches." I know. That's part of the problem. But something like this had better start happening, because church leaders don't just spring up; they must be carefully nurtured and tended so that they put down deep roots. Otherwise, we may be only one generation away from a basically leaderless church.

DEAL WITH SIN

Again, there is an earlier chapter devoted to this topic (see chapter 4). But I want to make a few follow-up observations about the need to deal with sin in the body of Christ.

People need to know that the church is serious about holy living, starting in the pulpit and moving to the pew. Every member needs to understand that God hates sin. His abhorrence of sin, His holiness, is one of His basic attributes.

Think of examples in Scripture that remind us how much God hates sin. He put Adam and Eve out of the Garden because He hates sin. He destroyed the world in the Flood as a judgment against sin. He allowed His chosen people to wander in the wilderness until an entire generation died because of their sin. God even put His Son to death on a cross to pay for our sin.

We like to rank sins according to human standards. Thus, murder is much worse than gossiping. Well, murder may be worse in terms of the human consequences, but not in terms of God's attitude. To Him, sin is sin.

If God takes sin so seriously, the church had better get serious about it too. If there's anyplace where the church can demonstrate to the culture that God's standards are different, it's in our attitude toward and treatment of sin. The world thinks sin is funny. We know it is fatal.

BECOME A COMMUNITY

To most people, the church is the building on the corner where Christians meet each week. But biblically, the church is a family, a fellowship of believers who share of themselves and their resources to address the needs of their members. The church is a community, not a building.

That's why biblical references to the church often use designations such as "the household of the faith" (Galatians 6:10) and "fellow citizens" (Ephesians 2:19). The church is a family that ministers to families. It functions as a family, models family life, and cares for the families within it.

But as families deteriorate, the role that the church should play becomes more important but also more difficult. Children need fathers, wives need husbands, and single-parent families need a variety of social service support systems. The church can offer God's solution to these and other family problems.

That's one thing that made the New Testament church so dynamic (Acts 2:44–45). It not only proclaimed the Word, but it modeled the Word to the world by the unique love between its members, demonstrated in the corporate meeting of needs.

In the early days in America, the church functioned as an extended family. Non-related church members became aunts and uncles to youngsters and were free to help them and to discipline them. Sharing common meals on a Sunday-by-Sunday basis was a norm.

Today, much of that has been lost. The church has by and large adopted the independence and material individualism that is so much a part of American society in general. This is one form of Americanism that must be removed from the church.

Unless the church helps to build whole families individually and corporately, we won't have strong churches and will never impact the society in which those families exist.

BECOME UNITED

In chapter 11 we looked at church unity particularly in light of the racial and cultural divisions now present among us. Let me make some additional observations.

When Jesus told Peter that He would build His church on the "rock," the word He used refers to a slab made up of many stones bonded together. This helps us understand that Jesus was saying all of His disciples would unite to form His church.

Nobody can build the church alone. If we're going to defeat our enemy Satan, we've got to work together. And it's obvious that we have a lot of work to do.

Churches across the country can ill afford to be divided over non-essential matters. Although we cannot compromise biblical truths, unity on the basis of the fundamentals of the faith will give us the strength necessary to oppose Satan and to accomplish God's will for the church. In other words, we need to find points of agreement instead of focusing on disagreements.

There are certain fundamentals such as the Trinity, the Person and work of Jesus Christ, salvation by grace, the absolute authority and inerrancy of the Bible, and the return of the Lord Jesus Christ that are central to our beliefs. We can't have fellowship with someone who denies these fundamentals.

But other areas of interpretation and preference simply aren't essential to fellowship and cooperation in ministry. If we can agree on our biblical responsibility, we can find fellowship and work together.

Although I realize that every church will not fellowship with every other church, if we are committed to the fundamentals of the faith and to living holy lives, we can show our unity cross-culturally and cross-denominationally much more than we do.

MOVE FROM PROGRAMS TO MINISTRY

The plight of our culture demands that we move beyond programs that are not tied to ministry.

Many churches put a lot of time and effort into programs that they've had for decades. No one can remember when the program started or why, but they still carry it out faithfully.

We might define ministry as an activity in which the needs of people are met by Christians in accordance with the Scripture. Events in themselves, if they do not qualify as ministries, do not help us address the crisis we are facing.

A great example of ministry is found in Acts 6. Because the Greek widows were being neglected in the daily giving of food, a complaint arose in the church at Jerusalem. When the apostles were told of the problem, they didn't turn to Caesar. The church handled it by appointing seven deacons to meet the need.

Notice the spiritual qualifications for the leaders of this ministry. They were spiritual men who had good reputations and were filled with the Holy Spirit and wisdom (Acts 6:3). Anyone with ability can head up a program, but not everyone can pull off a ministry that God can bless.

In too many churches, the pastor or staff members find themselves doing all the work of the ministry. This goes back to the need to help believers accept responsibility for the ministry so they can begin serving and find their areas of giftedness.

There is work for everyone. For example, our churches need programs that minister to single parents by providing godly big brothers and sisters for their children. They also need whole families who will serve as extended families to the single-parent home.

Children need opportunities such as athletic teams to learn discipline, determination, cooperation, and other elements of successful Christian living. Men's groups can be more than a chance to play table games together. They can become a network through which unsaved men are reached.

The list could go on and on. But my point is that unless some biblically based goal is being met by a program, it is not ministry. And ministry through believers, not simply programs, is a crying need in the church.

In addition, the ministry of the local church must be comprehensive, seeking to apply the whole Word to the whole world so that the culture can see the power of God at work on every level of human existence.

MOVE FROM MEDIOCRITY TO EXCELLENCE

People need to know that when they serve God, they must do so in keeping with His perfection. God is worthy of the finest service we can give Him, not the leftovers.

But some believers try to give God the junk. Only after they have taken care of their needs, and even their wants, are they ready to offer anything to God. Many believers give God whatever is left, handing it to Him with great ceremony and even a sense of sacrifice.

Do you know what the Bible says about that? Speaking through the prophet Malachi, God said He doesn't want the last and least of what we have. He wants and deserves the best, the firstfruits of our labor (Malachi 1:6–9).

How do you know if you are giving God leftovers? Here is the test suggested in Malachi 1:8: If you offered to the governor what you are offering to God, how would he react? If your gift would displease the governor (or the mayor, or the president, or your boss), God will surely not be pleased with it.

Giving God our best shows up in the little things. Some believers drag into church whenever they feel like it. But they show up on the job ten minutes early on Monday morning. Why? Because the boss holds their paycheck! What these people often don't realize is that God holds their lives.

Some preachers are guilty of giving God less than their best. If a man is called to preach, he must "be diligent to present [himself] approved to God as a workman who does not need to be ashamed, accurately handling the word of truth" (2 Timothy 2:15).

I believe this command can be expanded to cover all of our service for God. It's a reminder to take our responsibility seriously. God does!

Our culture needs to see that God deserves and demands our best. We as believers have a tremendous opportunity here to impact America for the Lord. Most believers work in the secular marketplace, rubbing shoulders with unbelievers every day.

The most effective open door for a witness you may ever have is when you do your work "heartily, as for the Lord rather than for men" (Colossians 3:23). Doing anything with excellence has become rare in America. When Christians live with excellence, people will take note and want to know what makes us different.

STOP DEPENDING ON GOVERNMENT

You have probably detected by now that this is a real hot button with me. Chapter 11 is the biblical argument for my position, but let me just restate here that God did not create governments to take care of the church, and the solution to our problems won't land in Air Force One. He made the church responsible for the church, so the world can see firsthand the divine household at work (Acts 4:32–35).

To put it another way, we Christians should be caring for our people so well that government experts come to us to find out how we do it.

See, Jesus could feed, heal, lead, and minister to people in a way that was a witness to the world. Because He was able to minister to their needs, Jesus turned the people's eyes toward Him and not toward the Roman government. His followers quickly learned to depend on Him for their needs rather than on the governing authorities.

One of the great problems in the black community is that many of our leaders have not recognized this truth. As a result, there has been an overdependence on government.

In our legitimate, biblical call on government to promote justice and mercy, we have become so dependent on its programs, grants, and assistance that we have failed to develop the means of addressing our own needs through the church.

Since the church is the most important institution in the black community, it would seem that we would have the wherewithal to meet our own needs. Unfortunately, that's not the case. We are supposed to represent God as His people, yet we are more dependent on the government than many other groups.

On the other hand, the white church, while complaining about the waste in government programs, has done little to equip itself to place charity back in the church where it belongs.

Like believers in the first century, we have to learn not to look to Caesar to solve our problems and care for our people.

Jesus Christ, not the government, has promised to build the church.

It is true that we live in a democratic society that provides certain benefits to its citizens. And as contributing members of society, we can expect to partake of many of those benefits. However, believers ought not be so dependent on government that when the benefits are withdrawn, we can't function.

I won't restate my earlier thesis, except to say that even well-meaning government programs often demean and demoralize their recipients. What we need is less dependence on government and its agencies and more reliance on God and His ability to work through His church to help it meet its own needs.

CONCLUSION

No doubt you can think of other areas that need renewal in the church in America. One thing is certain: Our culture is not going to show any signs of renewal and godly influence until the church of Jesus Christ is renewed and revived.

It's too late for business as usual in the church if we expect to see God reverse the trend of destruction that is the inevitable result of rejecting divine authority.

However, the Bible clearly teaches that when the enemy comes in like a flood, God will raise up a standard against him (Isaiah 59:18–19 KJV). The enemy indeed has come upon America like a flood. God has already raised up a standard against him, and it is called the church.

The standard, however, needs to stand firmer and higher above the world. "Secret agent" Christianity won't benefit the people of our culture. If the church ever becomes the righteous people of God in America, not only may God be pleased to spare our nation, but by His grace He can reverse the decay.

CHAPTER 15

RECLAIMING THE TERRITORY

We have covered a lot of territory as we try to answer the ques-tion, Are Christians destroying America?

Instead of writing off our culture as hopelessly secular and doomed, I'm convinced that God wants His people to have a redeeming and transforming impact on American society. In this closing chapter I want to outline a biblical strategy for reclaiming the cultural territory we have lost.

But before we get to that, I need to make a biblical statement about an issue that has been around for a long time and continues to be critical. This issue is the relationship of the gospel to social action. What is the Christian's responsibility in matters of social ills such as injustice, poverty, and hunger?

EVANGELISM AND SOCIAL ACTION

I need to deal with this first because I don't want anything I say in these pages to be construed as a theology of social action in place of the gospel. The very terms "social action" and "social gospel" have a negative connotation in many evangelical circles.

But the question remains, What does the gospel of Jesus Christ have to say to the poor and oppressed? Bible-believing Christians need to clarify the relationship of the gospel and evangelism to social action, especially since our attitude toward culture is an integral part of the whole discussion.

The Content and Scope of the Gospel

First, let me emphasize that the message of the gospel is narrow, not broad. The issue of social action is not a part of the gospel message. Whenever social action is made part of the gospel, two problems arise: It obscures what the gospel really is, and no one knows how much emphasis to give to the social aspect of the message.

Those who want to make social action a part of the gospel's content make the same mistake repeatedly in biblical interpretation. They apply the non-technical uses of the word *gospel* in the Gospels to its use in the Epistles, where the word has a much more limited meaning.

For example, when Paul spoke of the gospel, he limited it to the death, burial, and resurrection of Jesus Christ for sin (1 Corinthians 15:1–4). The social liberationists argue, however, that because Christ proclaimed and demonstrated social liberation as a part of His kingdom message, that too is part of the gospel's content.

But the term *gospel* is used in a variety of ways in Matthew and Mark. In Matthew 4, Jesus used the term to refer to the good news of the kingdom (see vv. 17, 23). Meanwhile, Mark used it to refer to the complete narrative of Christ's life and ministry (Mark 1:1), of which the proclamation of kingdom good news was only a part (vv. 14–15).

Luke never uses the noun form of the word at all. He uses the verb only ("to evangelize," "to tell the good news"), which places the emphasis on the proclamation of the gospel, not on its content. In Luke, the content varies according to the need of the audience, as we will see below. So in Luke there is no statement of content, only of proclamation.

So one extreme in the debate is to attempt to weave social action into the content of the gospel. I believe that approach is clearly unbiblical.

The other extreme is to eliminate social concern completely from the scope of the gospel. In this case, a person could believe the gospel and receive Christ, yet feel that his faith has absolutely no bearing on the needs in this world.

This is equally unbiblical. Although the content of the

gospel does not include social action, its broader scope and application insist upon it.

This is because the New Testament includes sanctification, the process of becoming more and more like Jesus Christ, in the scope of the gospel. For Paul, the gospel that saves is the gospel that sanctifies (see Romans 16:25; 1 Thessalonians 5:23). Ministering to the physical person is part of the sanctification process.

One major problem in America is that often Christians separate the personal message of salvation from its practical implications. As the gospel is proclaimed, a concern for human needs should flow naturally out of its effect on people and the community. A trait of our individualistic age is that people care little about the deterioration of our society.

When the gospel has permeated a group of people, there should be a shifting from social inertia to social sensitivity. This increases the importance of Jesus' statement, "By this all men will know that you are My disciples, if you have love for one another" (John 13:35). Our testimony is enhanced by the social interplay that takes place among Christians before the world.

A Gospel Prototype?

Those who hold strongly to the view that social action is a part of the gospel message lean heavily on Luke 4:18–21. They see this passage as not only the leading statement of Jesus' ministry of evangelism, but also as the prototype of what the church's ministry of evangelism should be.

So let's examine this crucial text. Jesus came into Nazareth one Sabbath day, entered the synagogue, and stood up to read (v. 16–17). He was handed the Isaiah scroll, and this is what He read:

The Spirit of the Lord is upon Me, because He anointed Me to preach the gospel to the poor. He has sent Me to proclaim release to the captives, and recovery of sight to the blind, to set free those who are downtrodden, to proclaim the favorable year of the Lord. (vv. 18–19)

Then Jesus sat down and said, "Today this Scripture has been fulfilled in your hearing" (v. 21).

In reaction to the view that this passage is Jesus' call for a "socialization" of the gospel, many evangelicals have over-spiritualized these verses. Thus, the poverty and blindness and oppression and bondage mentioned here are understood merely as a description of mankind's spiritual condition, not as real physical or social needs.

But a careful look at the passage belies both of these extreme positions. Notice first that Jesus claimed to be the fulfillment of the prophecy of Isaiah 61:1–3, the text from which He read. So we need to understand what Isaiah was referring to in his prophecy, since Jesus said specifically that He was fulfilling these verses.

As I turn back to Isaiah 61 and examine its context, I see two things that argue strongly for a physical understanding of the passage.

The first is that the background here is clearly the Year of Jubilee, that year set forth in the Law when all Israelite servants were to be set free (see Leviticus 25:8–55, especially vv. 40–41). That's what Isaiah meant by "proclaim[ing] liberty to captives" (Isaiah 61:1).

The phrase in verse 2, "To proclaim the favorable year of the Lord," is also an allusion to the Jubilee. According to Leviticus 25:8–12, in this special year when God's favor would be expressed in the context of liberation, the trumpet was to sound and liberty was to be proclaimed throughout the land.

Therefore, because Isaiah was expressing the fact that the Messiah would bring about Jubilee, it is natural to assume that what characterized Jubilee would characterize the Messiah's ministry. This kind of physical liberation was a natural outgrowth of God's spiritual relationship with His people. It followed the Day of Atonement (Leviticus 25:9) and expressed a deliverance by God of His people from Egypt so He could be their God (Leviticus 25:38).

So Isaiah viewed Messiah's provision of physical liberation as an expression of a spiritual reality. And when Jesus used this phrase, He was expressing the same understanding Isaiah had.

A second argument for the physical application of this passage is that Isaiah's prophecy was given to the Jewish exiles in Babylon. In Isaiah 39, the Babylonian captivity of Judah was clearly prophesied.

Since this physical captivity was in view, it is natural to

assume that the Jews would have been thinking about a temporal, physical restoration if the nation repented. They were in a physically helpless state, and they would have understood the prophecy to mean deliverance from their bondage.

What I'm saying is that those who spiritualize Luke 4 as simply talking about salvation from sin fail to take seriously the context of Jesus' quote from Isaiah 61.

But to say that Jesus was *only* referring to physical deliverance and social justice in Luke 4:18–21 doesn't stand up. We have to understand that in the Old Testament, physical salvation was always predicated on spiritual salvation. That is, the benefits of Jubilee were not received until the people had dealt with their sin on the Day of Atonement (Leviticus 25:9).

It was because the people had offered the prescribed sacrifices for their sins that they could expect deliverance from their slavery. Thus Jesus' statement about preaching good news to the poor assumed a response of faith to that good news, not simply a change in economic status.

In other words, the captives would be set free only when the people got themselves right with God and repented of their sins. Don't miss this point. The social effects of the gospel cannot be realized until the gospel is accepted. So even though physical and social benefits come from the gospel, the gospel itself is very narrow and specific in its content.

This explains why social benefits in the New Testament are almost totally limited to the church rather than to society at large. It also explains why those who argue for social action as part of the gospel's content rarely use the Epistles for their argument.

To argue that social action is an integral part of the gospel is unthinkable. But it is equally unthinkable that we who have received the gospel message would be socially insensitive, first to fellow believers in need and then to the world at large (Galatians 6:10).

A STRATEGY TO RECLAIM CULTURAL TERRITORY

Now we're ready to outline a biblical strategy to reclaim the territory we have surrendered to the culture. This strategy is found in Jeremiah 29:4–11.

The reason this passage is so relevant to our current culture is that the people to whom Jeremiah wrote were God's people in a pagan world. They were the Jewish captives in Babylon, a small group within a hostile society.

That's how Christians often feel today. As we congregate in our evangelical subculture while society becomes increasingly hostile to our faith, it's easy to develop a "captive" mentality. This tells us that all we can do is huddle close together and try to survive until Christ comes back for us and rescues us from the sinking ship of modern American culture.

Well, I want to propose an alternative to that way of thinking. I believe that our culture can be reclaimed if Christians will execute God's strategy in history. This will require that we get busy being God's people in the world.

By "in the world" I don't mean worldly, I mean involved in history in a Christ-centered, Bible-centered way. And I'm not talking about so-called reconstructionist theology, which teaches that Christians need to retake society and re-establish the Old Testament legal system with its prohibitions and punishments. That's something else entirely. America is not a theocracy, and even Christians are no longer under Old Testament legal regulations.

But the Jews in Babylon were in a pagan environment. The question they faced was how they should function. Should they just sit around and do nothing in the hope that this mess would all be over soon and they could go home?

Speaking through the prophet Jeremiah, the Lord said no to that idea. He had a better plan, as outlined in the letter that Jeremiah wrote to the captives in Babylon (Jeremiah 29:1–3). I see in verses 4–11 five principles or propositions for reclaiming society.

We Must Regain Our Spiritual Clarity

First, cultural territory will be reclaimed when Christians regain spiritual clarity. The letter from Jeremiah to the captives began with this "salutation": "Thus says the Lord of hosts, the God of Israel, to all the exiles *whom I have sent into exile* from Jerusalem to Babylon" (v. 4, italics added).

You can't get a much clearer statement than that. God told

His people, "The reason you are in this mess is that I sent you into this pagan culture." We know from our Old Testament history that God sent the Jews into exile because they had ceased being faithful to Him.

See, the exiles couldn't sit around feeling sorry for themselves. They needed their memory refreshed. They needed to be reminded that they had forsaken God. They had become as pagan as the pagans, so God had said, "Since you want to be pagan, let Me send you to live with the pagans."

It was the failure of the people of God to be His set-apart, unique people that caused God to bring them to judgment.

Christians in America today are not captives from a foreign land. We were born and raised here, for the most part. But we have been guilty of the same kind of compromise as Israel, so God has permitted the culture to fall into spiritual ruin around us.

This verse answers the question, Would God allow His people to get stuck right in the middle of a hostile culture? Yes, He would. That's where Christians are in America today. And it didn't just happen. The reason our culture is decaying is that the Christians are nowhere to be found except in church. And the world is following the lead of everyone *but* those in church.

So the first thing we need to do is clean our spiritual glasses so we can see clearly. America's decline is the result of God withdrawing His hand of blessing because Christians aren't being Christians in the culture.

Many of us are doing fine personally, but that's not enough. We now have a culture without a conscience. In urban areas like Dallas/Fort Worth, children can't go out and play anymore. A little girl was abducted from a soccer field on a Saturday morning with dozens of adults all around. A fifteen year old killed the owner of a hair salon simply because he thought it would be exciting.

When you have a culture without a conscience, that's what you get. And you can get a culture like this when there is no morality being transferred to the culture anymore. When my generation was growing up, even if your mama and daddy didn't give you a moral frame of reference, your schoolteacher did. Or if it wasn't the teacher, it was the people who lived next door. You kept bumping into solid morality. You couldn't get away from it.

Why? Because a basic moral code permeated the culture. Not because everyone was a Christian, but because most people embraced the Judeo-Christian ethic. That's no longer the case, because a godly influence is no longer being felt in the culture.

We Must Develop Economic Independence

Second, cultural territory will be reclaimed when Christians develop economic stability. "Build houses and live in them; and plant gardens and eat their produce," continued the letter from Jeremiah to the Babylonian exiles (Jeremiah 29:5).

I believe in the imminent, "any moment" return of Jesus Christ. But that has never been a reason for doing nothing. Jesus told the parable of the nobleman who went away on a long trip, gave his servants money, and told them, "Do business with this until I come back" (Luke 19:13). In other words, "Get busy in the culture using what I have given you."

In Jeremiah's day there were prophets going around telling the Jews, "Don't worry about making yourself at home because God is going to rapture you out of Babylon soon. In two years, you'll be out of here" (see Jeremiah 28:3, 11). They were false prophets giving false hope, because God had decreed seventy years of captivity.

I've said it before, but it needs to be said again. The reason God didn't rapture you to heaven the moment you were saved is that He has work on earth for you to do. Most certainly, at the heart of that work is evangelism, living holy lives to His glory, and building His church.

But we are also called to have a purifying and preserving effect on our world. We need to make this world the best possible place to live. That's not liberalism, it's part of the dominion given to mankind at Creation and lost through the fall of Adam and Eve.

So Jeremiah told the people to get a homestead because they were going to be in Babylon for a good while. We live with a tension. What do we do while we wait for Jesus Christ? Christians could be around for several more generations. How should we conduct ourselves?

Hold on to your hat for this one, but in Jeremiah 29:5 God

told the Jews to plant their own gardens and live off them. In other words, "Develop your economic independence. Don't depend on the Babylonians to fund your Jewish community." We as believers cannot become dependent on the pagans for the wherewithal we need to live in a pagan culture.

See, pagans are not going to fund Christians so that Christians can make a spiritual impact on them. God was telling the Jews in Babylon, "In order for you to do what I want you to do in that pagan culture, go out in your backyards, get on your knees, get out your garden tools, and plant your own seeds. Then if they cut you off, you can still eat."

This was not an exhortation to cultivate a few pretty flowers along the sidewalk. Jewish culture was agrarian. Raising food was the backbone of the Jewish economy. God was talking about their bedrock economic stability, the staples of life.

Like it or not, there is no discussion of ministry without a simultaneous discussion of economics. You can't talk about serving God without including economics somewhere in the discussion, because ministry costs money. So God says, "In order for you to pull off My program, you must have a measure of economic self-sufficiency."

One reason many of our urban communities are falling apart is that the people who have the wherewithal to sustain them don't live there anymore. When these people move out, the communities they leave behind are crippled economically. The people who remain can no longer sustain the quality of life their community once enjoyed because they had become dependent on others.

If the believers in the churches in these communities are also dependent on what other people do, and many of them move out as readily as the non-Christians, then their churches are going to decline and be unable to do the work of the kingdom. So today we have poor inner-city churches and rich suburban churches. We have churches with extra funds (or that would have extra funds if their members gave biblically), and we have churches with unmet needs. What could happen in America if wealthier churches teamed up with poorer churches to lend financial support? Paul wrote to the Corinthians suggesting this very thing (2 Corinthians 8:14–15).

Let me give you a heavy one here. Back when Israel was getting ready to enter the Promised Land, God told His people, "One way you will know that I have withdrawn My blessing is when you live in debt."

When Israel was experiencing God's blessing, they would be the lender and not the borrower (Deuteronomy 28:12). But if they disobeyed the Lord and fell under His curse, they would become the borrower (28:44). They would have to go to the pagans with their hats in their hands asking for the money they needed to live as God's people. Something is wrong with that picture.

God did not want the Israelites, even in captivity, being dependent on the Babylonians for their livelihood. He wanted them developing whatever measure of economic independence they could develop in the culture of which they were a part.

Christians could make a major impact on the economics of this country if they would either bank together at the same bank, or start their own banks with God's people controlling the wealth of the Christian community, taking this thing totally outside of non-Christian control.

There would be no churches that could not be built, no missionaries who would lack support, no ministries that could not be developed. Why? Because God would be in control of the funds again instead of us going to the Canaanites or the Babylonians for what we need. As long as you are dependent upon Pharaoh, as long as you beg your livelihood from him, he will never let you go.

Even though this issue of economic independence is a major one in the black community, I am not speaking about any one race here. I'm talking about the Christian community, be it black, white, Hispanic, American Indian, or Asian.

God told the Israelites through Jeremiah, "Plant your own gardens so you can feed yourselves." That's why at our church we have an economic development program. We want to teach people skills so they become employable and have the ability not to have to depend on government.

I'm not talking about Christians trying to make themselves rich. This is not prosperity theology. I'm talking about our ability and freedom to do God's business God's way because we are using God's resources.

I'm also not talking about a social gospel. We must win people to Christ first, because it doesn't matter how much money they have and how good their jobs are; if they die without Christ, they die without hope. So don't misunderstand me on this one.

But I'm saying that since Christians still have to live and carry out God's business in this world, we need as much as possible to be free of the whims and the control of the world. We've given up a lot of territory economically, but it can be reclaimed.

We Must Recapture Family Sanctity

A third way we can reclaim the territory we have lost is to recapture the sanctity of the family. Jeremiah's letter to the Jewish captives continued:

Take wives and become the fathers of sons and daughters, and take wives for your sons and give your daughters to husbands, that they may bear sons and daughters; and multiply there and do not decrease. (Jeremiah 29:6)

Can you imagine? Here were these Jews living in the midst of a pagan, debauched society, and God is telling them, "Go ahead and have children. Establish your families."

See, we hear it said all the time that this world is too evil a place to raise children. But God said, "Do not decrease." Why? Because the purpose of having children is not so that we can have look-alikes. The purpose of children is to stamp the image of God on future generations.

If you raise your children in the fear of God, when they leave home they will carry the image of God with them everywhere they go. So whether they move to New York, Miami, Los Angeles, or wherever, people should be able to see what God looks like by hanging out on the block where your kids have set up their homes. Our society doesn't think of children and families as a blessing. Kids are an inconvenience to many people, or a vehicle through which parents try to achieve all the things they couldn't achieve. But kids are the greatest investment in history because with children, we secure the future.

In biblical days, children were also the security of their parents in their old age. There were no nursing homes or Social Security checks to sustain people in their later years. Aging parents were dependent on their families. Having raised godly children, these parents would not have to worry about a place to live when they could no longer care for themselves.

Look how the world deteriorated from the first family. Adam blew it as the leader of his family. Eve blew it as his helper. They rebelled against God and lost His paradise. Then murder entered the picture as Cain killed Abel. Then polygamy entered because Lamech took more than one wife. By the time we get to Genesis 6, the whole world is debauched and God must destroy it with a flood.

Why? Because one family wouldn't do it right. When you mess up the family, you mess up the culture. Kids need some kind of family, so what they are doing today is joining alternative families called gangs. Gangs are like families to these kids because it's in the gang they find meaning and self-esteem and responsibility and accountability, although it is all twisted.

God told His people to increase and build families, even in the land of exile. A lot of their children and their children's children got to go back home to Israel and re-establish the nation. I don't know how God will use our children and grandchildren, but I know He can't use them if they're not there!

We Must Exercise Social Responsibility

Here's a fourth way we as believers in America can reclaim some of the cultural territory we have surrendered: by exercising social responsibility.

In Jeremiah 29:7, the prophet wrote: "Seek the welfare of the city where I have sent you into exile, and pray to the Lord on its behalf; for in its welfare you will have welfare."

This is an incredible statement. God was commanding the Jews in Babylon to do everything they could to improve the quality of life in that place. He was saying that unless His people did something positive in the culture, it would get worse and fall apart—and they would fall apart with it.

This hits all of us no matter where we live. The days when we could escape the deterioration and the violence of the cities by fleeing to the suburbs are over. Even if we don't live in the city, the overflow of our drug-and-violence culture has already caught up with the "burbs." There's nowhere to run, so we had better "seek the welfare of the city."

But if Christians are going to affect our culture, we need a comprehensive program. For example, there is no question that abortion is one of the most hideous things we are facing today, and God's judgment is on our culture for it.

It's not enough just to be against abortion. If we are going to preserve the lives of unborn children and bring them to birth, we have to have a plan that takes a person from the womb to the tomb, from the cradle to the grave.

The church is going to have to take responsibility for holding families accountable for their children who are falling through the cracks in the welfare state. We must see that these children are fed and clothed and discipled properly so they can go out and reproduce the image of God in their families instead of becoming long-term wards of the government.

This book is not the place to outline a comprehensive program, but it can be done. It *is* being done in churches all across America. And it *must* be done, because no other institution has our mandate from God, and no one else holds the church's potential for blessing. If Christians don't accept the challenge of a comprehensive agenda for restoring the culture, we can't look for someone else to do the job.

We Must Maintain Biblical Integrity

Finally, we can only reclaim lost territory as we maintain our biblical integrity:

For thus says the Lord of hosts, the God of Israel, "Do not let your prophets who are in your midst and your diviners deceive you, and do not listen to the dreams which they dream. For they prophesy falsely to you in My name; I have not sent them," declares the Lord. . . ."For I know the plans that I have for you," declares the Lord, "plans for welfare and not for calamity to give you a future and a hope." (Jeremiah 29:8–9, 11)

God is saying to us, "Church, let's do this My way for a change. Stop letting the false prophets of this world system tell you how it's supposed to be done. Stop letting the government tell you how it's supposed to be done. Try 'It is written.'"

Unless we do this God's way, it won't work anyway. God's way is infinitely better than anything anyone can come up with. Jeremiah 29:11 is a promise we could take to the bank if we would obey the Word.

One day, a man went to a mental hospital and noticed hundreds of patients out on the lawn, walking around and talking, with only one guard at the gate. He was curious, so he asked the guard, "There are so many patients out here, and you're the only guard. Aren't you afraid they will overpower you and escape?"

"Not at all," replied the guard.

"Why not?"

"Simple," the guard explained. "Lunatics don't unite."

It is lunacy if Christians in America don't come together and by God's grace get this thing turned around for our children and for our future generations.

I am not saying we can solve all the problems. I am not saying there won't be more crime. I'm not saying there won't be more social deterioration. I'm not saying any of that. What I'm saying is, it starts with us. Christians are the only people who can halt the deterioration of our culture.

The apostle Paul tells us to do good to everyone at every opportunity (Galatians 6:10). Obeying that command alone would be a powerful step we as Christians could take to reverse our complicity in the destruction of America!

EPILOGUE

The Mafia is an intriguing organization. It has no central-ized address, no identifiable zip code, and no central leader. Yet its influence and impact is felt worldwide. The presence, program, and people of the Mafia have infiltrat-ed every segment of society for evil. It is the power behind crime, drugs, and prostitution. It is a highly organized, fine-tuned, well-financed industry that operates from the lowest to the highest echelons of society. Its representatives camouflage themselves as well-dressed businessmen, entertainers, farmers, and politicians. They have successfully entered the mainstream with their craft while simultaneously presenting themselves as model citizens. There is not a person alive who does not feel the influence and impact of this worldwide criminal organization.

It has been my contention throughout this book that what the Mafia is to evil, the church should be to righteousness. What the Mafia is to hell, the church should be to heaven. We have no central address, for we are more than a building, and we are located everywhere. You can find us in factories, in offices, on farms, in schools, and in every neighborhood in society. We come in all shapes, sizes, colors, ages, genders, and classes. We, like the Mafia, are to infiltrate every segment of society with the message of Jesus Christ as we visibly reflect His character before a watching world.

Just as the Mafia brings misery to the culture because of the evil it multiplies, Christians should bring blessing to the culture because of the goodness and righteousness we promote. Just as a Mafia member is to never lose sight of the fact that his identity goes beyond the normal activities of life in which he or she is engaged, even so Christians are to see themselves beyond the normal secular human viewpoints of men. There must always be the overriding reality that we belong to another group. Our loyalties transcend our jobs, families, and personal goals. We are carrying an agenda bigger than ourselves and bigger than history itself. And just as commitment unto death is the understood code of the Mafia, Jesus Christ calls us to totally sacrifice all things for His kingdom.

Until Christians begin to view themselves in this light and function accordingly, we will not see the life-changing impact on the culture that we were redeemed to have. In the same way the Mafia has brought death, fear, pain, and immorality to the lives of countless millions, Christians should be bringing joy, peace, unity, hope, and love to the world in which we live. Since greater is He that is in us than he that is in the world, our presence should be an intimidating one for good in a culture that is desperate for answers. There is no time left for "polite" Christianity. Too much is at stake. We don't need nice Christians who live in nice homes and attend nice churches. What we need are committed Christians who are willing to show their true colors, Christians who are tired of the status quo and who want to be used of God to turn things around. If not you, who? And if not now, when? Our decaying culture needs men and women made of spiritual steel.

One of my favorite television programs as I was growing up was "Superman." I loved the superhero. As Clark Kent, he was a bumbling idiot. Lois Lane didn't like him, Jimmy Olson couldn't respect him, and old Perry White was always yelling at him.

But Lord have mercy, don't let that man find a telephone booth or go in that storage room at the *Daily Planet!* The criminals in Metropolis would be wreaking havoc and somebody would say, "Where's Superman?"

I sat on the floor next to my brother watching this thing. Clark Kent would take off his glasses and unhook his tie. I looked at my brother and said, "There he goes!" My man would step inside a telephone booth or a nearby closet and come out with a red-and-blue jumpsuit on.

He wasn't Clark Kent anymore. Now he was "faster than a speeding bullet, more powerful than a locomotive, able to leap tall buildings in a single bound." The man of steel would go streaking across the sky, and people would be hollering, "It's a bird! It's a plane! No, it's Superman!"

All of a sudden, the whole culture of Metropolis was transformed because this guy would bend steel in his bare hands and crumple the bad guys' guns like they were paper.

Do you know why Superman could do all of that? Because he wasn't from this world. He was from a place called Krypton. And when he got transferred here to Earth, he brought the power of Krypton with him and made it work down here. The result was that when Superman showed up, the environment in which he lived was transformed.

Do you get the idea? Too many of us Christians have been living like Clark Kent, apologizing for taking up space and breathing the air. We need to take off that old Clark Kent suit—that old way of thinking, that old way of walking, that old way of talking—and take a trip to God's telephone booth.

We need to come out with our red-and-blue jumpsuits on. We need to come out faster than speeding sin, more powerful than public unrighteousness, able to leap racism and other forms of cultural evil in a single bound! Christians must re-emerge into our contemporary culture with a big *S* on our chests.

The *S* doesn't stand for Superman, but it does mean we are saved. It doesn't stand for Superman, but it does mean we are sanctified. It doesn't mean we are Superman, but it does mean we are saints of the Most High God.

We need to get flying so that when people see us coming they say, "It's a bird! It's a plane! No, it's God's 'supersaint' on the move!"

It's time for us to go public for Jesus Christ and reclaim our culture in His name. It's time to take the power of heaven and bring it down to earth so that people see what a real Christian looks like when he or she takes to the sky for Christ. It's time for Christians to stop contributing to the destruction of America and take back our culture for the glory of God.

ABOUT THE URBAN ALTERNATIVE

THE PURPOSE

The Urban Alternative is a Christian ministry founded in 1982 by Dr. Tony Evans that seeks to equip, empower, and unite churches to impact individuals, families, and communities for the rebuilding of their city from the inside out.

THE PROBLEM

We are witnessing firsthand the internal destruction of our culture. Nowhere is that destruction more evident than in our urban centers where drugs, crime, teenage pregnancy, racial conflict, poverty, and family disintegration are combined to unravel the very structure of our society.

In spite of the increased education, funds, programs, and prisons, etc., these problems are getting worse, not better. This is because the real problem is not being addressed, namely the absence of a proper moral and spiritual frame of reference accompanied by a system of accountability to that standard. That standard is the Bible.

THE PHILOSOPHY

TUA is committed to the thesis that the only mechanism which can successfully address the problems of our society is

the church. This is because the church alone possesses the
resources to address the spiritual and moral causes that serve
as the basis for the existence of these problems in the first
place. We believe that there is a biblical solution to every social
problem and the church is the best institution that can apply
these solutions properly. Although churches cannot be expected to solve all the problems of the communities in which they
are located, they can model these solutions in their communities so that people will know where to go to find help God's way.

In order to successfully address the enormous amount of
need in our communities, there must be an intentional and
aggressive cross-racial and cross-denominational networking
between churches. TUA seeks to show churches how they can
minister effectively where they are and network with others to
create biblically based programs that not only accomplish the
goal of successfully addressing urban problems but that simultaneously promote reconciliation among Christians in the
process.

THE MODEL

Project Turn-Around (PTA) is TUA's comprehensive model
for the revitalization of your community from a moral and ethi-
cal frame of reference. We believe that in order to impact the
community, the church must holistically address at least the
seven areas listed below. These areas or components comprise
the *PTA Model*. The Urban Alternative uses this model as the
fundamental basis for consulting with churches and organizations that want to make a difference in their communities for
Christ.

THE BIBLICAL PRINCIPLES

Church and Leadership Development

God has ordained the church to be the entity to communicate His truth. He expects the church to use His truth to impact
the home, the community and the world for His kingdom.
Therefore, the church must be committed to developing
mature leaders who can oversee the dissemination and applica-

tion of God's truth (Matthew 28:18–20; 1 Corinthians 14:40; 1 Timothy 3:1–11; Titus 1:5).

Family Renewal

God's ideal family is modeled after how Christ relates to the church. Therefore, each member of the family, as with members of the body of Christ, must function effectively in order for the family to be strong and have a positive impact in the community (Deuteronomy 6:6–9; 1 Kings 17; Ephesians 5:22–6:4; James 1:27).

Housing Development

God desires that the basic needs of all individuals are met, one of which is shelter. He also expects the church to foster better living conditions and encourage community ownership (Nehemiah 2:3–5; Psalm 72:12–14; Matthew 25:34–46)

Health Revitalization

God is concerned about our entire being. A Christian's physical body is the temple of the Holy Spirit and the vessel God uses to carry out the work of His kingdom. Therefore, we must discipline it if we expect to run the Christian race to the fullest (Romans 12:1–2; 1 Corinthians 3:16–17; 3 John 2)

Educational Revitalization

God wants the church to be committed to instilling both intellectual knowledge and godly wisdom, from infancy to adulthood, in order to bring people to true maturity (Deuteronomy 6:6–9; Proverbs 22:6; Colossians 1:28; 2 Timothy 2:2; Titus 2).

Business and Economic Development

God expects laboring to be a part of every Christian's life, not only for the purpose of obtaining financial gain but also to produce greater quality in one's own character and the community at large (Proverbs 13:11; 14:23, 31; Ephesians 4:28).

Community Mobilization and Reconciliation

God commands that we truly love each other, since He is the Creator of us all. When this love is performed, it results in team work, which brings about a better return for one's labor. Therefore, churches must be committed to reconciliation so that we can labor together for the welfare of our communities (Nehemiah 3; Ecclesiastes 4:9–12; Malachi 2:10; John 12:34–36; Galatians 2:11–14).

PROJECT TURN-AROUND MODEL OF COMMUNITY REVITALIZATION

- **Church and Leadership Development** focuses on assessing, developing, and equipping the church for effective ministry resulting in maximum outreach to the community.

- **Family Renewal** focuses on rebuilding and strengthening the family as a whole according to the ideal biblical model.

- **Housing Redevelopment** focuses on stabilizing local communities through promoting affordable housing, fostering safe neighborhoods, property beautification projects, and encouraging relationships and community ownership.

- **Health Revitalization** focuses on assessing the elements that contribute to the deterioration of the physical and emotional health of the community and developing a plan to address them.

- **Educational Revitalization** focuses on enhancing and strengthening the community's educational systems.

- **Business and Economic Development** focuses on assessing the economic needs of a community and the options that one can effectively utilize to meet them.

- **Community Mobilization and Reconciliation** focuses on utilizing all necessary resources to promote racial, gender, class, and denominational reconciliation and coalition-building.

THE PRODUCT

To assist you in utilizing the Project Turn-Around Model, The Urban Alternative offers:

- Assessments for individuals, churches, and communities to help evaluate your present level of effectiveness considering where you are in ministry. The goal is to devise a plan for how you can develop your ministry for maximum impact in your community.
- Consultation on how to adapt and implement the PTA model in your unique community through the assistance of The Urban Alternative staff and other qualified ministry professionals.
- Training to equip churches and other organizations for effective ministry and outreach through TUA's annual Church Development Conference and regional workshops.
- Resources to aid in church and leadership development and the implementations of the PTA model.

THE RESULT

We believe that with the application of biblical principles and the implementation of the Project Turn-Around model, we will begin to see lasting change in our society and souls added to the Kingdom. These are some of the results:

- The Bible will be established as the standard by which society should function.
- The church will take leadership in establishing the moral tone for society at large rather than simply reacting to the trends of secular society.
- Specific programs will be in place that meet the needs of society and can be modeled by society.
- The oneness of the body of Christ will be demonstrated and a new atmosphere will begin to take shape in society.

For more information contact:
The Urban Alternative
P.O. Box 4000
Dallas, TX 75208
214-943-3868

Moody Press, a ministry of Moody Bible Institute,
is designed for education, evangelization, and edification.
If we may assist you in knowing more about Christ
and the Christian life, please write us without obligation:
Moody Press, c/o MLM, Chicago, Illinois 60610.